No Bugles, No Drums

An Oral History of the Korean War

Rudy Tomedi

JOHN WILEY & SONS, INC.

New York • Chichester • Brisbane • Toronto • Singapore

For the men and women who served in Korea—those who
returned and those who did not.

Copyright © 1993, 1994 by Rudy Tomedi
Published by John Wiley & Sons, Inc.

Library of Congress Cataloging-in-Publication Data:

Tomedi, Rudy
    No bugles, no drums : an oral history of the Korean war / Rudy
Tomedi.
        p. cm.
    Includes index.
    ISBN 0-471-57232-2
    ISBN 0-471-10573-2 (paper)
    1. Korean War, 1950–1953—Personal narratives, American.
    I. Title.
DS921.6.T66   1993
951.904'2—dc20   93-10569

Printed in the United States of America
10 9 8 7 6 5 4 3 2 1

Contents

CONTENTS

Author's Note

For a long time the fighting in Korea was euphemistically called a "police action," but make no mistake about it, it was a war. It lasted exactly three years, one month and two days: June 25, 1950 to July 27, 1953. Over 54,000 Americans died in it, and over 103,000 suffered wounds serious enough to earn the Purple Heart medal. It was a brutal, bruising, physical war, fought largely on the ground, over some of the most inhospitable terrain imaginable, in temperatures that ranged from a hundred degrees in summer to fifty below in winter. And when finally it ended, the men who fought it (to a draw) were brushed under a rug in the national mind.

Yet in lives sacrificed, wounds received, and Americans made prisoner by the enemy, Korea was almost as deadly for the United States as World War I.

It was also a strangely anachronistic war. During the last two years of the conflict the combatants fought almost exclusively from opposing trench lines, giving some of those who were familiar with the images of the 1914–18 trench warfare an eerie sense of deja vu.

Hand to hand combat was common, and it was in Korea that Americans drove home the heaviest bayonet charge since Cold Harbor in the Civil War.

I knew Korea only from brief visits as a journalist, and initially I was as ignorant of the war that was fought there as I suppose the average American still is. Then I met, almost by accident, three or four aging men who talked very articulately and movingly about their part in this curiously neglected conflict. Their stories piqued my interest enough to get me reading, and as a marine veteran of the Vietnam era I was immediately struck by the similarities of Korea and Vietnam: both unpopular, both largely misunderstood in their time, and both, in their aftermath, leaving thousands of combat veterans and at least an equal number of civilians wondering if it had all been worth it.

But as I began talking to other men who had served in Korea I found a fundamental difference between the two conflicts: almost to a man, the veterans of Korea believed then and still believe now that whatever their personal beliefs about the war, *it was their duty to go.*

To me, growing up in the Vietnam era of student deferments and antiwar protests, this was rather astonishing. Clearly these men were of a different generation, encompassing a different set of beliefs. And when I realized that I hadn't gotten that insight from my reading but rather from talking to the men who were there, I decided to do the book you now hold in your hands.

Based on the most articulate and insightful of the more than one hundred interviews I conducted, this book is an attempt to personalize the Korean conflict in a way that most standard narratives fail to do. Firsthand accounts have their limitations, but they also catch things that often fall through the cracks of a conventional history. And they do one other thing: they bring home the experience of combat as only personal reminiscence can.

As much as possible, I have tried to let these men speak for themselves, allowing small factual errors to stand, since the way a thing is remembered is often, in itself, a revelation of character. Where a precise fact or date was in my judgement significant, I balanced the erroneous statement with a footnote. When I edited by stringing sentences and phrases together to make a long discussion shorter and more coherent, I sent the edited transcript to the interviewee for review and approval. To all these men I again offer my thanks for their cooperation and in many cases their friendship.

—Rudy Tomedi

Prologue

The roots of the Korean War go back to World War II. By the last year of that war Japan had been exploiting Korea as a colony for forty years, but Japanese domination of the Korean peninsula ended with Japan's surrender in August 1945. A large number of Japanese soldiers, however, remained on the peninsula, and something had to be done about them.

After the Japanese surrender it was decided that the Americans, approaching from the south, would disarm the Japanese occupation troops in southern Korea while the Russians, hurrying down from Manchuria and eager for a share of the spoils, would disarm all Japanese troops in northern Korea.

But where did north end and south begin?

Obviously a line had to be drawn.

Meetings were held between Soviet and American officials, and at one of them an American military officer pointed to a map, indicated the 38th degree of north latitude, which divides the Korean peninsula almost in half, and said, "Why not here?"

The Soviets agreed, and it was done. Russian troops stayed north of the 38th parallel, and the Americans kept to the south.

But Korea in effect became two countries as the Russians quickly tore up all railroad tracks directly north of the parallel, blocked the roads, and placed armed guards along the entire length of the new "border." No one north of the parallel was allowed to go south, and no one from the south was allowed to cross into the north. Meanwhile a Russian-trained Korean communist named Kim Il Sung was put in power in the city of Pyongyang.

The United Nations attempted to sponsor elections that would allow all Koreans the chance to choose their own government, but north of the parallel any free expression of choice was ruthlessly blocked by the Soviets. The elections took place only in the south, and there a government was chosen, with an aging but fiery patriot named Syngman Rhee as president and Seoul as the capital city.

In reply, Kim Il Sung staged his own mock elections in the north, and when they were over he proclaimed himself the head of a separate state.

In 1949 both the Soviet Union and the United States withdrew their combat troops from Korea, but the two superpowers left behind two vastly different national armies. South of the parallel America left (abandoned, many critics would later charge) a poorly trained and equipped force of some 65,000 men, an "army" that had no armor, no air support, and less than a hundred heavy guns. North of the parallel the Russians left behind an intensively trained and highly motivated army of 135,000 men equipped with heavy artillery, tanks, trucks, automatic weapons, and almost two hundred combat aircraft.

But at the time both the strength and the fighting qualities of the North Korean army were vastly underestimated by the U.S. military. It was generally believed that the South Koreans, stiffened by a few hundred American advisors, would be able to hold their own in the event of an invasion.

By June of 1950 there were only five hundred American soldiers in the country, all advisors to various South Korean units. There were four U.S. divisions in nearby Japan, but all were understrength and most were made up of men and officers softened by occupation duty. Meanwhile, somewhere in the Pyongyang-Peking-Moscow triangle a decision had been reached, and the North Koreans secretly massed their artillery and armor and arranged themselves 100,000 strong along the 38th parallel in preparation for an all-out invasion of the south, a hammer blow that would reunite the country by force.

The attack came during a heavy rainfall early in the morning of June 25, 1950. Surprise was total, and within hours practically every South Korean unit in the field was in full retreat.

CHAPTER 1

First Blood

When the North Korean army crashed over the border into South Korea on that rainy Sunday morning in 1950, Robert Roy was still in bed. He was stationed at Camp Wood, near the city of Kumamoto on the Japanese island of Kyushu. Roy was a member of M Company, a heavy weapons company in the 21st Infantry Regiment of the 24th Division, and because June 25 was a Sunday, and he had no weekend duty, Bob Roy was sleeping late.

Roy had been in Japan since 1949, and the duty, up until now, had been good. "Everything was cheap," he recalls. "As a PFC I was only getting about eighty dollars a month, but that was plenty. That was more than enough to live good. You could live off the base in a Japanese house for ten dollars a month, with a girl to do all the cooking and cleaning and laundry. We had Class A passes. You could go on liberty every night. If you were off duty, you were gone. There were bars and movie theaters and cabarets where you could drink beer and talk with the girls."

The good life went on for almost a week after South Korea was invaded. During that week momentous events occurred: The UN Se-

*curity Council passed a resolution demanding North Korea's with-
drawal from the south; President Truman ordered U.S. air and naval
forces to support the South Korean army; Seoul fell; and finally, after
another UN resolution that called on member nations to go to the
aid of South Korea, Truman authorized the use of U.S. ground troops
in the fighting.*

*But almost none of this was known to Bob Roy, because he wasn't
paying much attention. He was a nineteen-year-old private and his
mind was on other things.*

*More understandably, since enlisted men are almost never told
anything in advance, Roy and his fellow soldiers were also unaware
that their regiment had already been chosen by the army's Far East
command to be the first to go to Korea.*

*Only one battalion of the regiment would go, because only one
battalion was immediately available. They were given the name Task
Force Smith—two understrength rifle companies, a headquarters
company, and a heavy weapons company (Bob Roy's M Company).
They were named after their commander, Lieutenant Colonel Charles
Smith, and they were being sent to Korea, all 420 of them, to delay
the onrushing Communists until the rest of the 24th Division, which
was scattered all over Japan, could be gathered up and sent into the
fight.*

*So Bob Roy would be going to Korea ahead of everybody else—
not because his unit was the best, but only because it was the closest.*

When we heard the news of the invasion we didn't pay any
attention to it. The officers did, but we didn't.

On the last day of June we got paid, and as usual the whole camp
cleared out except for the guys who had duty. Everybody else went
into town and stayed until the midnight curfew. At midnight we all
came in to the barracks pretty well feeling our oats. We'd just gotten
to bed when one of our lieutenants came in, threw on the lights and
said, "Pack your gear. We're headed for Korea."

That's when we knew the war was on.

I was on a 75mm recoilless rifle. Nine months before I'd been
in the Military Police. M Company was originally an MP unit. Then

2

one day they came around and said, "All right, you're all in the infantry."

How did I get on a 75? "There you are. This is what you're going to do. You're the volunteer."

The 75 is basically a big bazooka mounted on a tripod. Each gun has a five-man crew. It's an awkward weapon, because it gives your position away. It has a big backflash, and it also blows up a big cloud of dust. It's like saying, "Here we are."

There was supposed to be four 75s going over, but two got delayed. Two went through. I happened to be one of the lucky ones that went through.

From Camp Wood we rode up to the airfield at Itazuke in trucks. I remember the Japanese guard waving us out the gate. We'd left all our personal stuff in the barracks. We all thought we'd be back in a week or so.

I think the ride took three or four hours. I remember it was raining. When we got to the airfield we stood in formation in the rain with the two rifle companies. Brad Smith was there, talking to General Dean, the 24th Division commander. I guess Smith was getting his instructions. Then Smith saluted, and we were ordered into the planes.

I believe they were C-54s. Six of them. Our gun was already in the plane, all strapped down with the ammunition. On the flight over I thought we were going to hit the water. We flew at wave-top level to stay out of the radar. Add that to the fact that that was my first-ever plane flight, and you got one nervous kid sitting in that canvas seat.

A lot of the guys were writing letters, hoping to get them out somehow, because the families weren't notified. Nobody knew we were going. And of course nobody knew what the hell was going to happen when we got there.

We landed near Pusan on the first of July, and it took us four days to get into position. First we were put on a train and went as far as Taejon. At Taejon we loaded onto trucks, and from there we moved a little farther north each day. I had no idea where we were going. All I knew was we were headed for the front, wherever the

3

hell that was. I was only a PFC, and when they tell you to go somewhere, you go. You don't ask questions.

What I remember most about those four days was not getting any sleep. And the flies. The flies would carry you away. We were in this little Korean village, before we went up to our final position, and Marguerite Higgins[1] showed up and started interviewing us, and the flies . . . we were spitting them out of our mouths as we talked.

And the stench. The Koreans put human excrement in their rice paddies, and God did it smell.

We got to our final positions on July fifth, at two in the morning. The infantry started digging in. My 75 they put on one of the highest knolls. We got off our truck and went straight up the hill. The lieutenant told us where he wanted the gun, and up we went.

I learned later that while we were still moving north Brad Smith had gone up ahead and personally picked the position we were going to fight from. It was a good position. We were set up along a ridge that ran at right angles to the main highway that came south from Seoul. The infantry was dug in to the left and right of the road. My 75 covered the road, and the other gun was placed over near a railroad. From up where we were, when daylight came, we could see two or three miles ahead of us.

About seven in the morning I decided to open a can of C rations, and that's when we saw the tanks. I just dropped the can. What the hell was this? Nobody told us about any tanks.

Before I fired the first round I counted thirty-five tanks coming down the road. Everybody was shitting their pants. From what I understand now, the South Koreans had been running from the tanks, and they wanted somebody up there who wasn't going to run. But at the time we weren't told that. We weren't told anything. We were all eighteen, nineteen years old, a bunch of cocky guys. We didn't know what to expect, and we didn't think too much about it. I think if I'd been thirty years old I would've turned around and run.

We didn't realize what we'd gotten into until we saw those tanks. But by then we were in it.

---

[1]Marguerite Higgins was one of the first female war correspondents and already famous by the time the Korean War began. In 1951 her dispatches from Korea won her a Pulitzer Prize.

4

We had no armor-piercing shells, so we tried to stop them by hitting the tracks. We would've been better off throwing Molotov cocktails at them. Some rounds were duds, some were even smoke rounds. We could see them bounce right off the tanks.

We fired as fast as we could. As soon as we'd get a round into the breech we'd cover our ears and let it go, get another one in, fire that one . . . but they went right through us, right on down the road.

A round from one of the tanks hit right in front of my gun. I saw it coming. I saw the turret turn. We worked as fast as we could to try and get off another round, but the tank shot first, and all five of us were thrown back over the hill from the concussion and the earth hitting us in the face. Our ears were ringing. We were all disoriented, couldn't function at all for five or ten minutes.

But the gun was all right. The lieutenant, he wanted us to go back and get it. The tank was still there, with its turret pointed right at us. I said to him, "I'm not going up there until that tank moves." I disobeyed a direct order. I said, "If you want that gun, you go get it."

He didn't go. The gun just sat there, and the tank waited there for a while, and we kept peeking over the hill, watching the tank, until it moved farther down the road.

We stayed there for a while longer and just watched the tanks. A few had stopped alongside the road and were firing into our positions, into the infantry, but none of them stayed around for long. Then our officers moved us across the road and behind a hill where the mortars were.

By this time, eight, nine in the morning, it was raining like hell. The mortars were right behind us, firing for all they were worth. The North Korean infantry had come down the road in trucks, and had gotten out of the trucks and started moving around our flanks. I didn't actually see the North Koreans deploy, because our view was blocked by the hill in front of us, but we knew their infantry must have come up behind the tanks because the mortars and our own infantry were all firing like crazy.

Me, I couldn't see anything to shoot at. So we got under a poncho, me and another guy, and we sat there smoking a cigarette.

An officer came by and yelled down at us, "What the hell are you doing?"

"We're having a smoke."

He says, "You're about to die."

"Yeah," we said, "we're havin' our last smoke."

That's the way it was for us. That was our state of mind. We'd been told how the North Koreans were a ragtag army, couldn't fight worth a shit, couldn't shoot straight, all that baloney. And what did we know? A bunch of kids? We just believed what we were told. And it was raining like hell. And our ammo's no good. We had nothing at all to fight with.

We'd been in trouble from the beginning, only now we knew it.

Hell, it was even worse than we knew. By now all the radios were out. The tanks had run over the communications wire, and the ones in the jeeps got wet from the rain and just stopped working. The infantry was strung out along the ridge, and we were just behind them, and there was no communication between any of the units.

I heard Brad Smith give the order to withdraw. He was up on the hill behind us. He stood up there and gave the order verbally. Just yelled it out. I don't remember exactly what he said, if he said "Every man for himself," but they were words to that effect.

So we got the word, but I found out later that one platoon never did get the word to pull out. They were left there all by themselves. Some of those guys eventually got out, and some didn't.

As soon as we heard the withdrawal order we took off down the hill and crossed the road, but by now the North Koreans had gotten behind us. They had the high ground, and I was down in a rice paddy and all friggin' hell broke loose. It sounded like a bunch of bees. Friggin' bullets bouncing all over the place.

Everybody just kept going, as fast as they could. Slipping and sliding through the rice paddies. Like I say, I don't remember the exact words Brad Smith used, but by now it was definitely every man for himself. Nobody wanted to be the last one out of there.

We were supposed to destroy our gun, but we didn't have anything to destroy it with. There's a self-destruct charge you drop in the breech. We didn't have any of those. We didn't have any grenades. As gunners we didn't even have rifles. All we had was our .45s.

We just left the gun where it was.

Normally what you do when you have to withdraw is you set up a rendezvous point. Then you retreat in an orderly fashion toward that point. But there was never any rendezvous point. Nobody told us anything. So we all took off on our own.

I was with a squad of guys who all got captured. Every one of them except me. I went over a railroad embankment, running like a bastard, because the North Koreans were still firing at us from the hills. Everybody was with me when I went over the embankment, but after running three or four hundred yards I turned around and, Jesus, I'm all alone.

I'm in the middle of all these rice paddies, and I'm thinking, Where the hell is everybody?

I found out, forty years later, that everybody else went down the *right* side of the railroad tracks. They went due south, where the North Korean tanks were, and they got captured. Most of them spent the war as POWs. I went down the left side, kind of southeast, because I wasn't about to go where those tanks were.

I ran into some guys from one of the infantry companies. They told me what happened up on the ridge. They'd made a pretty good fight of it, but then their ammunition ran out. They were going southeast too, and I joined up with them, and we just kept walking. It was still raining. Just pouring down. We didn't know where we were going. We finally ran into some people from the 34th Regiment, which was deployed south of us, but we had no idea they were there. We were just trying to get away from the North Koreans.

Those people in the 34th had just gotten orders to pull back. They had a sergeant with them who was wounded, and I was O type and I volunteered to give him a pint of blood. I did that because they said they'd give me a ride. Well, I gave him a pint of my blood, and they all loaded up on a jeep, and guess what? There was no room for a ride. I had to walk. It wasn't funny, because I had to walk almost forty miles before we finally stopped and got reorganized. What was left of us.

We were on the Kum River waiting to be relieved by the 19th Infantry when General Walker[2] showed up. He stood next to his jeep and gave us a talk. "If they come across this river," he says, "you guys are to stay here and fight to the death." Then he jumps in his jeep and takes off.

And we're all saying, "Yeah, sure."

They got tanks, and we got nothing to knock them out with. I still had only a .45 at the time, and I think six rounds of ammunition.

You've got to understand what it feels like to be in combat and not have enough ammunition, or have a weapon that don't work. The feeling of helplessness. What I'm saying is, it's easy to sit back and say, Well, those guys ran. Sure we ran. But what did we have to fight with?

You read about a lot of the wounded and litter cases being left behind. But I saw guys who should've gotten medals. I saw guys carrying other guys who had been shot in the legs. There were a lot of guys trying to help other people out. I saw a buddy of mine stay behind to lay down covering fire, and I don't know to this day if he got out of there. Everybody was trying to help out the best they could.

I lost a lot of friends there. One of them was my best buddy, John Holland. We used to call him Baby Face. He was only seventeen. A seventeen-year-old kid from Ohio. He was my gun loader and my bunkmate. In Japan we used to go out to the cabarets and have a few beers together. He was taken prisoner by the North Koreans and died in captivity.

We were sent over there to delay the North Koreans. We delayed them seven hours. Don't ask me if it was worth it. We were a bunch of kids and we were just trying to do our jobs.

---

[2]General Walton Walker was the Eighth Army commander, Eighth Army then being made up of the four divisions stationed in Japan.

CHAPTER 2

The Long Way Home

Accompanying Task Force Smith to Korea was Battery A of the 52nd Field Artillery: six 105mm howitzers that supposedly would give the task force added punch. Early in the fighting one of the guns managed to disable two North Korean tanks, but that was about the extent of Battery A's contribution, because the artillery position was soon overrun by the remaining enemy armor.

At the battery's home base in Fukuoka, Japan, a nineteen-year-old private first class named Bob Fitzgerald had been the number one man for one of the guns. But when Fitzgerald got to Korea he suddenly found himself not only in unfamiliar surroundings, but in an unfamiliar job, because he was taken from his artillery piece and assigned to the infantry.

On each gun we had a number two man, who took coordinates from the forward observer, we had a loader, and the number one man. My job as number one was to open the breech for the loader,

9

and when the number two man had his sighting equipment ready and gave the word to fire, I pulled the lanyard and fired the gun.

But none of that meant anything when we got to Korea, because the word came down on the fourth of July that the infantry needed machine gunners, and I was taken off my gun before we even got into position and sent on up to where the infantry was digging in. Supposedly I volunteered, but it was "You, you, and you, on the machine guns."

I'd fired machine guns in Japan, I could break one down and put it back together again, so a machine gun wasn't alien to me. But I wasn't too happy to be going up with the infantry. That was a different outfit, and I didn't know anybody there. In the army the one thing you want to do is stay with your buddies, and I felt like I was getting kicked out of my home and thrown in with a bunch of strangers.

There were two hills where they were digging in, one on each side of the main road. By the time I got there, they were basically in position. I had a loader with me, and we got off the truck and carried our gun up to the top of the hill on the left side of the road. It was still dark, three or four in the morning, and it was raining. Just miserable conditions.

Once dawn came I could see I had a pretty good field of fire. I had an open field to the right of me, and more open fields and rice paddies in front of me. Around seven in the morning I could see a line of tanks coming down the road, which we never expected. Tanks were the furthest thing from our minds. Then I saw trucks pulling up, and the North Korean infantry getting out of the trucks. The trucks stretched back along the road until you couldn't see them anymore. I learned later that the truck column was six miles long. There was something like ten thousand North Koreans coming down the road.

They piled out of the trucks, and some came straight across the fields at us while more of them started off to the right and left to try and get around our flanks. I'm pouring rounds into them now, and I could see some of them dropping in the fields. I could hear bullets zinging past my head, I could see bullets kicking up the dirt in front of me, I could see mortar rounds coming in, exploding on the hill in front and off to the side of me, in among our positions. They got us zeroed in in a hurry, and they were pouring a hell of a lot of fire into us.

I saw these two guys with a 2.36-inch bazooka down by the side of the road. There was a North Korean tank down there, and they fired at it. But nothing happened. I could see the round explode against the tank, but the tank just kept on going.

The hair went up on my neck. I thought, What the hell do we do now? We got nothing to stop the tanks.

We held them off for seven hours, until our ammo ran out. But there was no pre-planned route of withdrawal, and there was no regrouping area. So when the time came to get out of there it wasn't a withdrawal, it was a rout. The only withdrawal order we got, and I'll always remember this, was somebody up on a hill yelling, "Every man for himself!"

That was it. We left the gun where it was and took off down the hill.

We ran down to the bottom of the hill, and there were some officers there, in a group by themselves. I can remember a couple of captains and one lieutenant. I overheard one of them say, "I understand they're not taking prisoners." It sounded to me like they were trying to decide whether or not to surrender, and I made my own decision about that. They could go their way and I'd go mine.

To the left of me there was a rice paddy, and I heard a sergeant say, "I'm going across this rice paddy, and I want every one of you to follow me."

Not everybody did, but I was right behind him. There were a couple of guys behind me. We crawled through the muck of that rice paddy on our hands and knees, trying to keep down below the level of the dike, because by now the North Koreans were firing at us from our old positions up on the hill. On the other side of the rice paddy there was a plowed field, and we ran across that, zigzag, with the bullets kicking up the dirt.

There was a woodline at the far end of the field and we hid there in the trees for a while. We picked up a few more stragglers, until there was about a dozen of us. There was a second lieutenant, two first lieutenants, and the rest enlisted men.

We spent the next eighteen days trying to get back to our own lines. We traveled only at night, always trying to head south, and every day we'd find a clump of bushes or some woods or some other place where we could hide.

Every so often we had to take chances to get food. There were still some friendly South Koreans around but they were skittish. They were afraid that if they got caught helping us the North Koreans would shoot them, which I believe happened in a number of cases. So they had good reason to be scared.

But we did manage every so often to get some rice. And water. Nothing else.

After eighteen days on the move we started to hear artillery rounds going off to the south of us, and small-arms fire, so we knew we had to be getting close to our lines. Early one morning, just as it was getting light, we ran into a couple of Korean civilians, a man and his wife, with a wooden cart packed with all their belongings. They spoke fairly good English so we asked them if there were any North Koreans ahead, in the direction of the firing, and they said no, no North Korean, you don't have to worry, everything's all right.

So one of our officers decided we'd move during the day. I didn't like the idea, but everybody else was going so I went along too. We were near a road, with a rice paddy off to our right, and after that more hills, and after the two civilians left we moved out into the road for a while and then started to cross the rice paddy.

We were about halfway across when a voice behind us yelled, "Come back! Come back!"

We turned around, and the entire back edge of the paddy was covered with North Koreans. They had machine guns, rifles, burp guns, everything aimed right at us.

We put our hands in the air and walked back toward them. They tied our hands behind our backs with commo wire, cracked us with a few rifle butts for good measure, and marched us away.

From then on it's hazy. We kept picking up more American prisoners. They kept us moving all the time, from village to village. This went on for weeks, until there were about seven hundred of us. Finally this North Korean colonel showed up. We called him the Tiger. He split us up into groups of fifty, and put an American officer in charge of each group, to keep order. If anything went wrong, or if somebody was caught trying to escape, the officer was responsible.

Something did happen in one of the groups, I never found out exactly what, and they shot the American officer. I was only a few yards away. They held this joke of a trial right there by the road, pronounced the death sentence, made the guy kneel, and shot him in the back of the head.

They marched us north. We slept in the streets of Seoul one night. That's the only time I knew where we were. They marched us all the way up into North Korea, and finally they turned us over to the Chinese.

The Chinese put us in a POW camp at Changsong, near the Yalu River. Camp Number Three. I was there for three years, until the prisoners were exchanged in August of 1953.

One fight. That's all I was in. But I ended up being one of the last guys to leave Korea. I was in the first battle, and there I was, the last to go home.

CHAPTER 3

Holding the Line

Even as the scattered survivors of Task Force Smith were being gathered together other American units were arriving in Korea. The 34th Infantry Regiment had gone in just behind Task Force Smith and had taken up positions around the town of Pyongtaek, about ten miles to the south, but its men would abandon these positions in much greater haste than the men of Task Force Smith had abandoned theirs. On July 6, as the lead tanks and infantry of the North Korean army, the same troops who had punched through Brad Smith's formation the day before, swarmed down on the 34th Regiment, many of the men simply stared in shock, unable to fire their weapons. Those who did keep their wits and who attempted to fire back often found that their rifles wouldn't work or that their ammunition was too old to be effective. When the order to withdraw came, discipline broke down completely. Many men bolted, leaving behind weapons and equipment and throwing away even their helmets and shoes.

Behind the 34th came the 19th Regiment, the third and last regiment of the 24th Division. Then came elements of the 25th Di-

15

vision and the 1st Cavalry Division, all from bases in Japan. The North Korean formations continued to pour down the peninsula, and the collective mission of these newly arriving American units was to try and establish a defensive line and hold it until the battlefield could be stabilized.

Uzal Ent arrived with the 25th Division. He was a young lieutenant in one of its regiments, the 27th Wolfhounds, a regiment that later would make itself famous in Korea. Ent had entered West Point in 1946 but had failed in German and had not survived his plebe year. After recovering from his disappointment, which was considerable, he applied for Officer Candidate School and was accepted. By 1950 Ent was back where he wanted to be—in the army. And he was just in time, as it turned out, to be thrown into the war in Korea.

On the fifth of July we got the word. We crossed from Moji, Japan, to Pusan on what I think was a Japanese fertilizer boat. It was jammed with troops. If enemy planes had attacked us, that would have been the end, because all we had for protection were a couple of .30-caliber machine guns mounted on the bridge.

We landed at Pusan on the tenth. We were lucky, I feel. Our regiment was in Korea from the tenth to the twenty-fourth of July before we actually experienced combat. We had two full weeks to get acclimated to the terrain, to the weather, to conditions in general—unlike the men of the 24th Division who went in just before us. Some of those units were there only four or five days when they got into some pretty tough fighting.

We moved around a lot during those two weeks. The defensive perimeter that was eventually thrown up around the port of Pusan had not been formed yet. Conditions were still pretty chaotic. We had no contact with the American units that had gone in just ahead of us. Our job was to backstop South Korean units, the ones that were still fighting.

Of course we'd heard about what had happened to Task Force Smith. We were surprised that they hadn't been able to stop the North Koreans. But I think what really bothered us was that the North Koreans hadn't shown any awe, any respect if you will, for the American units that had been put in their way. There had been a definite feeling, not articulated maybe but very much in people's minds, that the North Koreans would quit when they found out they were facing American troops. Of course they hadn't quit. Task Force Smith, and the 24th Division's other regiment, the 34th, had been badly beaten up.

On the twenty-third of July we moved to a place called Sangyong-ni and dug in there. We relieved elements of a South Korean division. I can remember them moving back through us in the evening, a column of small men in dirty faded fatigues, some of them barefoot, some without weapons. We were supposed to be relieving a division, but there weren't very many of them left.

My company took up a position on the right side of a road that ran through a series of low hills. There was no vegetation on these hills, none at all, and when the usual ground fog we had over there lifted in the morning, I knew the enemy would be able to see us.

But I remembered all this schooling I'd had about grazing fields of fire, so I thought if I had some of my men dig in on the side of this hill, the side facing the enemy, we'd have these long grazing fields of fire. So I had them dig in there.

That turned out to be a very serious mistake.

In the morning, as the haze was lifting, one of my BAR men saw a form running toward the platoon on my right, and he fired and killed the man. It turned out to an American. We found that out pretty quickly, when the other men in the platoon started swearing and yelling at us. As the fog lifted that platoon got into some pretty heavy fighting. In some instances hand-to-hand. All day long. My platoon was receiving mortar and long-range machine-gun fire. I didn't have visual contact with all my squads, so I didn't know what was happening across my platoon.

To add to the confusion, at one point the North Koreans came through with tanks. Some of the tanks got into our rear, far enough back to where they were firing into the battalion command post. By this time we had the 3.5-inch rocket launchers, which could stop a T-34 tank. Between the rocket launchers and the air strikes that were called in we knocked off six or eight North Korean tanks.

At the end of all this, just as evening was coming on, we were ordered to withdraw. And that's when I discovered that the men I had ordered to dig in on the side of that hill were dead. Every one of them. Twelve men. I had thirty-six men in the morning, and twenty-four at the end of the day. Those twelve men were all dead, and they were dead either in their foxholes or just next to the foxholes, killed as they were trying to crawl away. I'd put them in a position they couldn't really defend, or even get away from if they had to. Had I put them near the top of the slope, or on the reverse slope, some of them might have survived.

Well, that was pretty traumatic. But you learn things very quickly in combat. And one of the things you learn is to put your losses behind you. You can't dwell on losses or you become ineffective. I had the rest of my platoon to lead, and I had to go on from there.

We withdrew that night in a very orderly fashion. Just exactly the way the book tells you to do it. We did this very quietly and carefully. The North Koreans didn't know we had withdrawn, and the next morning they launched an attack against our old positions. Our artillery and air caught them out there in the open and just tore the hell out of them. Shot 'em to pieces.

I should mention that I did not feel any personal animosity toward the enemy. My attitude was that the other guy, whoever he might be, North Korean, Chinese, Russian, whatever, was serving his country and following orders, just as I was doing for my country. I will say, however, that I don't think that was the normal attitude. Many men fought with a visceral hatred of the enemy. Maybe the fact that they were Orientals had something to do with it. "Gooks" was the standard term for them, and it was easier to think of them as not quite human, as something beneath us.

After our first action we moved to another position, near Hwang-gan. That was about the twenty-sixth of July. And there I made another mistake. I had a rifleman in one of my squads who wore glasses, and he broke his glasses and couldn't see worth a hoot. So I told my medic to take the guy back to the aid station. But I had the medic leave his medical kit with me. Shortly after this we came under intense mortar fire. Really intense. The North Koreans were very good with mortars. Every time a round landed, people were killed or wounded. And where was my medic? I'd sent him off to the rear.

Well, I had his bag. So after every salvo I would run out to see what I could do. I went to this one hole and there were two guys in it. A mortar round had gone right into the hole. One of the guys was slumped over dead. The other one had half his face blown away. His throat was open and it was completely filled with blood. I couldn't save that guy. Others I was able to help, but it was the medic who should have been there.

The company finally got orders to withdraw. I was patching up a guy who had been hit in the leg, and by the time I was done everybody else was gone. Me and this wounded guy were the last ones out of there. We took off down the hill, went down along a creek, and on the other side of the creek I could see a warrant officer I knew, and a fellow with a BAR. And I could see this kid with the BAR is really hanging in there, firing away, holding his ground, trying to give the stragglers like me a chance to get away.

Back in Japan I'd been on what was called a Three Six Eight board. The board was throwing people out of the service. If you got a couple doses of VD and were AWOL once or twice, out you went. Well, this kid that was on the BAR was one of the cases that hadn't been completed yet. He was one of the guys we were going to throw out of the army. And I can remember this warrant officer, in the middle of all this chaos and confusion, standing up and yelling across the creek to me, "Hey, lieutenant, what do you think of this guy now?"

I said to myself, "Yeah." That's another thing you learn. You just can't tell ahead of time who's going to perform well in combat. Very often it's the guy who gives you the most trouble in peacetime.

After Hwanggan we reorganized and took up another blocking position. The North Koreans continued to advance, and there was still not a uniform line to stop them. There was an enclave of a battalion here, another battalion there, and there were huge holes all over the place. We were simply trying to slow the enemy down until we could get some organization.

19

I know now what was happening. I know now that Task Force Smith was supposed to delay the enemy until the 25th Division and the 1st Cavalry Division could get to Korea. I know now that even as we retreated all through July, General Walker knew exactly where he was going and what he was going to do when he got there. He was going to prevent the capture of the port of Pusan by establishing a perimeter defense around it, and he was going to hold this perimeter until he got enough men and supplies through Pusan to go back on the offensive.

I know all that now. But at the time, on my level, the troop level, there wasn't any sense of a coherent strategy. It seemed like we were continually falling back, and there was no indication where it would end. There was a real fear that we'd be pushed right out of Korea.

You have to imagine the chaos. All the roads were jammed with civilian refugees. Sometimes it seemed like everybody in the country was trying to go south. From one position we were on we overlooked a railroad, and we could see these trains coming through, with the outside of the cars just alive with people. They were hanging on the sides, on the roofs, they were jammed in over the couplings. And there were South Korean soldiers mixed in with the civilians.

It was early August before what is now called the Pusan perimeter began to solidify. And even after it did, it wasn't a solid defensive line. We didn't have enough troops for that. It was just a line on a map, running behind the Naktong River and then north and west through the mountains to the Sea of Japan.

The defense of that line was basically a series of violent, isolated fights. The North Koreans would attack in a particular sector, and we'd meet them with everything that could be pulled together. Whoever happened to be close enough.

Sometimes *we* attacked. On the second of August my battalion was involved in an attack toward the town of Chinju, and it was a piece of cake for a while. We moved along the road in trucks, jeeps and tanks. About halfway to Chinju the road made a hard turn and entered a long narrow valley between two hills. This was the Chinju Pass, and as soon as the lead company got in there they were hit. The North Koreans really beat them up. Lots of heavy machine-gun and rifle fire. My best friend was killed there. He was the CO of their weapons platoon. He was shot in the head.

We finally drove the North Koreans out of there. The artillery, which was farther back, just dropped their gun trails on the road and laid it on, and we counterattacked with elements from my company and pushed them off the hills.

We were forming up to continue when we learned that the enemy had closed around behind us. It was the same old story. It's what all the units fighting in those early days of the war experienced. The North Koreans would fix us in position with an attack, then envelop our flanks and get behind us. It was classic. And they did it over and over again. We simply did not control enough of the terrain to prevent it. We were always without flanks, out there on our own.

We turned around and went back to Chindong. Regimental headquarters was there, in a schoolhouse at the foot of a series of hills. They put us up on the hills, and early in the morning we were hit again.

It was havoc again for a while. I remember a 155mm howitzer battery was down in the school courtyard. The crews had scattered when the firing started, and the guns were facing in the wrong direction. But I thought that if I could get a couple of those guns turned around, we could really give the enemy fits. I went down there into the courtyard, and like a ninny I tried to turn one of the guns around by myself. All the artillerymen were hiding behind the school buildings, and I cursed and swore at them to come and help me, but I couldn't get a single one of them to move.

Our regimental CO, Colonel Michaelis, and some others finally got things organized, and we counterattacked and eventually killed about six hundred of the enemy.

We held the Pusan perimeter from the beginning of August to the middle of September. During that time fresh troops and supplies kept coming in through Pusan, until we actually outnumbered the North Koreans. By now the enemy was at the end of a very long supply line, with no air cover to speak of, and it's been debated whether the North Koreans could have exploited a breakthrough even if they'd been able to achieve one.

But at the time I had no sense of any of that. At my level we were simply trying to stay alive from day to day, and survive to the next day. At the platoon and squad level you're about as close as you can get to the enemy, and most times you have no idea what might be happening a thousand yards from your own position, let alone across the front.

I didn't feel I was defending the port of Pusan, or the rights of the South Koreans, or the interests of the United States. I was simply trying to stay alive. To survive from one moment to the next, to survive the day, to survive the next day. Some people are exhilarated by combat. They love it. They seem to thrive on it. I knew people like that. Most people though, ninety-nine percent of them, are scared to death. Including myself. It's only after it's all over that the grand design falls into place, and you begin to see what you had a hand in doing.

CHAPTER 4

All Glory Forever

What Uzal Ent's regiment had been doing, once it was inside the Pusan perimeter, was acting as General Walker's emergency reserve, a fire brigade that would rush from one breach in the line to another. Walker was in command of the Eighth Army, and it was his divisions that were being committed to the fight, and he was enough of a general to see, very early on, that the North Koreans would push for the port of Pusan, on the extreme southeastern tip of the peninsula, for by capturing Pusan they could sever his supply line into the country.

Walker's plan, appearances to the contrary, was carefully orchestrated: he would delay the North Koreans for as long as possible, in the meantime leapfrogging his units back behind the Naktong River, the last natural barrier before Pusan.

By the third of August everyone was behind the river, and the long, desperate struggle to defend this last line of defense began. In the meantime reinforcements continued to flow in through the port Walker was holding open. The 2nd Infantry Division arrived from Fort Lewis, Washington, the 5th Regimental Combat Team from Hawaii, the British Brigade from Hong Kong.

And the 1st Provisional Marine Brigade swaggered in from Camp Pendleton, California.

The marines arrived in a blaze of publicity, and they proceeded to live up to their press notices. They were tough, disciplined fighters, with an esprit that had been noticeably lacking among many of Walker's army units. Walker used them as another fire brigade, shifting them from one hotspot to another along the perimeter, wherever his thinly spread forces needed help.

Arnold Winter was a twenty-year-old PFC at the time, and he remembers how it was to be used hard in hundred-degree heat, to fight up and down hills only to be given more hills to take, to see friends die, to risk death yourself . . . and all with a reputation to live up to.

I was in Hawaii, in the middle of war games, when the word came that they wanted the marines in Korea.

My raider unit packed up and sailed for California that same day. They were forming the 1st Provisional Marine Brigade at Camp Pendleton, and they were doing it fast.

At Pendleton I was assigned to the 5th Marines, which was going to be the Brigade's rifle regiment. I was given a BAR, a Browning automatic rifle. Actually it's a portable machine gun. It's got an awesome rate of fire, five hundred rounds a minute on full automatic. And it's very dependable in the field. But it's heavy. I had to carry that big BAR and fifteen to twenty ammo clips, plus my pack, entrenching tool, canteen, C rations. I was carrying eighty pounds of gear, and I only weighed a hundred thirty-eight.

We left on troopships out of San Diego. Sixty-five hundred marines, and they'd gotten us together and moving in five days. The Commandant gave us a little send-off speech. Supposedly he told us, "You boys clear this up in a couple of months, or I'll be over there to see you!" But if he said that, I don't remember it. What I remember him saying was, "You're going over to do a service for our country, and some of you won't be coming back."

It was a long, slow trip. We were not allowed to write letters home. Back in Camp Pendleton we'd been told not to discuss anything about any of this with anybody. Not that we knew much. We knew we were going to Korea, and that the army was taking a beating over there, but for a PFC like me, that was it.

As we were crossing the ocean the Pusan perimeter kept shrinking, and I heard later that guys were making bets we'd be kicked out of Korea before the Brigade could get there, but personally I wasn't aware of that. I don't remember getting any news at all about what was happening. And I don't remember being very curious. I was more interested in what we'd be having for chow each day.

We landed at Pusan and they put us on flatcars on a narrow-gauge railroad. We rode the train for a while, then we loaded onto trucks. We rode the trucks only for a few miles, and then we got out and started walking.

We reached our positions very early in the morning. Right away we came under North Korean artillery fire, and I learned to dig a foxhole like you wouldn't believe. I'd dig, and when I'd hear a shell coming in I'd put what part of my body I could in the hole, to save that part. I kept digging, through rocks and roots and everything, until I had a hole big enough to get my entire body in. I could feel the hot wind every time a shell landed close by. Our captain was hit that morning. He got his arm all mangled up from a piece of shrapnel. The shelling lasted about forty minutes, and that was our initiation to the war.

We were never in one position for very long. The North Koreans never had a chance to attack us, because we were always attacking them. We would send out patrols along the roads to draw their fire, and once we knew their positions we'd call in our Corsairs and they'd drop napalm and white phosphorus and then artillery would come in and we'd really tear them up.

We had our setbacks. One patrol walked into an ambush and out of thirteen men in the patrol ten were hit. Not all of them were killed outright. When the rescue party got to the bodies some had their skulls smashed in, and some had puncture wounds. I don't recall during those first weeks having an opportunity to take prisoners, but after that I don't think it was likely we would have taken any even given the chance.

Also there were casualties from friendly fire. We would throw out flags for the Corsair pilots, and they would come in and strafe right up to the red flags. But sometimes they'd screw up and shoot our own guys. And a couple of times our own artillery hit us.

After three or four days we'd punched a hole about twenty-five miles deep in the line. Then we were ordered to give up all that ground and pull back. We thought that was crazy, but you don't question orders.

What we didn't know was that the North Koreans had punched another hole of their own. Up to the north of us they'd gotten an entire division across the Naktong River, which was our last line of defense. If they pushed out from where they were and captured the highway at Miryang, that was it. We'd have to withdraw from Korea. The army had already counterattacked several times and failed to get them out of there, so they called us.

We were trucked to the town of Miryang, given our first hot meal and our first full night's rest since we'd landed, and in the morning we formed up for the attack.

To push the North Koreans back across the river we had to kick them off a series of ridges. Air strikes and artillery had pounded those ridges until they were bare of vegetation, but the North Koreans were still up there when we jumped off.

It was straight uphill. No cover. There were machine guns, mortars, grenades going off. The volume of fire was terrific. They were pouring everything they had into us. Guys were cursing and yelling and dropping all around me, and I was never so scared in my life. I don't think even our commanders thought we were going to make it, but we kept going and pushed right up to the top. Somebody from *Time* magazine was there, watching us charge up the ridge through all that fire, and we got written up in an article. I haven't looked at it in a while, but I remember a line that guy had in his story. "All glory forever to the bravest men I ever saw."

But I can't say I was brave. That's not why I charged up that hill. There was the fear of disobeying an order. In the marines, even an order from a corporal is like an order from a general. When they gave you an order to go, you went, in spite of everything. And there was also the fear of letting your buddies down. There's an almost

26

unbelievable loyalty among men in a rifle company, and you don't want to be the guy to break that bond. You didn't want to die, but you also didn't want to embarrass yourself by failing your buddies.

We charged over the first ridge and down into a valley, and this machine-gun fire started. It went through my pack and through my trouser legs and finally I hit the ground and played dead until the gun stopped shooting at me. Somebody must have knocked it out, because my sergeant yelled for me to get up and get across the valley, which I did. I ran across the valley and up the next ridge, and then artillery came in on us. I jumped into a ditch where there were some trees still standing, and the explosions started blowing the branches of the trees down on top of me. All I could do was pray like hell.

When it started to let up a little I got out of there. Another machine gun opened up. One of my buddies got shot through both legs and both arms. Through the bones. He was screaming his head off. Somebody called for air support, and a Corsair came over and dropped a five-hundred-pound bomb right in front of our positions. My ears came out of my head when that bomb went off. They were ringing like sirens. I couldn't sleep for three days and nights after that.

By noon of the second day we took the second ridge, the highest one, and when the gooks lost the high ground they started running. My sergeant ordered me to shoot at them with my BAR, but they must have been a thousand yards away by then. I shot at them anyway, because that's what I was ordered to do, but I couldn't tell from that distance if I hit any. Some of them fell, but they could've been playing dead, the way I did.

We drove them back into the river, and that's when the real slaughter started. Swarms of them were trying to swim across, and our Corsairs and artillery caught them out there in the open. Some of the pilots reported that the river actually turned red.

We handed those positions over to an army unit, and then we moved again.

A lot of what happened later blurs in my mind. The exact sequence of things. Because we were moving all the time. What I do remember is the heat. We'd climb these long hills . . . first we'd have to assault and capture them, then we'd have to go back down, load up with rations and ammunition, and climb back up again. A lot of guys went down with heat stroke. They gave us salt tablets, but it seemed like the salt would come right out of you. It would crystallize on your forearms and face like a thick crust.

Several times we moved into positions where the dead had not been taken away. They were usually army positions that had just been overrun or fought over. It wasn't necessary to dig in, the foxholes would already be there, and we'd move in and spend the night among hundreds of corpses. Some would be ours, but most would be theirs.

I had no sympathy for the North Koreans. I never saw any of their atrocities myself, but there were quite a few reports of American GIs who were found shot in ditches with their hands tied behind their backs. Apparently they took no prisoners. They also practiced a tactic where they would herd hundreds of Korean civilians ahead of them when they assaulted a position. It didn't happen to my unit, thank God, but we understood there would always be women and children mixed in with the North Korean soldiers.

Eventually we made four separate counterattacks against four different enemy positions, and the story went around that a captured North Korean officer, when he was being interrogated, refused to believe that the same unit had made all four attacks. He thought there were four marine divisions in the area.

They used us hard. Those were desperate days. We were hanging on to that perimeter by our fingernails. The only thing that kept us going was our discipline. And for me personally, my faith.

By the end of it most of my original platoon was gone. Killed or wounded. Those of us who survived simply went on to another operation. I didn't notice it at the time, but toward the end of August, while we were still patrolling out of the Bean Patch,[1] they started moving some of our heavy equipment back to Pusan and putting it on ships. A week or two later we were quietly pulled off the line. We weren't told anything, but one thing we knew, we weren't going home.

---

[1] The Marine Brigade had established a rest area near the town of Masan, in what had originally been a large bean field.

CHAPTER 5

Chromite

Holding the Pusan perimeter was only one part of General Douglas MacArthur's grand design for winning the war in Korea. The other part was an amphibious landing deep behind enemy lines that would cut off and destroy the entire North Korean army in the south.

With his headquarters in Tokyo, MacArthur had been the Supreme Allied Commander in Japan since the end of World War II. Shortly after the United Nations passed its historic resolution on June 27 calling on member nations to come to the aid of South Korea, officially making this undeclared war a UN effort, MacArthur was appointed Supreme Commander of all UN forces.

Even before his appointment MacArthur had flown to Korea for a firsthand look at the fighting. According to his own account, he stood on a hill overlooking the Han River and watched as the shattered South Korean army retreated from Seoul, and as the retreat washed around him he conceived the idea of an amphibious assault at Inchon, a coastal city thirty miles to the west that served as a seaport for Seoul.

MacArthur's original plan for the Inchon landing proved to be wildly unrealistic. He had wanted to make the assault by the middle of July, using one of the Eighth Army's divisions then stationed in Japan. But MacArthur, like everyone else, had vastly underestimated the professionalism and fighting qualities of the North Korean army. Throughout July the North Koreans smashed through every American unit that was placed in their way, until it appeared they would take over the entire peninsula before the month was out, and it soon became obvious that an amphibious landing behind the lines would have to be put off until the North Koreans were checked and the fighting in the south stabilized.

When it appeared that the defensive perimeter around Pusan would hold, MacArthur went forward once again with his plans for an Inchon landing. He set a new target date of September 15. The army's 7th Infantry Division would go in, along with the 1st Marine Division, with the marines as the spearhead.

Part of this marine division, the 5th Marine Regiment, was already in Korea, fighting as the Provisional Marine Brigade in the Pusan perimeter. So the 5th Marines were quietly pulled out of the line early in September. Meanwhile the call had already gone out to the rest of the division, which was scattered all over the United States, to prepare to go to war.

Ed Simmons, who would spend thirty-six years of his life as a marine and eventually retire as a brigadier general, was a young major in command of a weapons company when the order came to ship out. Simmons was then stationed at Camp Lejeune, the big marine base in North Carolina, and from there he had watched the progress of this new war in Korea (which the newspapers were still calling a "police action"): the invasion late in June, the introduction of U.S. ground forces in July, their steady retreat to the defense line thrown up around the port of Pusan, the fight to hold the perimeter. But Inchon was a closely guarded secret, and what Ed Simmons could not know was that he would not be a part of anything that had gone before. Instead, he would be at the spearpoint of one of the boldest and riskiest amphibious landings ever attempted.

When the word came we moved immediately by train from Camp Lejeune to Camp Pendleton in California, where we got the replacements we needed to build the division up to war strength. These men came to us mostly from the Reserve, and they proved to be excellent replacements. Most were World War Two veterans. They were experienced combat marines, and that's a fact that can't be made too much of. That single fact, the quality of the men who were called back to active duty and who made up the bulk of the marine units sent to Korea, had a lot to do with the outstanding performance of the marines over there.

Not to say there wasn't any grousing. Most of them didn't like the idea of being called back in. After World War Two they had stayed in the Reserve really as a kind of social thing, like a fraternal organization. Nobody was expecting that we'd have another war five years later.

By late August we were in Japan. Our troops in Korea had by this time fallen back behind the Pusan perimeter. We knew the situation was critical, and we thought we'd be used to reinforce the perimeter.

Then we were made aware that there was going to be an amphibious landing at Inchon.

The field-grade officers of the regiment were gathered aboard this transport, which was serving as regimental headquarters. In the wardroom we were briefed on the landing we were going to make. We would have this fourteen-foot seawall to go over. There were these treacherous tides that would make the landing extremely time sensitive. We would not have tactical surprise, because there were two small islands at the harbor entrance that would have to be reduced first. We would be going into a narrow winding channel with no room for maneuver. There would be no time for rehearsals.

We started looking around at each other. The whole thing looked like an invitation to disaster. I didn't know it at the time, but the leadership of the Marine Corps had great reservations about it. The navy flat out didn't want to do it. But MacArthur had brought everyone around. His personal powers of persuasion were incredible. And of course his confidence knew no bounds. There was that famous meeting held on the twenty-third of August in Tokyo, with all the top military people, that ended with MacArthur going to the map and saying, "We will land at Inchon, and I will crush them."

Our regimental commander was the legendary Lewis B. Puller, probably the most battle-scarred and decorated marine in the history of the Corps. And after we'd listened with the gravest of reservations to the briefing, Chesty Puller got up and gave one of his famous inspirational speeches. It went about like this: "I don't give a blank how many blankety-blank Koreans are defending the blankety-blank beach. We'll find out what's on the beach when we get there. And as far as you people are concerned, I had to wait twenty years between wars, while you get one every five years. You've been willing to live by the sword, and you'd damn well better be willing to die by the sword."

With that reverberating in our heads, we were sent out to start loading for Inchon.

From the transport we boarded this rusty travesty of a landing ship. The landing ships turned out to be old surplus LSTs that had been used by the Japanese for interisland trade and whatnot. They were not at all seaworthy. Ours kept breaking down. The crew had been patched together at the last minute. The navy lieutenant who commanded it couldn't get his mind off that orange grove he wanted to retire to in California.

The invasion started on the morning of September 15 with the assault on Wolmi-do, a fortified island just outside the harbor. Wolmi-do had to be taken first, and the plan was to take it on the morning tide with one battalion of marines, who would then hold it until the rest of the invasion force came in on the evening tide to take Inchon itself, one segment landing on Red Beach and the other on Blue Beach.

The two beaches were four miles apart, at opposite ends of the city. I was assigned to Blue Beach, and I was on the bridge of our LST for most of the day, listening to what I could of the radio traffic, and trying to see what I could. It was a misty day with light rain, and with the smoke of the naval gunfire and the burning city, it made for a very heavy smog over the landing area.

Wolmi-do was taken on schedule. The morning tide went out, and as we waited for the evening tide the navy continued to fire on Inchon. The Corsairs flew in all day strafing and bombing. One of the most awesome sights was the rocket ships, the "floating shotguns" as they were called. Within a space of about ten minutes one of these ships could release a thousand rockets, and I remember how they would go off with a terrific whoosh, practically all at once, and streak off into the gloom with fiery red tails.

At about three in the afternoon we loaded into our amtracs, and when we pulled away from the LST the first thing I looked for was a guide boat. These were vessels equipped with radios and various other gear to keep the landing boats from getting lost.

When we found one I went up onto the bridge and asked for directions to Blue Beach Two. A semi-hysterical ensign pointed to where the smoke was the thickest and said, "That way, I think."

So we started off in that direction, and presently an LCVP came alongside my amtrac. I thought that was our wave guide, but it turned out to be a boatload of Koreans who were being parceled out as interpreters.

Two of these Koreans tumbled into my boat. Well, whatever language they knew, English wasn't one of them. We couldn't make ourselves understood.

I had a map, and finally I decided I'd have to figure things out for myself. But I didn't have a compass, so I asked the amtrac driver if there was one in the amtrac.

He looked at his instrument panel and shrugged. "Search me," he said. "Six weeks ago I was driving a truck in San Francisco."

That's generally the way things went. It was a scene of almost total chaos. Various waves of the invasion force were wandering around in confusion, trying to find their way to the beaches through this immense pall of smoke. And by this time it was also getting dark. There were nowhere near the number of guide boats there should have been. I've said many times that if those beaches had been defended by Germans or Japanese of World War Two caliber, we would not have gotten ashore at Inchon. But they were defended by second-rate troops. And not very many of them.

We finally did manage to find our sector and get ashore. What the boats in the first wave did was come in against the seawall, throw ladders against the wall, and it was up and over the ladders as other marines in the boats lobbed grenades over the wall. But by the time I landed there were big holes in the wall, and we went through one of those.

In front of us there was an open stretch of about a hundred yards, well pockmarked by shell craters, and then some partially destroyed warehouses. Occasionally bullets whined by, but there wasn't a lot of enemy fire, and we were able to move quickly to our assigned positions just outside the town.

Once we secured the beachhead the army's 7th Division, which was landing behind us, was to move through us and continue the advance. This is the way we understood it at the time. What actually happened was that the 7th Division landed behind us and then wheeled south to link up with the Eighth Army, which was hopefully breaking out of the Pusan perimeter, leaving it up to the marines to capture Seoul.

It was about twenty-five miles from Inchon to Seoul. The road was narrow, hard-surfaced, and paralleled by a railway. That road became the axis of our advance, and we moved forward in school-solution manner, in a series of well-coordinated attacks, capturing successive pieces of high ground. There was excellent support by marine air. The landing itself may have been confused, but not the advance on Seoul.

During the week it took to fight our way to the city we could feel the resistance stiffen. But the North Koreans were not attempting to hold any piece of ground to the bitter end. It was clear they were fighting a delaying action. We would attack, they would withdraw.

At Yongdungpo we had our first really hard fight. The town is on the opposite bank of the Han River from Seoul, roughly the same position that Brooklyn occupies relative to New York City, and we had a very tough fight there.

All three battalions of our regiment were involved in it. My own weapons company was on the high ground overlooking the town, supposedly in reserve, but everyone was called into the fight, and we came down off the high ground and crossed some dried over-grown rice paddies to a canal. The 1st Battalion came across those rice paddies at an angle to us, and watching them come was like watching a scene from World War One, the companies moving forward in a long line through the waist-high grass, with shot and shell going off all around them.

We had a hard time getting across the canal. We were up against this dike, and again it was like World War One, one rifle platoon after another going over the top, right into the teeth of heavy machine-gun fire from the other side. A lot of the men were hit. I remember one big red-headed marine falling back dead about ten feet away from me.

I tried to bring in mortar fire on the enemy machine guns, but my mortar lieutenant screwed up. Instead of carrying his mortar ammunition with him he'd left it on a trailer that was back on the road somewhere. He'd been trying to make it easier on his men, not having them carry those heavy mortar rounds, but now we suffered the consequences of this guy allowing himself to get separated from his ammunition.

Well, we had to reduce that machine-gun fire that was tearing us up. So I brought up all my own heavy machine guns and had the crews set them up on the brow of the dike. And we had a shootout. Water-cooled Brownings on our side, water-cooled Maxims on the other, blasting away at each other across this narrow canal.

They quit first. The North Koreans pulled back out of their positions, and we crossed the canal.

Once we crossed the Han we were given Ma Po Boulevard as the axis for our advance into Seoul. My battalion, the 3rd, had a series of objectives we were supposed to take. We were supposed to take the railroad station. We were supposed to take the National Palace.

We made this day-long attack. It was house-to-house fighting. House to house, building to building. Very bitter fighting. As soon as a particular stretch of the boulevard was taken, patrols had to be sent into the side streets and alleys to clean out snipers and hidden machine-gun nests and even tanks. I don't believe we passed a single building that somebody didn't fire into, or toss in a few grenades.

In the streets the North Koreans were fighting from behind rice-bag barricades, big bags made out of rough rice straw and filled with dirt, stacked up four and five feet high, and we had to reduce these positions one by one. By now it was clear to everybody that these were not the same type of troops we had met at Inchon, or on the way in to Seoul. These were hardcore regulars, well led and often quite fanatical. These people were not going to give up any ground. They were going to throw us back or die in the attempt.

How and George Companies were spearheading the attack for the battalion. How Company finally reached the railroad station, but they couldn't make anybody believe it. George Company, ordered to take the National Palace, was not as far along Ma Po Boulevard as they thought they were. They were about a quarter of a mile off in their map reading. They'd reached this stream, and there was a bridge across the stream, and then there was this big compound, which they thought was the National Palace.

But something was wrong, because over the radio How Company kept saying, "Hey, you're shelling us." And George Company was saying, "No, we're not."

Our units were shooting at each other, and it was clear nobody knew where anybody else was.

I was with the battalion commander, and he told me to go up and see where George Company was and get them straightened out. So I went up and found the George Company commander, and the poor man was distraught. He couldn't get across this stream. He'd tried several times but the enemy fire was too intense, and he was bogged down.

By this time we were under intense pressure to attack. I didn't know it at the time, but General Almond [the overall commander of the Inchon landing] had promised MacArthur that he would capture Seoul by September 25. That was the three-month anniversary of the North Korean invasion, and Almond, who was well aware of MacArthur's love of the grand gesture, knew it would please MacArthur no end to be able to go into the city on that day and ceremoniously hand it back to the South Koreans. It was now the afternoon of September 23, and time was running out.

So there was this intense pressure to push forward, to keep going, with no reason given. But we all felt it.

I told the George Company commander, "You've got to make another effort. You've got to get across that stream. I'll give you the best mortar preparation I can, but you've got to get across."

Well, he couldn't get across. I don't want to disparage the man, but he was about at the end of his rope at that point.

So I radioed the battalion commander and said, "We're not getting anywhere." And he said, very sensibly, "Okay, stay there for the night."

We formed a defensive line along the stream. I also set up a roadblock on Ma Po Boulevard itself, using heavy machine guns and antitank rocket launchers, and all three companies, George, How and Item, buttoned up for the night.

Then, around midnight, we were told we were going to make a night attack.

Immediately we protested, because we hadn't been able to get across the stream even in the daytime.

This was heavy pressure. We were under very heavy pressure now to attack. We didn't know the reason why, but as far as we were concerned this was insane. Because we weren't doing any of the things you're supposed to do in a night attack. You're supposed to have well-delineated objectives, you're supposed to rehearse it, you're supposed to know where you're going, you're supposed to have means of identification. And there was none of that. We were just told that we're going to attack, and that we're going to attack straight ahead.

I learned later that the attack order had come directly from General Almond. All the senior marine commanders protested the order, but Almond [who was army] was insistent. Almond had what he thought was good aerial intelligence that the North Koreans were withdrawing from the city and moving north. Well, they were probably refugees that had been spotted. The North Koreans were still very much in the city. They were right out there in front of us.

The jumpoff was delayed once or twice. Finally it was scheduled for two in the morning. I was standing in front of this Korean house that I was using as a command post, right by the cellar steps, and a few minutes before two I heard enemy armor clanking down the boulevard toward us.

My first feeling was one of relief. I thought, We're not going to have to attack after all. They're going to attack us.

I flashed a warning over the radio: enemy armor attack. And as I flashed the warning I dove for the cellar steps, kind of all in one motion, as the lead tank fired its first round. I heard the round crack by me, and I looked back for my radioman, PFC Vargas, and half of him was on the wall. That first round had gone through his stomach. It was an armor-piercing shell, which was lucky for me, because if it had been high explosive it very likely would have killed me too.

So my radioman is dead and his radio's smashed, and I'm scrambling around in the dark, and I get another radio and manage to come up on the right frequencies. I called down to the roadblock below me, and they said, "Yes, we see them. We're engaged."

I called battalion and said, "Let's have artillery. Let's have everything they can shoot."

The artillery fired all night long. And every time they'd stop shooting the tanks would start coming forward again. We're engaging tanks with everything, even machine guns. I could see the tracer rounds from the machine guns pinging off the front plates of the enemy tanks. The North Korean infantry got within assaulting distance of us, within burp gun range, but we were solidly dug in and we stopped them rather easily.

That proved to be the climax of the battle for Seoul. With daylight the North Koreans were either dead or withdrawing. There was another two days or so of mopping up, and we were still conducting these mopping up operations when we were told to prepare for MacArthur's entry into the city.

The idea was that the Americans were to be in as little evidence as possible. South Korean soldiers would be along the route of march, and also cheering and happy South Korean civilians. MacArthur and his party were to land at Kimpo airfield, cross the pontoon bridge over the Han River, then move up Ma Po Boulevard to the National Palace, where Syngman Rhee would be reinvested as the president of South Korea. The marines were to form a cordon, but to be as inconspicuous as possible.

Of course that just added to our bitterness about the whole thing. Operation Chromite was a success, Seoul had been retaken, and it was the marines who had done most of the fighting. And now they wanted us out of sight.

Chapter 6

Breakout

It took a few days for the news of the Inchon landing to reach the North Korean troops farther south who were still trying to capture Pusan, but once they realized that a large enemy force had landed in their rear it was the beginning of the end.

By September 20 the fighting around Pusan began to change from a hang-on defense by the UN to a breakout and pursuit as one after another of the North Korean divisions left the line and headed north, hoping to get back across the 38th parallel before the UN forces that had landed at Inchon could block their escape. But this meltdown of enemy resistance was quite uneven, and for Bill Glasgow and many other men who had been fighting in the Pusan perimeter the breakout was not a sudden push forward. "It was more like push and shove," Glasgow recalls. "We pushed, and once we got across the Naktong River they damn well shoved back."

I arrived in Korea with the 2nd Infantry Division from Fort Lewis, Washington, around the middle of August, and as soon as we got there they busted us down into battalions so they could spread us around and put us where we could do the most good.

My first real hard fight was on the thirty-first of August, in front of the Naktong River. I was a first lieutenant and I had an infantry platoon, about forty men, and with those forty men I was supposed to hold twenty-six hundred yards of front.

So what I did was occupy these four little hilltops. There was no other way to do it. You can't stretch forty men along almost a mile and a half of front. The only chance I had of holding that sector was to hold onto the high ground.

That night the better part of two North Korean regiments walked through my positions. We knew they were coming. We could see the Naktong River from our foxholes, and the rafts that were hidden just under the water on the other side of the river. And toward dusk we could see all these little pointed heads moving around in the rice paddies. So we knew we were going to be hit that night.

They came through about midnight, but before they came across we saw a strange torchlight procession in the hills across the river. I tried to get my artillery forward observer to fire on it, but he wouldn't call in the fire mission because he thought the North Koreans had lined up a bunch of refugees and were making them march around by torchlight. So I finally got Colonel Freeman, our regimental commander, on the line, and he said to the forward observer, "Do you see all that stuff Glasgow's reporting up there?" And the artillery guy says, "Yeah, sure, but—" And Freeman just cuts him off and says, "Well get some damn artillery fire going."

So we had all the division artillery firing for us, the 105s and also the big 155s. The shells from the 155s would pass just above our foxholes before landing on the other side of the river, and they'd make this terrific freight-train noise going over.

At about nine o'clock we lost all communications. Probably the North Koreans had already infiltrated and cut the telephone wires. Around eleven o'clock the order went out to withdraw, but of course my platoon never got it. We were still there at midnight when the two regiments of North Koreans came across the river.

It was two and a half days before we got out of there. Once I realized we were behind the enemy lines, that they'd gone right through us and were behind us, I had everybody leave their positions and start back. The North Koreans knew we were there, because that first night we had a sharp fight with some of them. For the entire two and a half days they had patrols out looking for us, but we managed to avoid them all and link up with one of our own units, except that the battalion we linked up with was also surrounded. So we weren't out of it yet.

We got a tank platoon together and with the tanks in the lead we lined up and busted out of there finally, after some hard fighting. Once we got out they put us on trucks and hauled us back up around Yongson. That's where we joined the French Battalion. By now both Britain and France had sent troops to Korea, and they were fighting with us in the perimeter.

We were on the line in front of Yongson for about a week before the breakout finally came. You'd have the mosquitoes and the flies and the heat pestering you all day, and the North Koreans pestering you at night. When they weren't coming at you head on, they were constantly trying to infiltrate the line. I remember a kid we had with us named Forner, who probably weighed ninety-eight pounds soaking wet. We gave Forner a carbine to carry instead of an M-1, because a carbine was lighter. Lucky for him, you can also get off more rounds a lot faster with a carbine. One night Forner jumps up and yells "Gooks!" and sprays 360 degrees around his foxhole, and the next morning we found three dead ones right there, one with his hand draped over Forner's hole.

The breakout came on September 16. It was timed to the Inchon landing. But I only learned that later, after the war. For guys at my level, you don't get that kind of information. Nobody came around at the time saying, "All right, we're going to start the breakout today."

We were kind of expecting it though, because for one thing, we'd heard about the big landing up at Inchon. And about that time our division's 3rd Battalion came up and joined us. They were fresh troops, and the only reason they'd put a battalion of fresh troops on the line was for a big push.

And we had already begun to feel a difference in the way the fighting was going. We could feel their initiative slowly turning into our initiative.

We jumped off on the sixteenth, but as soon as we got across the Naktong River the North Korean resistance really stiffened up.

I was hit the first night after we'd crossed the river. We were nearly overrun by a heavy counterattack and I took a round through my helmet. It knocked the helmet off my head and scraped the scalp and I bled so much I thought for sure I'd been shot through the head. But actually it was just a grazing wound. Anyway I couldn't stop to think about it, because at night like that they'd get in on us real close, only ten or twenty yards away, and I was standing there holding my damn helmet with a hole in it in one hand and firing my machine gun with the other.

The next day I got hit for real. I was kneeling on the ground, yelling over to some forward observers from a 4.2-inch mortar to put some fire up on a hill, when *whop*, I got hit in the right lung by a round from probably one of their .28-caliber sniper rifles.

It picked me up and spun me completely around. There was this terrific burning feeling, like a hot poker going through me. After the bullet went through my lung it hit the ribs on the right side and spiraled down the rib cage and went through the tip of my liver and finally came out my back through a kidney. I learned all that later, from the doctors. At the time all I knew was I'd been hit really bad. My right side was on fire, the inside of my boots were soggy and there was blood all over my fatigues.

I was lying on the ground in the open, between two groups of my men, and to this day I don't know how I did it but I got up and ran until I couldn't run anymore. When I collapsed I was pretty close to some of the men, and they put me on a poncho and carried me out of there.

When they got me down the hill one of the medics started putting plasma into me. Then they put me on a jeep and took me to the regimental aid station. The regimental surgeon came out and took one look at me, then turned to the medic who was putting in the plasma and said, "Keep it going."

42

They got me back across the Naktong to the division collection station at Miryang, and that ride was sheer hell. I thought the pain was going to break me apart. It felt like my whole body was on fire. They gave me morphine but it didn't seem to have any effect at all. Every time we hit a bump it felt like somebody was sticking hot ice picks into me. I prayed I'd black out, but I didn't. I didn't think it was possible to feel that much pain and not black out.

By the time I got to the collection station I had a raging thirst, but they wouldn't give me anything to drink until I urinated and they saw it was almost pure blood. Then they realized it was one of my kidneys that had been hit and not my stomach, and I finally got something to drink.

From Miryang a helicopter took me to an army field hospital. They performed some operations there, stuck a bunch of tubes in me, and the next day I was taken down to Pusan and put on a Swedish hospital ship, and from there I was taken to Japan.

I never went back to Korea. That was September, and I didn't get out of the hospital until the following February, and when I did, I was sent back to the States.

So the big push went on without me.

CHAPTER 7

Death All Day

*Eighth Army's breakout from the Pusan perimeter was not dramatic,
it was slow and hard and uneven, with some units meeting less
resistance and making better progress than others. In fact the breakout was really a matter of the North Korean divisions voluntarily
withdrawing from the fight because of their fear of being trapped,
rather than being pushed out of their positions.*

*But once the North Koreans did begin to withdraw they wasted
no time abandoning the battlefield. As they streamed north in great
haste, pounded incessantly by UN air strikes, Eighth Army's pursuit
turned into a roadmarch. The challenge now was just to keep up
with the fleeing enemy. One unit near the west coast, an armored
column from the 1st Cavalry Division, covered 105 miles in three
days, finally linking up with some 7th Division soldiers who were
moving south from Seoul.*

*By early October the headlong UN pursuit was getting all the
attention in the newspapers, but something was already happening
in the wake of the victorious UN forces that would later generate*

even bigger headlines, and for many people in the West, an enduring and implacable hatred of the enemy.

A gruesome discovery was being made. A young sergeant from Texas named Bill Chambers had a hand in it and he remembers being shaken by what he saw, at a time when he didn't think anything you could show him on a battlefield would bother him. Chambers was with a graves registration company, and every working day he was required to look upon death in all its forms.

It was funny how they tried to set you up for it. When we were in Yokohama, on our way over to Korea, an officer came up to us and said, "I'm taking you to see the army mortuary." Because at that point none of us had ever seen a dead body before. They wanted to break us in, get us used to seeing these things. So they took us to the army mortuary, and we went up and down the aisles. There were gurneys on both sides, with dead bodies on them. They pulled back the sheets to give us a good look. The army mortuary at that time handled all the American dependents in Japan, so there were not only GI bodies but women there too. And we got a good look at all of them. But let me tell you, it didn't help. You thought it helped, until you saw what bodies looked like on a battlefield.

Our real education started after we got over there. We landed at Pusan and the next morning we got into some trucks and we were taken to the military cemetery at Taegu and shown what to do. How to go about identifying the bodies. That was our job: identify the battle dead, collect all the personal effects for shipment home, and see that the bodies were properly buried.

There was still heavy fighting going on up along the Pusan perimeter, and they were bringing the dead in by truck. We'd leave work at night with the collection tent empty, and in the morning the tent would be full of bodies, with more bodies stacked all around. They'd come in all through the day and all night. Swollen, smelly, some with the faces all black, some with limbs missing, hands and feet missing, sometimes with the heads missing.

There was a river near where we were working, and sometimes we'd find bodies floating by us in the river. Some of these guys were killed maybe thirty or forty miles upstream. They'd been in the water for days. Once me and another fella found a body that was swollen up so much you couldn't make out the features, and as we were pulling it out of the river and trying to get it on a stretcher, to carry it over to our work area, it kind of cracked open, and all the gas sealed inside just whooshed out and hit us in the face. Talk about two sick individuals.

That wasn't typical, though. We had a routine procedure. A man comes in, first thing you do is open his mouth. You got a dental chart, and you check all his teeth. Then you go through his clothing, find his dog tags, take everything from his pockets. Everything that you find, you write down.

Sometimes we found men with grenades still in their hands, with the pin pulled. The grenade would be frozen in their hand. Then we'd have to slide a pin back in that thing and pry the fingers off of it. It used to scare us a little, because one mistake and there'd be two dead bodies there instead of one.

You take all the personal effects. Then you take all the ammunition off of him. The personal effects you put in a bag. Everything except pornographic pictures. We had an order: if you find any pornographic pictures, just tear 'em up and throw 'em away.

All the bags went to a personal effects tent. There were two clerks in the tent, and they made a list of everything that was going to be sent home. Especially money. You wouldn't think it, but some of the dead had a lot of money on them. There was an officer in the tent, and a sergeant, standing there watching. So there was no way you could steal anything. But I've never heard of a graves registration man stealing anything off a dead man. A live GI has a lot of respect for a dead GI. Besides, if you stole even a penny from a dead man, you got five years, no questions asked.

After we took care of the personal effects we buried the body. At first we were burying them in mattress covers. This was a throwback to World War Two. But mattress covers, after so long in the ground, they rot. When it comes time to dig up the body, to move it to a permanent cemetery, you got your hands full picking it up. So we started using canvas shelter halves. Now they have plastic body bags. But those things weren't around when I was in Korea. So we used canvas.

After we were at Taegu for a while the 1st Cavalry Division asked for eight graves registration people to follow our troops up into Korea, to help gather evidence for war crimes trials later on, when the war ended. This was after the breakout from the Pusan perimeter. We were chasing the North Koreans back to the 38th parallel, and some of our infantry units were finding GIs who'd been shot with their hands tied behind their backs. So me and seven other guys volunteered to go up there. We'd heard rumors about a death march, where the North Koreans just herded this big group of American prisoners along, trying to get them up into China, and shooting and killing and starving them all along the way. And then we discovered evidence that it was true.

South Korean kids, we found out, were the best source for finding out where American dead were. They wandered all over, and for a few sticks of candy they'd tell you everything. The adults wouldn't tell you, because they were scared you'd blame them for what happened.

So the kids would tell us where these graves were, and we would dig them up. And in one of them we found a chaplain. And in his Bible we found the names and serial numbers of people who had died on the trip. The chaplain had written down all the names in the margins of the pages.

That's when we started asking Koreans about what they knew. Some of them had seen columns of Americans being clubbed and shot. We kept finding more graves. It wasn't the North Koreans who buried them, it was the local people. The North Koreans couldn't care less about dead Americans.

Some of these guys had been in the ground a long time. They were hard to get out. Sometimes you could reach down and take them by the shoulders and pull them out, but most times you'd reach down and pull and they would come apart in your hands. Then you had to pick up all the pieces. We had big rubber gloves that came up to our elbows, but they were too clumsy to work with. We had to write things down, and with the gloves on you couldn't handle a pencil. So we usually worked with our bare hands. The smell was horrible, but it's funny how quickly you got used to it.

We got up above Pyongyang, up in North Korea, and we were digging up some of the prisoners who were shot in the Sunchon tunnel massacre. The North Koreans had put the American prisoners on railroad cars, to move them faster, because by then we'd landed at Inchon and recaptured Seoul, and we were pressing them hard. When they saw that we might be able to capture these prisoners and get them back, they stopped the cars in a railroad tunnel and shot everybody. We never found everybody they shot, but we found some. You could see they'd been starved. There wasn't a speck of flesh on the corpses. Almost every one we found had second wounds. Some had their skulls split open, like they'd been hit with an axe. Others had bayonet wounds. Some had a second bullet hole, usually right over the heart. The 187th Airborne was supposed to jump in and save these people, because we knew at the time where they were, but the jump got delayed four hours, and when the airborne got there it was too late.

I was in graves registration for fifteen months. Identifying the dead. Burying people. All day long. Day in and day out. I never minded it. Once you got used to certain things, it was just a job. But following the trail of that death march, seeing what the North Koreans had done to those people, I never got over that. Because those weren't battle deaths. That was more like wholesale murder.

CHAPTER 8

Into the Tunnel

Lloyd Kreider was twenty-three when he arrived in Korea, on the verge of making corporal. He was a medical aid man with the 34th Infantry Regiment, which landed right behind Task Force Smith in July 1950. After its first disastrous encounter with the enemy early that month, the 34th pulled itself together and went on to fight in the Pusan perimeter and to join in the pursuit of the North Korean army as it fled north after the Inchon landing. But even though he remained in Korea, Lloyd Kreider missed all that. Early in August he was taken prisoner, and as his regiment was fighting, Kreider was wandering among the living dead, lost to his old unit and to the world.

It was about the third or fourth of August. We were in positions along the Naktong River, and one evening I was taking care of a wounded man after the North Koreans had cut through our lines. He was shot through the chest. I really didn't know what I could do for him, if I could save him. He had a sucking chest wound. It was a mess. And I didn't have any battle dressings left. Nothing big enough for the hole he had in him. So I tore off a piece of his shirt and used that.

I don't know how long I worked on him, talking to him, trying to figure out how to get him out of there. But as I was working on him he died.

I got up to leave. To get to this guy I'd had to go way up front, ahead of everybody, and when I looked around I saw I was alone.

It was getting dark. I heard Korean voices behind me, it sounded like hundreds of them, and I realized I was cut off. I didn't know what to do then. Which way do I go? How do I get out of here?

I wandered around a little in the dark, not knowing for sure where I was, until I saw a bunch of GIs. I could just make them out. I could hear them talking. "Where's our company? Where's the company?"

I don't know why, but I didn't approach them right away. There was more talking, and this time I heard Korean voices too, and the next thing I knew these GIs were being pushed to the ground and shot. One after another.

I knew the Naktong River was close by, and I thought that if I followed the river south I'd get back to our own lines. So I found the river and walked along it for a while. I ran into some North Korean soldiers, but I was able to hide in a rice paddy until they went by.

A little later I stumbled over a body. It made a noise when my foot touched it, and I looked down and saw this star on the cap. What happened, I'd walked into a bunch of North Koreans who were sleeping. I thought that was the end of me, but the guy I'd kicked didn't come awake. He just grumbled and tossed around on the ground and then went back to sleep, so I kept going. I walked right through all of them.

I was desperate for water, because I hadn't had any all day, and later during the night I found a well and managed to get some. As it was getting light I came to a ditch. There was a high bank on each side, and along the bottom of the ditch I saw what I thought was a communications wire.

So I followed this wire, thinking it was ours. I followed it for at least a mile, until finally, up on the bank above me, I saw what looked like American soldiers. They had soft caps that looked like our forage caps. I came up out of the ditch and started walking toward them. I was so sure they were Americans.

Then four or five of them suddenly raised their rifles. I dropped to the ground and started rolling back down into the ditch. Now they were shooting at me. I was still wearing my Red Cross arm band. I wasn't wearing a helmet, I was wearing a fatigue cap at the time, and that wasn't marked, but I had the Red Cross band and I still had my medical aid pack with me.

I'm sure they noticed the band. What I didn't know was, they didn't believe in the Red Cross. I learned that later. The only Red Cross they recognized was the People's Red Army Red Cross. The International Red Cross was supported by capitalists.

They were shooting at me, and I was rolling down into the ditch like I was shot. I was hoping they'd stop firing. They didn't, and as I tried to get up the other side, *pling*, I got hit.

It felt like my head exploded. I saw a flash, and then I passed out. When I came to, there was blood pouring out of my eye. I thought I was shot through the eye. I thought my head was all gone. But it turned out I was only grazed in the head. I was bleeding a lot, but I wasn't shot. What I figure is a bullet ricocheted off a rock and cut across my forehead, or maybe a rock fragment.

The North Koreans were standing over me. They had their bayonets fixed. I thought they were going to shoot me, but all I could think about was getting a drink of water. I was so tired and thirsty I really didn't care if they shot me. All I wanted was a drink.

I asked them for water. I asked them in Japanese. "*Mizu ga hoshii desu.*" I could speak Japanese. I'd studied it in the Armed Forces Institute in Japan, and also learned it from a Japanese professor while I was on occupation duty. Most Koreans could speak Japanese. Korea was a Japanese colony for forty years, and under the Japanese it was against the law to speak Korean.

There was a small stream nearby, and they let me drink from it. They kicked me to make me stop.

One of them asked me, "What happened to your head?"

I just shrugged and pointed at his rifle.

They took all my clothes, everything but my pants. The shoes especially they wanted. They didn't have very good footwear, just a kind of tennis sneaker, and they were after American equipment.

They kept me with them, right on the front line, for about a week. They made me carry water for them. I carried their rice for them. They tried to give me a rifle, tried to get me to fight against my own people, but I just threw it back. They made me carry all their packs. I was weak, I'd had no food for days, and whenever I'd fall they'd kick me or punch me or bang me on the head with a rifle butt. I was hit so many times on the head it's a wonder I didn't go crazy. They'd jump on me with their boots and snap my back. I didn't even have my pants after a while, just some rags around my groin.

My big mistake was letting them know I spoke Japanese. Every time we ran across a new group of North Koreans, an officer would come over and interrogate me. They wanted to know how many planes we had, how many tanks we had. I was only a private first class, and a medic, but I guess they thought I knew about those things. I'd tell them anything. Five. Ten. Twenty. A hundred.

They knew I was lying, but they kept asking me. Sometimes they'd beat me. One day one of them put a pistol to my head and said he'd shoot me if I didn't tell him how many planes we had. They were really afraid of our air force. They had no planes of their own. We controlled the air, and during the daytime they were always afraid of being caught out in the open. It had happened a few times while I was with them, and I think they were mad. And for a while I was the only American they could take it out on.

I figured this guy was going to shoot me no matter what I said, so I told him a crazy story about having my own plane. When he asked me where it was, I told him I'd wrecked it.

He didn't shoot me. And they stopped asking me about those kinds of things. They got off the military angle, and started in on the political angle. What my father did. What kind of job he had. If it was people's work or capitalist's work. I told them he was a carpenter, and they said, "That's good. That's people's work."

Then they asked me what *I* did, and I told them that I was a carpenter too, but that was a mistake, because they felt my hands for callouses, and when they didn't find any, they beat me.

About a week after I was with them we picked up two more American prisoners. About fifteen to twenty, as I recall. Most were badly wounded. They started moving us north toward Seoul, and every night they would beat these wounded men with their rifle butts. Every night we traveled.

We picked up more prisoners along the way. Most were wounded or sick. We traveled mostly at night, and during the day they'd keep us in churches and schoolhouses. In every building, even in the churches, there were pictures of Stalin and Kim Il Sung, the North Korean premier.

It took us about two weeks to get to Seoul. We walked all the way, except for a few miles above Taejon where they put us on a train. During the march we got very little food. They gave us no water. We'd drink out of any mud puddle we could find. We had no shoes. A lot of us didn't have any clothes.

The wounded and the sick were continually beaten. We were not allowed to help them, and when they collapsed or couldn't walk anymore they were taken off to the side of the road and shot. The only reason they didn't shoot all of us was because the United Nations had already started complaining about North Korea shooting prisoners of war, and the North Koreans wanted to show everybody that they actually had prisoners. They were saving some of us so they could say they had prisoners and not be lying about it.

In Seoul they put us in a big schoolhouse and kept us there for two or three weeks. We got one meal each day. A cup of soup, which was just fish bones and water. That's what they called a meal.

During that time we sat through a lot of lectures and propaganda films. They were trying to teach us communism. They said one day we would go back to the States, maybe in five years, and we would go back and broadcast and teach Marxist doctrine. The good way of life, to their way of thinking.

We were questioned a lot individually. Mostly it was political. They wanted to know what you did, what kind of background you came from. All the boys turned out to be farmers or carpenters after a while. They figured that was the only way they could stay alive. They wanted to shoot me once when I told them I had a car, so I forgot about the car.

Sometimes the guards would have bayonet practice with some of the prisoners. It was a way of executing them. I don't know if they were picking out certain prisoners deliberately, or if it was just "You, you, and you," but they'd take two or three prisoners out to the courtyard and tie them up and stab them with bayonets. Whenever they did this, they would make the rest of us stand at the windows and watch.

A lot of the prisoners had been shot before they were captured and had festering wounds. The North Koreans knew I was a medic, and one day they gave me a handful of maggots and said, "Here, you're a medic, heal them." That's what they gave me. A big handful of maggots. You put the maggots on the wound and they would eat the rotten flesh. But these guys had fevers and blood poisoning and dysentery and all kinds of infections. Putting some maggots on the wound wasn't going to save the guy's life.

They put a radio in our room, and every evening for half an hour we listened to this propaganda about how they were winning, how the North Korean army was conquering all of Korea, and all that. Nobody believed any of it, but we had to listen to it every night. Then one night, it might even have been during one of those broadcasts, we heard this terrific bombardment. It wasn't close, but we could hear it very clearly, like a rumble of thunder just going on and on and on.

It was the Inchon landing. Inchon was only twenty or thirty miles away. We didn't know at the time exactly what it was, but we knew it had to be some kind of big American attack, because right away they moved us out of Seoul fast. About seven hundred of us. There was close to a thousand when we first got there, but men died every day and we were down to about seven hundred when they moved us out.

A lot of men couldn't walk, so the North Korean guards prodded them with rifle butts. When men fell, they wouldn't allow us to pick them up. They didn't want us to carry them. As we went along, each man got weaker and weaker, until none of us could walk anymore.

We had to help each other along. That's when they started taking away groups of men. I could hear rifle fire, and I thought they might be shooting these people, but I didn't know for sure until about halfway between Seoul and Pyongyang, when this one fellow who had been shot in the leg managed to get back to us, and he said they were shooting everybody who fell behind or was taken out of the column.

I figured they were going to shoot us all sooner or later. But I was close to the point where I didn't care. I'd been a prisoner for a month and a half by now. I was sick and starved and beaten down to the point where I thought I really might be better off dead. That's the way the mind works. I didn't see any end to my misery except by dying.

The road to Pyongyang was the real death march. As soon as a man fell out, he was shot or bayoneted. We were never given any food or water. Few of us had any clothes, just some rags around the waist. I think about three hundred fifty of us reached Pyongyang, out of the seven hundred that left Seoul.

In Pyongyang they put us in another school building. Men continued to die each day, and we would take them out to a graveyard and bury them. One day at the graveyard we found some leaflets that had been dropped by UN planes. One of them had a picture of General MacArthur on it, and he was appealing to the North Korean premier to end the needless bloodshed as the North Korean army had already been driven from the south. That's the first time I knew that the UN was taking over the country, and for the first time I began to think I might make it back.

We were in Pyongyang for about a week when we saw flares over the city and knew the UN forces were close by. The North Koreans moved us out again and the same way as they did in Seoul, in a hurry. I would say at least a third of the men couldn't possibly stand up, they were so weak. These men were bayoneted. A few we managed to carry out, but most were bayoneted or hit on the head with rifle butts and just left there. They obviously couldn't make the march, and the North Koreans didn't want them liberated.

We walked five or six miles, and then they put us on a train. We rode the train north through Sunchon City. When we got to the other side of the city they took us off the train and put us in a field. UN planes came over, and they put us back on the train, back into the coal cars. We were too weak to stand up, let alone run away. There was no way we could escape. Many of the men were so sick in spirit they didn't care if they lived anyway. They would as soon be dead as go through any more torture.

On the morning of the twentieth of October we pulled into a tunnel near Sunchon. The train stopped in the middle of the tunnel, and we just stayed there. It took us a while to figure out what was happening. They'd decided to kill us all in that tunnel, and they were hoping we'd suffocate from the smoke from the engine. Some of the boys did die, but it wasn't working for them. We weren't dying fast enough. There were a lot of UN planes going over, and the North Koreans were afraid we'd be liberated. So when they saw that the smoke was taking too long, they began taking us off the train in groups of forty. I could hear the burp guns firing after the first group left. I knew my life was over, but I was already as close to death as a live person can be. I had no feelings. My senses were numb. I had no mind left anymore. I was too weak to run away. I was too weak to even walk. I thought, just shoot me and get it over with.

We stayed in the tunnel until it was our time to go. I believe I was the second or third group of forty. We went down along the railroad track and turned to the right, along a ditch. They lined us up along the edge of the ditch, and then six or seven North Korean soldiers came up and pointed their burp guns at us. I knew what was going to happen, and just as they started firing I dropped, and they missed me. It looked like I'd been shot, because the guns were actually firing when I dropped, but I wasn't hit.

I dropped down into the ditch, and another man fell in on top of me, and pretty soon I had blood running down my face and all over my hands. This other guy's blood. And at this point I remember thinking, "Well, I might even get out of here alive."

After the shooting stopped the guards went around sticking everybody with bayonets, to make sure we were dead. They only got me in the kneecap. There was somebody on top of me, and I think the guards were in a hurry to leave by then. It was getting dark, and the UN forces were pretty close.

It turned out there was one other guy still alive. I could hear him crying for his mother. I found him and put my hand over his mouth to shut him up. This guy was a master sergeant, and he was too weak to walk, so I dragged him into a corn shock, and the two of us stayed inside the corn shock all night, it was so cold.

Early the next morning I saw a North Korean boy walking by, and I yelled to him in Japanese that we wanted some food. He didn't understand Japanese, he was too young, but he brought back an old man who took us down to the house and gave us food. Then he took us to Sunchon and turned us over to South Korean forces, and the South Koreans turned us over to the 187th Airborne. By now it was almost the end of October. I'd been a prisoner for only three months, but I looked like a walking dead man.

The first thing they did was spray us with DDT. We were covered with lice. Then they fed us C rations. They took us to Seoul and then we flew to Tokyo and then back to the States, to Letterman Hospital in San Francisco, where I stayed for three or four days while they gave me these psychiatric tests.

I had some problems after I got back. I started drinking. I kept having visions. Every time I saw mountains they reminded me of Korea. But I never talked about any of this before. You can't understand this kind of experience unless you've been through it.

Most people's troubles, they're petty. People think they have problems, but most people don't know what real suffering is. People like that aren't going to understand what I went through. They say, "Oh yeah, I know, I read about that." Well, you can read about it all you want, but you're not going to understand how it was.

CHAPTER 9

A New Enemy

By the end of October 1950 what remained of the North Korean army had retreated far above the 38th parallel. The units of the U.S. Eighth Army that had been fighting so desperately to hold the Pusan perimeter only two months before now found themselves facing almost no organized resistance as they raced up the western side of the Korean peninsula toward the Yalu River, the border between North Korea and China. Meanwhile the marines and soldiers of X [Tenth] Corps, the men who had landed at Inchon and recaptured Seoul, had been put back aboard ships and taken around the peninsula for another amphibious landing on the eastern side of the country. From there X Corps was also moving north toward the Yalu. Accompanying both the Eighth Army and X Corps were five divisions of South Korean troops.

Victory was in the air. Once the Yalu was reached, all of Korea would be in UN hands, and everybody could go home.

That's what Sherman Pratt remembers just about everybody thinking. Pratt had arrived in Korea at the time of the breakout, as an individual replacement officer in the 2nd Infantry Division, and his first experience of the Korean fighting was this exhilarating race to the Yalu.

But Sherman Pratt was no novice to combat. He was a decorated veteran of World War II, where he had been commissioned on the battlefield and had experienced a meteoric rise from sergeant to captain in three months, which may well be a record for the U.S. Army. And so his enthusiasm for the chase was tempered by a veteran's knowledge that in war things always go wrong. And very often they go wrong precisely when you least expect them to.

But even his cool professional skepticism did not prepare Sherman Pratt for the shock of what was about to happen next. Even people in a position to know better didn't see it coming.

The Chinese.

How, in retrospect, could anyone have ignored the Chinese? Korea was a next-door neighbor. Imagine a hostile army streaming up from Central America and heading straight through Mexico for the Rio Grande. Wouldn't the United States be concerned?

In late September and early October of 1950 there were definite signals that China would intervene in the Korean War if UN troops crossed the 38th parallel. But the signals were either misinterpreted or ignored at the top, which translated to a general indifference at the bottom. If MacArthur isn't worrying about the Chinese, many of the troops thought, then why should we?

It was arguably the biggest mistake of Douglas MacArthur's career. Because once the Chinese came into it the war would never be the same. It would no longer be winnable, although few people recognized that or would admit it at the time.

But all that is hindsight, while the reality of the time is more closely mirrored in the experiences of a soldier like Sherman Pratt, who was there, on the ground, when the Communist Chinese Forces hit the UN head on and abruptly turned the war around.

When I got to Korea in early September I was given command of a rifle company. Baker Company of the 23rd Regiment. I hadn't been with my company for more than a few days when we went on the attack all along the Naktong River. At the same time MacArthur landed at Inchon in the north, and within a week the enemy broke.

All through September and into October we pressed forward with great speed, and almost before we knew it we were at the 38th parallel. The North Korean resistance had collapsed. Our main problem in those days was trying to keep up with them.

We crossed the parallel and raced up to Pyongyang, the North Korean capital. The city was hardly being defended. When we cleared Pyongyang and moved into the high ground to the north I looked back and saw the sky filled with hundreds of paratroopers. I was puzzled. Everybody who saw it was puzzled. Why were they dropping in our rear, in an area that had already been captured? It turned out that the front was moving so rapidly that the drop zone was captured while these guys were still loading and getting airborne, and they never got the word.

We stopped finally when we were almost at the Yalu River. As I recall, we were about forty miles away. And it was here that we had our first brushes with Chinese troops.

Our intelligence reports had been telling us they were in the area. We were well aware that the border was only fifty miles away. But the intentions of these Chinese were by no means clear to us. In fact their actions were rather puzzling. They did things that led us to think they wouldn't fight unless we advanced too far. They even showed signs of friendliness. I remember taking a patrol out one day and having Chinese appear on the hilltops all around us. We were surrounded. I put out the word that under no circumstances were we to fire the first shot. They had us, and it would have been a massacre. Then a couple of my men waved, and lo and behold the Chinese started waving back. We turned around very slowly and went back the way we came, and nobody fired a shot. Colonel [Paul] Freeman was at the battalion CP and he grilled me over and over for details. He just couldn't believe it.

The next day I saw the Colonel again, and he had more strange news. He'd sent out a follow-up patrol, with instructions to push farther north to see what the Chinese would do. They got as far as we had without any problems, but when they tried to go farther the Chinese opened fire.

In the confusion the patrol left some wounded behind, and that was the most bizarre aspect of the whole matter. When a third patrol returned to the area they found the wounded men all bandaged up and warmly covered with blankets, lying comfortably on litters by the side of the road where they'd fallen.

We just couldn't figure it out. What were they up to? And just how many were out there? Of course, at the time we had no inkling they were out there in the hundreds and hundreds of thousands.

Around Thanksgiving word came that the Eighth Army was going to launch a general attack all along the front. We were told that theater intelligence believed the Chinese in the area would fall back into Manchuria. My own attitude was optimistic. We understood that the UN objective was to push on to the Manchurian border. Over on the eastern side of Korea General Almond's X Corps had landed and they had in fact already reached the Yalu River at certain points. It looked like this would be the final stage of the war, and that we'd all be home by Christmas.

That same night, the night the UN offensive was supposed to be in full swing, all hell broke loose. My company was in reserve just behind the lines, and there was heavy fighting to our front, to our right, to our left. And then we began to see American troops pouring back through our positions, some at a dead run. They were pathetic, scared-looking men. The panic began to spread contagiously among my own men, and it took close supervision to keep them under control.

We grabbed some of these guys who were running back through our positions and asked them what was happening, and they said the Chinese were attacking, that they're all around us, and that they were going to overrun us. Then A Company to our left got into a big fight, and shortly after that my own company was hit.

During the rest of the night we were engaged in almost continuous firefights. It was total confusion. We'd fire at the Chinese, and they would withdraw. They were trying to avoid a direct confrontation with American units, we found out later. Trying to avoid our heavier firepower, and instead hit South Korean units, or work around American units and hit them from behind.

All during this time stragglers from the front continued to filter back through our positions. Pitiful guys. Dazed, bewildered, most with no weapons, many of them with their clothes frozen stiff from splashing through rice paddies and across rivers, some with no shoes and their feet already turning black from frostbite.

At dawn the Chinese broke contact, and later that same day we were ordered to take a hill called Chinaman's Hat, but that was called off when casualties got too heavy.

Finally we got orders to withdraw. So the division and the regiment and our battalion started leapfrogging back out of the area. Because by then the only word we were hearing was, "Boy, all hell's broken loose. The Chinese have hit us with an ocean of manpower all along the front."

This was the great bugout. In ten days I believe the Eighth Army retreated one hundred thirty miles. It was not an orderly retreat. I hesitate to call it a complete rout, because some units did hold their ground under the most appalling conditions. But just about everybody had only one thing in mind, and that was to get out of the trap the Chinese had sprung on us.

My company was ordered into a blocking position along the main road near a village called Kunu-ri, and most of the 2nd Division passed through us on their way south. For a day and a night the troops and vehicles streamed through. Equipment had been tossed on the trucks haphazardly. Tanks had clusters of infantrymen on them, haggard, bearded men who looked just like the characters of Willie and Joe in Bill Mauldin's World War Two sketches. Many of the men retreating through us had no weapons or helmets or packs. Some didn't even have shoes. Some were wounded. Some died right there on the road. At times traffic was so heavy that the motor column would come to a complete halt. Of course we were hoping everything would keep moving, because we knew everybody else would have to clear our blocking position before we would be ordered out ourselves. By then that was the big fear: that you would be left behind in this big retreat, that you'd be the last one out and end up getting captured by the Chinese.

The withdrawing columns finally thinned out, and we received our orders to pull out ourselves, as soon as the last of the retreating units had passed us. By now we had collected about fifty Chinese prisoners. We were keeping them in a rice paddy near the company CP. I wanted to get rid of them, because by the time we moved out there would be nothing between us and the Chinese army except empty space, and the prisoners would slow us down. So I tried to persuade one of the units passing through us to take them to the rear.

Nobody would take them. No one wanted to be slowed down. I remember one infantry officer in the column saying, "Just shoot the bastards," tossing the comment back over his shoulder as he walked away.

I'm thankful today I didn't follow his advice, although I must have been tempted.

Shortly after moving out of the first blocking position we were ordered into another one. We were told to hold the pass on the south bank of the Chongchon River, just outside Kunu-ri, until the rest of the 2nd Division could get out. We were still the rear guard. And it was while we were on that hill above Kunu-ri that I saw something I don't think I'll ever forget.

One morning, just after we'd thrown back a Chinese attack the previous night, a runner from one of the forward platoons came rushing up and said, "Captain Pratt, it looks like the Chinese are attacking again!"

Now I thought that was strange, because the Chinese never advanced in broad daylight directly against our positions. They always attacked at night. So I went over to the forward edge of the hill, and through my field glasses I could see troops moving in the valley below us. But they were still too distant to make out. It was clear though that they weren't organized. They were moving around in bunches, this way and that, like chickens in a barnyard, with no clearly discernible direction.

We watched them for a while through our binoculars, and as they got closer one of my lieutenants said, "My God, Captain, I think they're GIs!"

Black GIs, I might add. We could recognize their American uniforms, but most had no helmets, and few had any weapons. Even at that distance they looked thoroughly disorganized and terrorized.

From up on our hill we could see them running and stumbling over the frozen ground. Some would fall and not get back up. Here and there we could see one of them stop, look back and fire. Although there wasn't much of that, because so few still had their rifles.

Then we noticed that mixed among these black GIs were Chinese. They were running in among the Americans, grabbing them and trying to pull them to the ground. We could see fistfights as the GIs tried to throw off the Chinese. We saw other GIs hitting the Chinese with what appeared to be clubs or sticks. The wild melee continued, off and on, for two or three hours. Watching it, we felt helpless and frustrated. It was too far below us to go out and help, and we couldn't fire on the Chinese without the risk of hitting the GIs.

We learned later that those black troopers had been overrun and bypassed in their positions northwest of Kunu-ri. They were what was left of the 3rd Battalion of the 24th Infantry Regiment, which was one of the last all-black units in the army. For a long time it was generally believed that the battalion had "bugged out." That was a term that had come into use about that time, to characterize a unit where the men would panic under attack and run for the rear without putting up much of a fight. There was no shortage of units in the Korean War who were accused of bugging out.

But of course with the 3rd Battalion there was the racial thing. A lot of people wanted to believe that black troops simply couldn't fight. But the 3rd Battalion, it should be remembered, had white officers, and poor leadership on the battlefield can cause a unit to break as much as anything else.

That same day we finally got our orders to pull out. All day we could see the Chinese moving around our flanks. By then we must have been the northernmost unit in the entire Eighth Army. Everybody was to the south of us, including a lot of Chinese. It seemed they had just about blanketed the countryside. But they also seemed disorganized. Sometimes we could see small knots of them just milling around. I had the feeling they were as confused as we were.

During that retreat the cold was our enemy as much as the Chinese. That should be kept in mind by anyone trying to understand the Korean War. We suffered constantly from the cold. Painfully. It dulled our senses. It made us move slow. It made us *think* slow. Wounded men who otherwise might have survived died because they couldn't be kept warm. Our vehicles wouldn't start. Batteries gave out. The grease on our rifles turned to glue and they wouldn't fire. Our rations would freeze solid. Men would carry cans of food around inside their clothes, under their armpits, trying to thaw them a little so they could be eaten. When the wind blew over those Korean hilltops the chill factor must have been twenty or thirty degrees below zero.

We retreated from Kunu-ri in a motorized column, got through the Chinese, and by the third of December we were in bivouac around Munsan, just below the Imjin River.

We were south of the parallel again.

But now we faced a new enemy. We had an entirely new war on our hands.

CHAPTER 10

FO

The initial Chinese attack had hit the Eighth Army across its entire front. During the first three weeks of October almost two hundred thousand Chinese troops had crossed the Yalu River from Manchuria undetected by U.S. air reconnaissance.

The Chinese were able to achieve this remarkable feat because theirs was a peasant army where everybody marched on foot. There were no vehicles even to move supplies. There were only pack animals (including camels) and the backs of the soldiers themselves. But precisely because it was not mechanized, this huge army was able to move in great secrecy. Roads were not necessary; the Chinese simply walked overland in their canvas sneakers, traveling only at night and hiding during the day in North Korea's numerous railroad tunnels and caves and mine shafts.

But this first great Chinese offensive did not hit every unit of the Eighth Army at once. Some were not hit at all. Others, like Andrew Barr's heavy mortar company, were surrounded first and then subjected to intensive small-arms and mortar fire in an attempt to annihilate the encircled defenders.

Andy Barr had been in Korea less than two weeks when the Chinese steamroller crashed out of the North Korean mountains, but he reacted like a veteran, earning a Silver Star for gallantry during the chaotic retreat that followed. But it is doubtful that anyone who knew him at the time would have been surprised by that. Barr had arrived in Korea in an uncommonly upbeat frame of mind, and even the retreat of an entire army failed to dampen the excitement he felt at just being in the show.

I arrived in Korea in the middle of November 1950 as an individual replacement for a mortar company. At this point, I guess I was twenty-one then, I was a very good officer. I'd been a lieutenant for three years. I was plenty good, plenty sharp, I knew what it was about. My morale was high. I didn't mind at all going to Korea. It was an adventure. That's the very word I used when I walked away from my family and my girlfriend. I said to myself, "Here's another adventure."

I'd gone into the service strictly to get the GI Bill, to be able to go to college at the army's expense after I got out. I kind of dogged it for a while, but by the time the war in Korea started I'd gone from a Reserve to a Regular Army commission, and I had it all wired together.

I flew over to Japan from the States. Then I spent five days on the Yellow Sea on a troopship. I puked every day. The ship went around the Korean peninsula to Inchon, and from there I got a ride into Seoul.

In Seoul a jeep picked me up, me and another lieutenant who was also reporting to the 2nd Chemical Mortar Battalion. We had to go up to Pyongyang, the North Korean capital, which had been captured by the UN and was being used as a replacement center.

Pyongyang is about a hundred thirty miles from Seoul, and we hadn't driven more than thirty or forty miles when we came to this big mound of bodies. They were all black GIs, and they were stacked up like cordwood. There must have been at least fifty of them.

I said to the driver, "What the hell is this?" And he tells us that these guys were ambushed by guerrillas, by North Koreans who had been bypassed after the Inchon landing in September and who were still operating behind the American lines. "But I wouldn't worry," he says. "It isn't likely they'd show themselves just to ambush a jeep. A two-and-a-half-ton truck maybe, but not a jeep."

I didn't believe him, and neither did this other lieutenant I was with, but we did make it all the way up to Pyongyang without being shot at.

At Pyongyang I was sent to C Company, 2nd Chemical Mortar Battalion, as a forward observer. Captain Paul Morton was the CO. Very rigid. Very hardnosed. The men didn't like him, the officers didn't like him, but I liked him. He'd been through World War Two, and I liked his experience. And he immediately liked me, maybe because I didn't even try to get close to him.

I remember one man who wanted to kill Morton. He kept saying, "I'm gonna kill Captain Morton." I asked him why, and I never got a good reason, but there was no question he was serious. Over a period of about a week and a half I talked him out of it. Later on in life this guy was one of the FBI's ten most wanted men. Yet we went through that awful November 26 night together. And I'll tell you, he was fearless. This guy was absolutely fearless. He wasn't afraid of anything. Just sort of a wild guy.

Now this was the first time I'd been in a mortar company. I didn't know anything about mortars. I'd never had anything to do with them. I was in the Chemical Corps when I was first commissioned, as a decontamination platoon leader. We would take a truck and fill it with water and pretend that mustard gas or whatever had been spewed down on something, and instead of using bleach we would use plain water and decontaminate everything. We'd try and think of different ways to make it interesting, but it was a screaming bore.

I'd gone into tanks after that, but in Japan, at the replacement depot at Camp Drake, they changed me back to the Chemical Corps and assigned me to a chemical mortar battalion.

These mortars had nothing to do with chemicals. They were standard 4.2-inch heavy mortars. The name "chemical mortar" was a throwback to World War I, when these things were there to lob poison gas shells at the enemy if the need arose. They were big, powerful weapons, great weapons, because a 4.2-inch mortar round kills everybody within fifty yards of its impact. In Korea we used them like artillery. They were the perfect weapon for use in mountainous country.

But as I said, I'd never been in a mortar company before, so I went up to Captain Morton, this stern, strict, very formal officer, and I said, "Look, I don't know the first thing about being a forward observer. I don't know how the system works."

I don't know what I was expecting, a chewing out maybe, but he couldn't have been nicer about it.

He put a hand on my shoulder. "It's real easy," he said. "I'll show you how it works."

So the first night or two we walked all over the mountains, way the hell out along the front lines. And he explained to me about triangulation, how the target I'm shooting at is one point of the triangle, the fire direction center where the mortars are is the second point, and I'm the third. It wasn't difficult. You could pick it up in one night.

So I became a forward observer, an FO, the guy who looks for targets and calls in the mortar fire. And I absolutely loved it. I was out there all by myself, literally calling all the shots. There was a real sense of power involved, the power of life and death.

But at the time I joined the battalion, the middle of November, there was hardly any fighting going on. Every day we'd get in our jeeps and drive north, to keep up with the infantry. There was no resistance. The North Koreans weren't fighting anymore. The Chinese had entered the war briefly in October, and then they'd pulled back. One of our mortar companies had fought them. I learned much later that they'd left a message through the Indian Embassy or through diplomatic channels somehow that if the UN got up any closer to the Yalu they were going to enter the war for keeps, but our government didn't believe it.

At the time, though, at our level, the feeling was this: they came in one time and they left. A few companies, maybe a battalion. So we didn't take them seriously.

The mood was, we were going to get up to the Yalu and we were all going to be home by Christmas. That was the mood. People were going lickety-split north, nobody gave a shit for nothing, we were winning the battles, there wasn't much resistance anyway, and the Chinese just weren't a factor.

On Thanksgiving Day, November twenty-third I think it was, we had this unbelievably huge meal that was served to all the troops in Korea. Hot turkey, cranberry sauce, mashed potatoes, all the trimmings, everything brought up by truck from the rear. A big hot meal. I sat there eating it, watching these four marine Corsairs strafing the side of the mountain not more than five hundred yards away, when suddenly one of them gets shot down right in front of my eyes. Down it comes, trailing smoke, then *boom*, a big ball of flame. But even with that happening, I was concentrating on eating that wonderful meal.

It was the last hot meal any of us got for a long time.

November 26, 1950. My eighth day in Korea. That was the day we moved four different times to catch up to where the infantry was. And every time we stopped Captain Morton would say, "Okay, dig foxholes." And nobody ever would, because the ground was frozen solid, and we figured we'd only be moving again anyway. So we'd just kind of stall and fumble around, and sure enough the word would come to move out.

About six that evening we got to a schoolhouse. There was a big courtyard there where we parked our jeeps, thirty-nine of them. About three hundred yards away was a big river. It was zero degrees at six in the evening, and we weren't allowed any fires, so we did what we always did in that kind of situation. We went to bed.

I left my clothes on, took my boots off, had my rifle right next to my sleeping bag. About a quarter to nine I'm almost asleep in the schoolhouse when Captain Morton calls up on the little telephone right next to my head.

"Lieutenant Barr," he says, "alert your men."

"Sir?"

"Didn't you hear me? I said alert your men."

Then he hung up on me. I got up, got everybody else up, and of course all the men wanted to know what was going on. I didn't know, so I walked over to Captain Morton's CP and asked him what was happening.

Turned out he'd sent back a wire party, a communications staff sergeant and two other men, to try to find a break in the phone line somewhere in our rear, and they were coming back now with the sergeant wounded. He didn't know why the sergeant was wounded, but there was obviously something going on behind us that we didn't know about.

They laid the sergeant on the floor of the Captain's CP. He had three wounds in his stomach and a bullet hole next to his right eye. Everybody was holding back, afraid to look. I'd never seen a wounded man before either, but I decided then and there that I was going to examine this man's wounds and see what my reaction would be. So I knelt down next to the guy and looked closely and very deliberately at all his wounds, and I was all right. I didn't have any reaction, and I never had any from that moment forward, even after seeing men torn apart and wounded in all sorts of ways. It just never affected me.

The story the wire party told was that there were Chinese troops to the rear, and that we were completely surrounded. And as if to confirm the story, mortar rounds started dropping all over the schoolyard. We started taking rifle fire from the hills around us, and artillery fire. Five of us tried to set up a mortar to shoot back, but as we were setting the thing up, an enemy round landed practically in our laps and knocked everybody down. I jumped back up, none the worse for it except for the ringing in my ears, and I yelled to the others, "Come on, let's get this goddamn thing set up!"

But nobody got up. All the others were either dead or badly wounded.

We were taking a lot of casualties, but that wasn't the worst of it. Men were starting to sneak out of there. I didn't notice it at first, because after I saw I couldn't get a mortar working I grabbed my rifle and started shooting, trying to defend our perimeter. But all along the perimeter men were leaving their positions and sneaking away to the rear, trying to get out of there. It was happening all up and down the front that night, guys bugging out, retreating without orders.

It never entered my head to leave. We had wounded men there. And we were taking more casualties all the time, because the fire from the Chinese was constant.

Two other guys who stayed were my sergeant and the guy who'd threatened to kill our captain. The three of us returned fire all night long. My sergeant, who also won the Silver Star that night, was firing a .50-caliber machine gun from the back of a truck. He held off the Chinese for hours. They would rush the truck in waves, six, seven, eight men at a time, and he'd mow them down with the machine gun. But he didn't have a loader. He had to change the belts [of ammo] himself. And finally he had trouble getting the belt in. While he was fooling with it the Chinese rushed him, and he was shot across the torso with a burp gun and killed.

Meanwhile me and this other guy are firing our rifles in every direction. We'd shoot from one position for a while, then run somewhere else and shoot from there, to make the Chinese believe there were more of us around. There were a few others, but not many. By midnight, one in the morning, most of the guys in the company had bugged out. In the meantime, whenever we could, those of us who stayed would put some of the wounded and dead on the jeeps, a jeep or two at a time, and send them out of there, until there was not a wounded man or dead body left inside the perimeter.

I remember praying for dawn all night long. It was very dark, and we were shooting at anything that moved. I'm sure that at times we were shooting at our own men. Remember, we were a mortar company, not the infantry. Mortarmen don't usually come into direct contact with the enemy. You don't expect to have to fight them off at close range. That's the infantry's job. But suddenly there wasn't any infantry. We were all alone, and we had to do it ourselves.

I kept thinking, *Dawn. Dawn. We'll be all right if we can make it to dawn.* I had faith in the dawn, because I thought that when we could see again we'd be able to sort things out.

But when dawn came I saw that our situation was worse than hopeless.

There were only six of us left, out of a hundred fifty men in the company, and we were totally surrounded on all sides.

We were hiding in a ditch, and to keep the Chinese from rushing us we'd move up and down the ditch and fire our rifles from different places. That worked for a while, but it wasn't going to fool them forever, not in broad daylight, and so we decided we'd have to try and work our way to the rear, back to our own lines, wherever they might be.

We left the ditch as the sun was coming up and ran across a little stream, one at a time. And as we ran across the stream the Chinese started shooting at us with a machine gun. I was the last to cross, and I can remember seeing the bullets hit the stream all around me. I can remember thinking: Either I'm going to get wet or I'm going to get killed. So I dropped down and flattened myself in the water. And the temperature, remember, was close to zero.

But it worked. The machine gunner missed me, and when he stopped firing I jumped up and ran to a bomb crater, the same hole the other five guys were in. The machine gun started up again, the bullets kicking up dirt all around the hole. In between bursts we jumped out of the hole, one at a time, and ran to the next point of cover. We kept doing that, hiding, running, hiding, running, until we were out of the enemy gunner's range. But always we were moving toward the rear.

We passed a battalion aid station. That's the first place they collect the wounded. Dozens of men lying on the ground, unable to move. I remember seeing one man lying on his stomach with half his rump blown off. There was nothing we could do for him. We were alone, just the six of us. We couldn't help. We were struggling to get out ourselves. I never found out what happened to all those wounded men, but it's almost a certainty the Chinese got them.

A tank finally rescued us. We were still walking, trying to find our lines. My clothes were soaking wet and my feet were getting numb. When we first saw the tank it was crossing a river, and we didn't know at first if it was Chinese or American. Luckily it was American, and we climbed onto it and it carried us straight through the Chinese positions. No fancy heroics. The driver just barreled down the main road as fast as he could, until finally we met up with the other two companies in our battalion.

Our colonel, Clancy Briggs, came up to us and asked us about it, what it was like, and we told him, and he said, "Well, it was like that all up and down the front. It wasn't just here. We're getting the daylights kicked out of us all along the line."

That's when I realized that this was something really big, not just another company or battalion-sized intervention by the Chinese, but a really massive attack. But I don't think any of us realized *how* big, that there was something like a quarter of a million Chinks out there and that they weren't messing around anymore.

The very day I escaped that trap I was assigned as a forward observer with another company, and for the next six nights I didn't go to bed. We got overrun every night. Finally the battalion commander leapfrogged everybody back, unit by unit, to where my old mortar company's jeeps were. These were the ones we'd sent out our dead and wounded on. We climbed into those jeeps and drove south all night. We kept driving south for seven straight days, and in those seven days I never went to bed, never slept except for little catnaps, never had a warm meal. The roads were like a crowded highway in a big city. You'd go four or five miles an hour, in a long convoy, starting and stopping. People were falling asleep at the wheel and it would stop the entire convoy.

I don't remember being afraid. I don't remember fear, ever. There was just an overwhelming craving for sleep. An hour's nap. Half an hour. You'd give anything for just a little sleep. You can be cold, you can be hungry, but I think the need for sleep is the most overpowering human need.

At the end of the seven days we had retreated well over a hundred miles. When we stopped I fell asleep immediately, in a cornfield next to the road, and when I woke up I saw thousands of infantrymen walking along the road, long long columns of them, retreating from the north.

A lot of the men were pretty demoralized by now, but in all honesty I wasn't. I figured we'd lost that one battle. A lot of people were saying, "Fuck this place, I want to go home." But I didn't feel that way at all. I thought: Nope, we have a battle to fight, we're going to win it, we're not going to get thrown out of here.

CHAPTER 11

Frozen Chosin

Over on the eastern side of Korea, separated from the Eighth Army by the central spine of North Korean mountains, X Corps had also been moving toward the Yalu River. The 1st Marine Division and the army's 3rd and 7th Infantry Divisions had landed in late October and early November at two different places along the east coast and had started north in widely separated columns, experiencing at first only scattered resistance from North Korean guerrillas. Then came a sharp fight with Chinese troops, who promptly faded back into the hills.

The marines got as far as the Chosin Reservoir, an enormous man-made lake seventy miles from the sea over a narrow twisting mountain road, when on the night of November 27 the enemy descended on them: three Chinese divisions against three scattered marine regiments. But the marines were hard and fit, led by officers and noncoms with World War II combat experience, the ranks leavened with tough young men who had not waited around in the States to be drafted but who had joined the Corps to fight.

Two hundred and forty of them were in Fox Company, 2nd Battalion, 7th Marine Regiment, and when the 5th and 7th Marines, caught on the western side of the reservoir, turned around to fight their way south out of the trap, Fox Company was given the job of holding Toktong Pass, through which the rest of the marines would have to withdraw.

Pat Scully had been with Fox Company from the day it was formed. He was one of the old hands, a twenty-four-year-old sergeant in his second hitch in the Corps.

I remember we had Thanksgiving dinner in Hagaru, a little town at the southern end of the reservoir. I believe they gave all the troops in Korea a hot meal that day. From Hagaru the rest of my regiment and the 5th Regiment went another fifteen miles up to the village of Yudam. We were kept back to defend the road.

Our skipper, Captain Barber, went out in a jeep and selected what later became known as Fox Hill as our defensive position. Fox Hill overlooked Toktong Pass. The pass was about halfway between Hagaru and Yudam, and everything going up or down the road had to go through the pass. If the 5th and 7th Marines up in Yudam had to retreat, they would have to come back through the pass. If the gooks got the pass, you'd have two marine regiments trapped up there at the reservoir. We'd had a big fight with the Chinese on the way up from the coast, but then they'd disappeared into the hills, and nobody was sure if they were gone for good or if they were still out there.

At Fox Hill we took up our positions in the dark. I got out of the truck, gathered up the guys in my rocket section, and yelled to the skipper, "Where do you want us?"

He says, "You're gonna be the roadblock."

So I set up my position down along the road, at the base of the reverse slope. Meanwhile the three rifle platoons dug in along the opposite side, facing north. They were only about a hundred yards away, but they might have been a hundred miles. I couldn't see them in the dark, didn't know exactly where they were, and I didn't have any radio.

About one thirty in the morning the sound of gunfire woke me up. We were sleeping in a couple of huts just off the road, and I stuck my head out the door of the hut and saw all these gooks running by our position laterally, just spraying the area indiscriminately with their submachine guns. They were waving the guns around like hoses. Why they didn't hit us frontally I'll never know, but if they had, we wouldn't have gotten out of there alive. There were a lot of them and only sixteen of us—the eleven guys in my rocket section and five guys from an artillery forward observer team.

After the firing slowed down I stuck my head out the door again and hollered up the hill to Captain Barber: "Where do you want my men now?" Considering that we'd been hit on the *south* side, on the reverse slope, opposite his primary position, I thought he might want to rearrange his perimeter. But I had no idea what his perimeter was like, or where the various platoons of the company tied into each other. I also had no idea that the main attack was at that moment hitting *him*, up there on the north side of the hill.

He yelled back: "Spread them anyplace you can."

So I moved everybody up along a path behind the huts, which put us about twenty feet above the road.

Well, the next thing that happened, they're calling out for us to surrender. An Oriental voice, but pretty good English. "We want you to surrender. We will honor the Geneva accord. We are only interested in your equipment. We will treat you properly under the Geneva accord."

I hollered up the hill, "Skipper, there's somebody down here wants us to surrender."

Captain Barber came down, and they yelled out the surrender offer again. Then I heard the click of a BAR, and the captain's runner let loose a burst.

That was our answer.

I found out later that there were two full regiments of gooks out there only five hundred yards away.

Nothing much happened the rest of the night. Even the north side was quiet, although they'd had a terrific fight up there. Waves of gooks came in on them. There was hand to hand fighting with shovels, bayonets, rifle butts, fists. One guy, Hector Cafferata, later

81

got the Medal of Honor. They lost twenty guys, and had something like fifty wounded, but they held the hill.

In the morning we found bodies all over the place. Up on the north side they counted five hundred dead Chinese. But the daytime was quiet. Just some sniper activity. The mortar and CP tents were down near the road, and we moved those farther up the hill, into the middle of a bunch of pin oaks. They became our hospital tents.

On the second night we didn't get hit at all. I could hear a lot of firing on the other side of the hill, but I had no communications with the rest of the company. My first indication of how hard they'd been hit was at about three o'clock in the morning, when the gunny came down and asked who was in my position. I told him, and he said, "All right, I want you to get up here."

We walked back up the hill, and he said, "We're down to a fifty-yard perimeter. Come daylight we're gonna take our positions back, and I want some guys up here who can kick ass."

What happened was, the gooks were in our own foxholes. They had hit the guys up there as hard as on the first night, only this time they pushed our lines back almost to the middle of the hill.

We got all the survivors together from the three platoons, and all the wounded who could stand up, and at the crack of dawn we went at them, screaming like hell, running forward and firing as we ran. We swept right through their positions and shot them in the holes. It didn't last long, and as soon as we got our old perimeter back I was told to get back to my rocket section.

The next day was quiet. The worst of it was not having any food. There was one can of rations for six men, and I was eating I guess a spoonful of food a day. Later the skipper was surprised to hear we didn't have any food on the south side of the hill. He had plenty up where he was. I was smoking four packs of cigarettes a day. I had a cartridge belt filled with nothing but cigarettes, and I'd smoke them and pretend I was eating warm toast. We managed to boil some instant coffee, and that was it: coffee and cigarettes and a spoonful of food each day.

My hands and feet were frostbitten, but a lot of the guys had that. The corpsman put a tag on me, "Frozen extremities," and I went on about my business.

On the third night the gooks came at us head on. We had a .50-caliber machine gun sitting down below us in the snow. The gun was set in against the base of the hill, with a 180-degree traverse. The gun team hadn't fired at all up to this point, and the gooks didn't know it was there. When they came at us across the road the machine gun opened up, and the whole thing was over in a matter of minutes. That one gun broke up the attack. When daylight came we went down there and found all the gook rifle stocks shattered into splinters, so you can imagine what the bodies looked like. There was just a tangled mass of corpses.

But I don't think it was more than a company that hit us. And whenever they were hitting us, they left the other side of the hill alone. I think that was their big mistake. If they had hit us at two different positions at once, they could have taken that hill, there were so many of them out there. Thousands, against only two hundred marines. But they didn't seem all that organized.

The next two days were quiet. The skipper kept sending out patrols, trying to find out where the gooks were. All we were getting was sniper fire. I spent a lot of time trying to help out in the hospital tent. There were so many guys jammed in there. I helped give morphine, the little that was left. Only the really bad cases got it. One guy had both his hands blown off. Another guy I remember was shot in the eye. I don't know how he was still alive. There was nothing really that you could do for them.

We were on that hill something like five days by now. We were completely surrounded, and out of contact with the rest of the division. But I don't recall being anxious about getting out of there. I really wasn't giving a lot of thought to getting relieved. The basic attitude was, Hey, the Marine Corps takes care of its own. When the time comes, we'll get out.

On the morning of the fifth day I saw a tank coming toward us through the pass, and I thought, Shit, now they're coming at us with tanks. There were people riding on the tanks, and as I watched through my binoculars I gradually made out the parkas with the hoods over the helmets, and the helmets half on the side.

Unmistakably marines.

I saw Captain Barber go out onto the road and shake hands with Ray Davis, the officer who was leading the rescue force. And then Barber comes back and says, "Sergeant Scully, get this area squared away. We're getting out of here."

We formed up and walked the six or seven miles down to the marine positions at Hagaru. Frozen, dirty, starved, and exhausted. Just before we got to the perimeter there one of our officers, Lieutenant Peterson, turned to us and said, "All right, you guys, square yourselves away. We're gonna go in like marines."

And don't you know, everybody did. We straightened our helmets and gear, straightened our shoulders, somebody started counting cadence, and we marched in like marines.

The defense of Toktong Pass was later written up as one of the most dramatic actions of the war. How Fox Company held the pass for five days until the rest of the two marine regiments could get out. When we'd learned what we'd done of course we were proud of it, but at the time I had no sense of that. None at all. And I think most of the guys felt the same way. We were just holding another position. They told us to keep the pass open, and we kept it open.

CHAPTER 12

Fight for Life

On December 1, 1950, with Fox Company three days into its defense of Toktong Pass, the ten thousand men of the 5th and 7th Marine Regiments began their fifteen-mile fighting retreat from Yudam to Hagaru.

Exactly three days earlier, on November 27, the two regiments had been ordered to attack west, toward the beleaguered Eighth Army on the other side of the peninsula. The order had come directly from General MacArthur in Tokyo, and in retrospect it was almost a death sentence, since it was sending ten thousand men to try to put a stop to an enemy offensive involving at least ten times that number. MacArthur, who had already blundered badly by dismissing Chinese intervention in Korea as unlikely, was now compounding that error by underestimating the number of Chinese troops opposing him.

The marines at Yudam had no more idea than MacArthur how many Chinese were really out there, but they did know they were being ordered to attack across an almost trackless wilderness of snow-

covered mountains, in bitter cold, with only one narrow tortuous road behind them over which supplies could be brought forward.

"Under those conditions," Fred Lawson recalls, "it wouldn't have taken all that many Chinese to stop us."

Lawson was a rifleman with Item Company, 3rd Battalion, 7th Marines. He had been wounded several weeks earlier at Sudong, where the marines had had their first sharp fight with Chinese troops, and on the morning of November 27—the day the marines at Yudam began their ill-conceived attack, and twelve hours before the Chinese launched their own massive assault against X Corps—Lawson was riding up from Hagaru in the back of a supply truck, looking to rejoin his company.

Yudam was a little village on the edge of the Chosin Reservoir, about fifteen miles above Hagaru, and when I got up there I couldn't find Item Company. I reported in to battalion headquarters, and when I asked where the company was, one of the guys in the tent pointed out at the mountains and said, "That way."

It was late afternoon by the time I found them. They'd moved out that morning as part of the general offensive, and when I got there they'd already gone into defensive positions for the night. Item had about two hundred men in its rifle squads, and they were strung out along a ridgeline high above the reservoir, two or three men to a position, with the individual positions so far apart most of them were out of visual contact with each other. The snow was hip deep. The wind was blowing. Flurries were still coming down, and you couldn't see anything.

I looked around and thought, If we get hit, there's no way in hell we'll ever hold a position like this.

One of the sergeants told me to get out on the left flank. I stumbled around for a while, until I found the hole in the snow I was supposed to occupy. There was a guy already in it. "Goddamn, am I glad to see you," he says. "I'm out here all by myself."

That night the Chinese really hit us. We knew they were out there somewhere, because we'd already had a fight with them at Sudong a couple of weeks before, but nobody thought there'd be so many. We had no idea what was happening over on the other side of the mountains, that the army was getting the shit kicked out of them over there by hordes of Chinese. We had absolutely no idea what we were doing. As far as we knew we were still headed for the Yalu River, and if we got there quick enough we'd be home for Christmas.

It wasn't too long after dark, eight, nine o'clock, when we heard the bugles. At the same time we started taking mortar and artillery fire. Then lights came on. The Chinese lit up the whole side of the hill with searchlights, and then charged into the light, and Jesus, what a sight. They looked like a bunch of sheep swarming up the hill.

None of us had ever seen anything like it. They didn't seem to have any training at all. They just came straight at us, like a mob. You couldn't help but hit them. And we were really stacking them up. But there were so goddamn many. And they just kept coming.

Pretty soon we were in it hand to hand. Gun butts. Knives. Fists. After I ran out of ammo I conked a couple with a helmet, swinging it by the strap. A lot of the positions got overrun, but nobody retreated. Unless somebody comes around and tells you to pull back, you have no choice but to go on fighting, because all you have in a situation like that is your buddies. You're depending on them, and they're depending on you, and it doesn't even occur to you to leave a position without orders.

We fought all that night, but it wasn't continuous firing. There was a kind of rhythm to it. For an hour or two it would be constant. The gooks would come in waves, one after another, each wave maybe six or seven hundred yards apart, and if you could bust up one you got a little breathing space before the next one hit. After a couple hours of that they'd stop attacking for a while, and you could get more ammo up, get the wounded taken care of, maybe get a little rest. Then you'd hear the whistles and bugles, and the mortar and artillery rounds would start coming in, and they'd come at you again.

Around dawn, when things calmed down a bit, we started counting noses, and we came up with only thirty-seven guys. That's out of almost two hundred.

The Chinese didn't do any attacking after dawn, and during the morning we fell back toward Yudam. Over on our left George Company had been all but annihilated, and so they combined what was left of our two companies and that same afternoon, after we got ourselves together, we moved back up near our old positions.

There were Chinese bodies still lying around. Hundreds of them, all stiff as boards. We suffered a lot from the cold, but those poor suckers were *really* in bad shape. They were wearing tennis shoes, and you could tell when they were attacking that some could hardly walk. Some didn't even have weapons. I don't see how in the world their officers ever got them to go up that hill. I really felt sorry for some of those Chinese.

That night was like the first night all over again. I honestly didn't believe I'd live through it. A lot of us felt that way. By now we knew we were into something big, and we felt we were up there to be sacrificed, to give the marine units still to the south of us time to get out.

Of course that wasn't the case. Everybody else was under attack too. But down there at the foxhole level you don't get told anything, and so you don't know anything except what goes on right in front of your eyes. And at the same time you're ready to believe every rumor you hear.

I take back what I said. That second night wasn't like the first, it was worse. The main thing on my own mind was, where the hell are they all coming from? Our own artillery and mortars were firing constantly, and we had air strikes coming in by the light of flares and dropping bombs and napalm, and the Chinese would come right through it. We were stacking them up like crazy, but they always seemed to have plenty of men.

I ran out of ammunition three times that night. Didn't get any sleep. The only food we had was frozen C rations. Ever suck on a frozen can of beans? All night long I just stood waist deep in snow, shooting at Chinese or waiting for them to come.

Lieutenant Al Thomas, who was Item Company's weapons officer, had been made the CO of our combined company, and he was the guy who brought us through. He was just a hell of an officer. He was all over the place, constantly giving us encouragement, holding everything together. I saw him a number of times actually pulling Chinese off of people, or running up with his .45 and personally cleaning out a position that had been overrun. Grenades would go off right next to him. Bullets were flying all around. By morning he looked like a walking sieve. His field jacket and trousers were full of holes, but he never got scratched.

That morning we got the order to withdraw, and both regiments formed up for the march down to Hagaru, where the marines were holding a perimeter around a little airfield. The combined company I'd been with was broken up, and I went back to Item Company. There were only sixty or seventy men left in Item, mostly headquarters and artillery people. Practically all the guys in the rifle squads had been killed or wounded.

We got assigned to the rear guard. Second Battalion of the 5th Marines was in the lead. We got together everything that would run, that had wheels and a motor, loaded up the dead and wounded, and what supplies we could, and set off.

It was just moving, stopping, moving, stopping, for a day and a night and another day. The Chinese would throw up a roadblock, or blow a little bridge somewhere, and when the column stopped they would hit the flanks with rifle and mortar and machine-gun fire. We could see them moving with us along the ridgetops, groups of little figures five hundred to maybe a thousand yards away. We had people out on both flanks, and there were always little fights going on to clear a ridge or a hilltop so we could move forward again. Our air support was constantly hitting them, but the Chinese kept up a sporadic fire all the way to Hagaru.

Hagaru was a mess. It looked like a staging area. Tents were up, vehicles were parked side by side and bumper to bumper, supplies were piled up wherever there was an open space. Everything was crowded in close together, because the perimeter was so small.

There was a little airstrip there, and planes were taking out the wounded and bringing in replacements. They were C-47s I believe, and I remember how big and slow and fat they looked coming into that field. The Chinese were in the hills all around Hagaru, and they shot at every plane coming in and going out.

When we got in there we didn't get a chance to rest, because we had to help hold the perimeter. We came in off the line in shifts, ate, and went right back out again.

The Chinese kept hammering at the perimeter. They were all around us, and I'd already made up my mind that it was going to be a miracle if we got out of there. We'd had such an awful time just getting down to Hagaru from the reservoir, and that was only fifteen miles. We had another sixty to go, and I just couldn't see any way we were going to make it.

CHAPTER 13

Escape to the Sea

The marine commander, General O. P. Smith, had it all worked out.

On the night the Chinese struck, two of his three regiments (the 5th and 7th) had been caught in an exposed position as they were attacking west from the Chosin Reservoir (just as Smith had feared they would). But his remaining regiment (the 1st) had been carefully outposted along the upper section of the seventy-mile-long road that led from the reservoir back to the sea.

One battalion of this regiment was holding Hagaru, at the foot of the reservoir. Another battalion was holding the village of Koto, eleven miles below Hagaru. And a third battalion was at Chinhung, ten miles below Koto.

All three garrisons were surrounded by overwhelming numbers of Chinese, but all three were holding firm, and so O. P. Smith would use these three fortified positions as stepping stones.

First the two lead regiments up at Yudam would turn around and fight their way back to Hagaru. Then the combined Yudam-

Hagaru force would fight its way down to Koto. Below Koto, at Chin-hung, the remaining marine battalion would attack north to seize a vital bridge as the main body at Koto moved south.

At the bridge Smith's division would be whole again, and from there it would fight its way south to the town of Hungnam, on the coast, where the navy would be waiting to take them out.

That was the plan, and so far it was working. By the fourth of December the 5th and 7th Regiments, along with the marines who had held Toktong Pass and what remained of some army units that had been on the eastern side of the reservoir, were safely inside the Hagaru perimeter.

The next step was to push down to Koto, and this movement began two days later, on December 6.

But during the two days the column spent gathering itself at Hagaru a number of important things happened: several enemy assaults were repulsed, over four thousand casualties were evacuated from the tiny airstrip inside the perimeter (thus relieving Smith of an enormous burden), and five hundred marine replacements were flown in.

Bringing in reinforcements was a bold move on Smith's part, because at this point the success of the withdrawal was by no means certain. In fact, to the outside world, watching the drama unfold daily in the newspapers, Smith's position looked utterly hopeless. But O. P. Smith, tall and courtly and soft spoken, but with the nerves of a gambler and a will of iron, was determined to bring his marines out fighting.

And so the call went out: men were needed to fly into Hagaru and join the desperate fight.

Richard Suarez was one marine who heard the call, and as he remembers it now, he experienced not a moment of hesitation.

I'd just landed in Japan from San Diego as part of a replacement draft. We were all lined up, getting assigned—some guys going off to supply, some getting desk jobs, some the infantry—when an officer came in and asked if anyone wanted to volunteer to fly into Korea as a replacement.

"The marines are in trouble at the reservoir," he said "They need men. Anybody wants to go, raise your hand."

So I raised my hand. What the hell did I know? I was nineteen years old, a private. And some marines needed help.

About twenty of us volunteered. We were taken down to Itazuke Air Base, where there were more volunteers waiting.

We flew over on C-47s. When my plane landed on the airstrip in Hagaru we immediately came under small-arms fire from the Chinese, who had the place surrounded. As I got off the plane the first thing I saw was another C-47 that had crashed at the end of the airstrip. It was just a burned-out hulk with its tail stuck in the air. And when the plane I came in on flew out again with some wounded I could see tracers from the Chinese machine guns streaking up at it.

Seeing that burned-out plane on the runway, and the plane I came in on getting shot at like that, I think that's when it finally sank in. Hey, Richard, you're really in some deep shit here.

I reported in to Three Seven[1] headquarters and was immediately assigned to the train moving out. The column was already formed up and Item Company, the unit I was assigned to, was leading the way out.

One guy, a sergeant, grabbed hold of me and said, "Stay here with the column, because if you go out there on the flanks you won't come back."

As we moved out from Hagaru I saw what he meant. There were high snow-covered hills on both sides of the road, and the Chinese were up there shooting at the column, so they would ask for volunteers to work the flanks, and whenever we started taking enemy fire the guys on the flanks would have to climb the hills and clear out the Chinese.

I volunteered anyway. On my first patrol we had to clear a ridge. We split up, one squad going up the front slope to hold the gooks' attention while the rest of us tried to slip around and take them by surprise. It was a long slow climb. In some places the snow would be waist deep, while on the saddles it would be almost bare and icy.

---

[1] 3rd Battalion, 7th Marine Regiment

We grabbed at any rock or shrub we could find, and sometimes we had to make a human chain and pull each other along. Guys would slip and fall and go rolling and clanking back down. But finally we got up there above the gooks and then we just shot them up.

There turned out to be more dead ones up there than alive. We found dozens of them frozen in the snow without a wound on them. They were just lying around like they were sleeping. They were all wearing sneakers. Most didn't have any gloves. Some didn't even have hats. The GIs in Korea always bitched and moaned about the cold, but I believe the Chinese had it much worse than we did.

They weren't up on those ridges in great force. They might have been when they first moved into the area, but I think a lot of them froze to death before they saw any action, or died of wounds from our air strikes and artillery. We pounded those ridges constantly, all during the six days it took for us to walk out of there.

From Hagaru one battalion from the 7th Marines went ahead of the column to clear the road. We started out the next day. It was clear and cold, and all day it was just moving, stopping, waiting, with the little fights on the ridges going on, and the air strikes coming in, and men leaving the column to go out on patrol, and other men coming back in. The column was all strung out along the road. Artillery, jeeps, trucks, tanks. There was one section where they had a dead marine tied to the hood of every jeep. The trucks were filled with dead. They were even tied to the running boards. Marines don't leave their wounded behind, and if they can help it, they don't leave their dead either.

By nightfall everybody was inside the perimeter at Koto. That's where we finally had to do something about the dead, because by now they were taking up space that was needed by the wounded and the guys with frostbite. There were more and more frostbite cases as we went along, guys who couldn't walk anymore, and it became a question of who we wanted to take out, the dead or the wounded. Because we could no longer take both.

The ground was too frozen to dig in, so the engineers blew a big hole in a rice paddy with TNT, and the dead were buried, right there at Koto.

I think it was a day or two later that we started south again. We had to wait until they replaced a bridge down near Chinhung. By now almost the whole division was together, and we made a column nearly ten miles long. Over fifteen hundred vehicles. As we moved south sometimes I was up on the ridges, sometimes down with the column. On one patrol I was on we found thirty or forty Chinese in foxholes near the road. We went around just pulling them up out of the holes. They were alive but they were so frozen they couldn't move. Some of them looked like they were wearing gloves, their hands were so black. It must have been gangrene, because you could smell it even in the cold.

There was fighting all the way to Chinhung. The usual thing: sporadic machine-gun and rifle fire from the Chinese, mortar rounds coming in and blowing up in the snow. If they hit a vehicle you'd see a ball of flame and a big column of black smoke going up. Then the whole column would stop until whatever got hit was pushed off the road.

Basically that's all it was, walking every day, and waiting while the planes or one of our patrols blew the Chinese off the ridges or out of a roadblock.

Not everybody was John Wayne up there. Our battalion had three self-inflicted wounds. SIWs. Most of the guys who had been up at Yudam, they were just trying to make it back. A lot of them were at the limit of what they could take. I saw one officer sitting by the side of the road crying. I guess he just cracked under the strain. Everybody has a breaking point, and everybody's breaking point is different.

You take the company I joined. Item Company. There was practically nobody left from the original company. Maybe fifty, sixty guys. They'd been decimated up at Yudam, and most of the ones that were left didn't think we were going to get out. But I think that says a lot about those guys, that they fought the way they did, and kept their discipline even when a lot of them thought the situation was hopeless.

I never had any doubt that we'd get out of there. None whatever. That's one thing the Marine Corps did for me. I believed all the bullshit. I believed one marine was worth ten Chinese, that when the Chinese surrounded the marines up at the reservoir, it was the Chinese who were in trouble. If marine training teaches you one thing, it's not to quit. That a man has in him more than he knows. Not every marine gets the most out of himself, but with the training they give you, and the way they indoctrinate you, you end up doing things you never thought you could do.

When we got over the bridge at Chinhung we knew we were in the home stretch. And the closer we got to getting out of there, the more the rumors flew. Back and forth along the column. Some of them were amazing. There were all these girls waiting for us in Hungnam. We were all going to be sent to Japan for a month's leave. Anybody with frostbite was going to be sent to Guam to thaw out. Everybody was going to be sent home for Christmas.

None of these things were true. But I think everybody at least half believed every one of them.

Hungnam was on the coast. That's where the navy was waiting to take us out. An army division was holding a perimeter around the port, and on the sixth day of the march, in the morning, we could see all these trucks coming toward us up the road. They had big white stars on them. That's when I knew we were out of it, when I saw all those GI trucks coming to take us out.

But a lot of marines didn't want the trucks. They were army trucks. We walked this far, we'll walk the rest of the way in. Dumb, right? But that's the way we felt.

CHAPTER 14

Shielding the Storm

While the marines were still fighting their way out of the North Korean mountains and back to the coast, an important but little-known action was taking place near the town of Sachang.

A regiment of the army's 3rd Infantry Division had been sent out toward Sachang, some twenty miles west of the road to the Chosin Reservoir, to protect the left flank of the advance to the Yalu. When the Chinese struck and the retreat began, this became the right flank of the withdrawal—and now more than ever it needed protection. Sachang was well south of the retreating UN forces, and if the Chinese broke through there and cut the road from the reservoir, nobody was going to make it out.

George Zonge was at Sachang. He was an army lifer, a thirty-year man. Korea was neither his first war nor his last, but he has no trouble remembering how it was. In particular he remembers something others seem to have forgotten or have never known—that a regiment of army troops fought long and hard to protect the lower end of the road that the marines used in their escape from the Chosin Reservoir.

"Everybody says the marines saved themselves. Especially the marines. And after all this time you can't argue with people because they won't believe you. But I know. I was there. It's been my little secret."

I was at Fort Lee, Virginia, when the war in Korea started. I was a master sergeant. I was in charge of the Office of the Quartermaster General photo lab, but I had a lot of troop experience, and I figured I'd be sent over there if the war lasted long enough, because my basic job in the army was still the infantry.

I was still at Fort Lee when President Truman let all the prisoners out of the army stockades. Truman promised all the stockade prisoners that if they went to Korea and fought well, they would be exonerated.

I got orders to go to Korea myself shortly after that. I don't recall worrying much about it. I thought, Hell, we'll knock Korea off in a week. They weren't even calling it a war. They were calling it a police action.

I went to Japan first, and joined the 7th Regiment of the 3rd Infantry Division.

I was put in charge of a weapons platoon. Recoilless rifles and 60mm mortars. We trained in Japan. Half my troops were Koreans. The other half were the guys from the stockade at Fort Lee. I caught up with them in Japan, and helped train them. And they were damn good soldiers too.

We only trained for three weeks. Strictly on how to use the weapons. I couldn't understand the Koreans. We needed an interpreter for everything. But they were good people, the ones I had. I think I got the smarter ones, because they had to learn to use the sights, learn about trajectories, things like that. The riflemen I didn't think a whole lot of.

After three weeks we shipped out and landed at Wonsan, right behind the marines. I'm kind of foggy on the date.[1] There was the 7th, 15th, and 65th Regiments in our division, and they all got to

---

[1] It was November 17, 1950.

Wonsan on different days. The 65th was all Puerto Rican. Our regiment and the 15th was both kind of slapped together, half American and half Korean. But the 65th was a good outfit. Those Puerto Ricans were well trained.

Shorty Soule was commanding the division. Colonel Robert Soule. He was a good man. He was like Patton. I served under Patton in World War II, and Patton would always talk to his NCOs. That's the way you find out how things really are among the men. Shorty Soule was the same.

No, I didn't know about his reputation for drinking. But I do know I never saw him drunk. And I saw him a lot.

The port of Wonsan had already been captured by the time we got there. It was captured before even the marines got there. It was captured by the ROKs. Even Bob Hope was there before we were. So we weren't expecting any resistance. Inland we were, but there turned out not to be any resistance there either. The ROK army was so far ahead of us, they had cleared out the countryside.

We moved north and then west, over on the left flank of the marines. Along the way our company commander got promoted and moved up to division, and we got a guy took his place who later went crazy. This guy was not a good CO. To be blunt, he didn't know what the hell he was doing. He gave at least two orders that I disobeyed. I was almost court-martialed, but I wasn't going to obey those orders. In both cases they would have resulted in people getting killed for nothing. Anybody who knew combat wouldn't have given them.

We got all the way up to the town of Sachang without any real fighting. There was some sniping, and some harassing attacks at night by North Korean guerrillas, but no big battle until the Chinese came in.

Then it was fighting, day and night.

I think the first time they hit us was about eight o'clock at night. It was the damnedest thing I ever saw—they came swarming over the hills making all kinds of noise, blowing bugles and rattling cans and shooting off flares and yelling their heads off in these high-pitched sing-song voices. They had no armor. No vehicles of any kind. It was like one of those old-time infantry charges you read about in the Civil War.

They were shooting burp guns and rifles but I'll tell you, they were lousy shots. What caused us the most trouble was grenades. And the fact that there was so goddamn many of them. Just wave after wave. You'd shoot down a whole line of Chinamen and another line would be right behind. They'd stop to pick up the weapons of the ones that had been shot, and then they'd come on like the first ones. We'd shoot them down, and there would be another line right behind them.

Also, by this time the weather had turned cold. At night it was ten and twenty below zero. The men didn't have foxholes dug. You couldn't dig a foxhole, the ground was too hard. What you did, you chipped a little depression in the ground, just enough to lie down in. Some fellas couldn't do even that much. Their hands were frostbitten and they couldn't hold an entrenching tool. They had trouble holding their rifles.

The Chinese who hit us were trying to cut the road between the Chosin Reservoir and the coast. They were trying to trap the marines and the 7th Division, which was also up around the reservoir. Personally I didn't know about any of that. I found that out later. All I knew at the time was that we were ordered to stay where we were and hold our positions.

We were on a series of low hills. Three or four times the Chinese broke our forward defenses, but we always beat them back. We learned to listen for their attack whistles. We'd pile all our grenades in the empty ammo boxes and hold our fire until we heard the whistles, and then we'd shift positions so that all our firepower was concentrated in the direction of the whistles. That way, they'd hit a new spot along the line, it would be just as strong as the place they'd hit before. They'd try spot after spot, and we'd beat the hallelujah out of them.

They had an awful lot of manpower but not much firepower. Once we got over the shock of having all those people coming at us out of nowhere, we were all right. Not to say we didn't lose men. But they didn't cut that road. They didn't even get close.

When we got the word to pull out we still didn't know much about what was going on, except that now we were retreating, and we still had to fight all the time. The marines were flying support for us, strafing and bombing, trying to keep the road open. They'd fly their Corsairs so low, the spent cartridges from their wing guns would bounce off our helmets.

Being in a weapons platoon, mostly I was up on the ridges, to support the infantry down on the roads. A 57mm recoilless rifle is really a small cannon, but it's light enough for a man to carry. It's got a range of about seven hundred yards, and my boys were good. They were always calling on us. We'd blow the Chinese out of caves in the hills. We'd shoot up their roadblocks.

We got down to the port of Hungnam, where the navy was evacuating everybody.[2] Hungnam was just one big swamp of slush and mud, from all the vehicles and troops going through. The air was full of smoke from the factories and warehouses that were burning.

I think they evacuated the troops alphabetically. I helped set the charges on the docks, and the guy helping me was named Zimmer. Zimmer and Zonge. I don't believe that was a coincidence, because he was a captain and I was a sergeant.

It was a spectacular explosion. We piled up cases of frozen dynamite and all the extra ammo and gas drums and wired it together and set it off with primacord. I was on an army transport out in the bay when it went off, and the explosion almost capsized the ship.

We went by boat to Pusan and retrained there. We were taking on a lot of replacements. We got new clothes. I don't believe we changed our clothes all the time we were up in North Korea.

We wondered what was going to happen next. A month before, up near the Yalu River, we thought the war was almost over. Now we were right back where we started, back below the 38th parallel.

Christmas of 1950 was a bad time. We were back in reserve, we were retraining, but for what? There was no morale left worth talking about. Most of the men wanted to leave Korea to the Koreans.

---

[2]In all, the U.S. Navy rescued 110,000 American and South Korean troops and 90,000 Korean refugees from Hungnam. The navy also took out 20,000 vehicles and more than a quarter of a million tons of supplies.

Let them work it out. They didn't think it was worth it, what they were going through. The Chinese coming in like that had really affected everybody. It was a terrific shock.

Personally I didn't feel like a beaten man, but I was part of a beaten army. I can't deny that. Wherever you want to put the blame, on MacArthur or whoever, we'd taken a real beating from the Chinese. And the worst part of it was, we didn't know where it was going to end. We didn't know but that there were a million of them out there, and not one of them afraid to die. You had to ask yourself, Was it worth it? And for a lot of the troops, the answer was no.

CHAPTER 15

Ridgway

Two days before Christmas of 1950, General Walton Walker was killed in a jeep accident near Uijongbu. Walker had been in command of the Eighth Army, that same collection of fighting men who had held the Pusan perimeter and who had then pushed north all the way to the Yalu River only to be pushed quickly south again as the Chinese crashed down upon them. A "European" general who was never completely comfortable in Asia and who had been looking forward to retirement, Walton Walker went home at last, leaving behind him a very shaky and badly demoralized army that faced, for the second time in less than six months, a very real danger of being thrown off the Korean peninsula.

The man chosen to replace Walker was General Matthew B. Ridgway. Ridgway arrived in Korea in January of 1951, and the changes that immediately began to take place could not have been more electrifying.

Harry Summers was a young enlisted man at the time, and he saw and felt those changes personally. He would have occasion, much later in his life, to dedicate a book to the memory of Matt Ridgway. Or more precisely, to what Ridgway accomplished in Korea.

Harry Summers went on to a distinguished service career of his own, including duty in Vietnam as both soldier and negotiator. He has written extensively about Vietnam, and he edits Vietnam *magazine. "But Korea was my defining war. It was in Korea that I really learned what war was all about. And it was in Korea that I witnessed what I still regard as the most remarkable accomplishment in our military history."*

I enlisted in the army in June 1947. I was only fifteen, but I told them I was eighteen. I enlisted in the engineers, hoping to go to Europe, but when I finished basic training I found I had orders for Korea.

I didn't know where Korea was. I'd never heard of it. So I went to my first sergeant, and he'd never heard of Korea either. We got out the atlas in the orderly room, and there was no Korea in the atlas. It was still shown on the maps as Chosen, the old Japanese name for it.

I was there from the end of 1947 until 1949, when we broke up the occupation. As was the case with most U.S. personnel, I was transferred to Japan. A brand-new tank company was being formed, and I ended up in that.

I was still in Japan in June 1950. As a matter of fact, I was in a hospital in Fukuoka with a stomach ulcer, at age eighteen, if you can imagine that. I'd had three-quarters of my stomach removed, and I was still in the hospital on bed rest the day the Korean War started. The first of the evacuees came through that hospital. They were mostly civilians, the wives and children of U.S. advisers. Then suddenly the medical orderlies came through and marked all the patients fit for duty. All of us had to go back to our units. They were clearing the hospital for casualties.

My unit shipped out through Shimonoseki, a town just across the straits from Korea. All the new people, all us kids, were afraid we weren't going to get there in time. We just couldn't wait to get into the fight before it was over. All the World War II veterans, which were the majority of our sergeants and officers, knew what we were getting into, and they weren't quite so eager.

We had sixteen light M-24 tanks in the company. The guns on our tanks were not powerful enough to stop a T-34, the Soviet-built tanks the North Koreans were using. We didn't know this as we headed into combat, but we soon found out. One of my platoon sergeants put something like twelve rounds into a T-34, and every one of them bounced off.

Eventually we were resupplied with better tanks. Actually they were tanks from World War Two that had been sitting in Japan, but they had a bigger gun that could stop the T-34.

After the breakout from the Pusan perimeter we just road-marched north and ended up on the Chongchon River in North Korea. The North Koreans had all but disappeared. We thought the war was about over. We were fifteen miles from the Yalu River. We had no inkling that the Chinese were about to come in.

It was a surprise to us when we got orders to pull back. The Chinese had hit Eighth Army hard, but not every sector saw fighting. We saw no Chinese at all, and for a while the withdrawal was puzzling to us. We didn't know what was going on in some of the other sectors. We actually had a pretty easy time of it. The 2nd Infantry Division was blocking for us, and they got decimated. There were hundreds of thousands of refugees streaming south. It was the most pitiful thing I've ever seen. If they got within a hundred yards of the road they were shot. There was only one road to move Eighth Army on, and the road had to be kept open.

We spent Christmas of 1950 in a blocking position south of the 38th parallel. My tank unit was broken up and I ended up in an infantry rifle company, and at first I was scared to death. You know, you get put in the infantry, you're a goner for sure. But it turned out to be a good company. Good officers, good sergeants.

I was with this company, L Company of the 21st Regiment, when General Ridgway arrived in Korea. Ridgway made an enormous impact, just unbelievable, and he made it right down to the troop level. We had been sitting around in these defensive positions ever since Eighth Army's withdrawal from the north, doing much of nothing, and within a week of Ridgway taking over we were on a combat patrol thirty miles behind the Chinese lines. It was the most remarkable transformation I have ever seen of turning an army around, on the strength of his character alone.

What Ridgway did primarily was get us off the roads and up into the hills. Walton Walker was a tank man, and maybe because of that he showed an inclination to stick to the roads. While Walker was in command the American troops were roadbound, and they stayed roadbound, and when the Chinese came into the war they used the ridgelines to get around and behind all those road-hugging American units. But Ridgway was pure infantry. He knew the value of the high ground. After Ridgway arrived on the scene, I don't remember being anywhere near a road. We stayed up in the mountains, meeting the Chinese on their own terms.

When he got to Korea the first thing Ridgway did was go out and talk to people. He talked to every corps commander and every division commander. He would stop soldiers along the road and talk to them. And he came to the conclusion, and rightly so, that Eighth Army's most serious problems were not physical but mental. Men were disillusioned and disoriented, they were not sure of their mission, not sure what they were doing in Korea. So Ridgway composed a message that was read to every man in Eighth Army. It asked, and answered, two questions: "Why are we here?" and "What are we fighting for?"[1] After that no one had the slightest doubt why they were in Korea.

Ridgway had a real empathy for the GI, and also a firm belief in the effectiveness of leadership. The tendency of too many commanders, when things went wrong, was to blame the troops. Ridgway knew there was always a great reservoir of squad-level courage in the American army, and that if the frontline soldier was led effectively he would always go out and get the job done. So he concentrated on the leadership, and heads rolled over there for a while. Walker had been very forgiving of officers who were in reality too old or too inexperienced to fight a war in Korea. When Ridgway came in he immediately identified these officers and got rid of them.

---

[1] What Ridgway did, essentially, was explain in very clear language that the American army was in Korea to contain the spread of Communism, which posed a threat to world peace and to the security of the United States.

He brought in or promoted younger men who had demonstrated their competence on the battlefield.

And it was also Ridgway, by the way, who was instrumental in getting the army in Korea truly integrated. And believe me, that was quite a job. The resistance to integration was terrific. Truman had signed an executive order in 1948 that supposedly integrated the army, but nothing had happened.

When they first started talking about integration, white soldiers were aghast. They would say, How can you integrate the army? How do you know when you go to the mess hall that you won't get a plate or a knife or a spoon that was used by a Negro? Or when you go to the supply room and draw sheets, you might get a sheet that a Negro had slept on.

Well of course that's ludicrous. But it wasn't ludicrous in 1950. That was a very common attitude among the troops then.

I remember a night when my rifle company was scheduled to get some replacements. I was in a three-man foxhole with one other guy, and they dropped this new replacement off at our foxhole. The other guy I was in the foxhole with was under a poncho, making coffee. It was bitterly cold. And pitch dark. He got the coffee made, and he gave me a drink, and he took a drink, and then he offered some to this new replacement, who we literally couldn't see, it was that dark.

And the guy said, "No, I don't want any."

"What the hell are you talking about, you don't want any? You got to be freezing to death. Here, take a drink of coffee."

"No," the guy said, "I don't want to."

"What's wrong with you, man?"

"Well," he said, "you can't tell it now, but I'm black. And tomorrow morning when you find out I was drinking out of the same cup you were using, you ain't gonna be too happy."

Me and this other guy kind of looked at each other.

"You silly son of a bitch," we told him, "here, take the goddamn coffee."

That was our first black replacement. And it really struck me then, what a terrible, terrible thing we'd done to ourselves, and to our society. That a man would come to us with an attitude like that.

Of course integration wouldn't immediately change the way whites and blacks looked on each other. But I think Ridgway realized that an integrated unit usually performed much better in combat than a segregated one.

One other thing Ridgway did, largely through his battlefield tactics, was disabuse people of the notion that the Chinese were supermen. They relied a lot on massive human wave assaults, but that could play right into our firepower. And that's the approach Ridgway adopted. He did not concentrate as much on capturing territory as he did on killing the enemy. And it worked. The Chinese simply couldn't take the kind of casualties they were taking indefinitely.

Our artillery especially would really wreak havoc on them. I remember once being up on the edge of the Chorwon Valley, and looking across the valley and seeing this enormously long Chinese supply train on the far side. They had camels and horses and donkeys and everything else. Everything except trucks. I don't think they had a single motorized vehicle. Our artillery forward observer, a guy by the name of Hardy, called in a TOT, a Timed On Target, and this mile-long supply train, this whole thing just disappeared. It was the most awesome, and at the same time the most terrible sight I think I've ever seen.

But probably the most remarkable thing about Ridgway was the speed with which he turned things around out there. He transformed an entire army within a matter of weeks. In early January of 1951, shortly after Walker's death, the Chinese launched another offensive. Eighth Army was pushed back again, and morale went so low it dropped off the scale. But by the end of that same month Ridgway had them on the attack, and by February he was launching counteroffensives of his own—the kind of big, brutal, punishing attacks that are not carried out by men with bad morale. In my opinion Ridgway's arrival in Korea marked the turning point of the war.

CHAPTER 16

Cold Steel

Matthew Bunker Ridgway got things moving again. The new Chinese offensive that had begun on New Year's Day of 1951 had pushed the UN forces sixty miles below the 38th parallel, but by the middle of January another lull had descended over the battlefront, and Ridgway used it to regroup his forces in strong defensive positions, from which they could launch aggressive attacks against any further Chinese buildup. It was the first stage in returning the Eighth Army (which now included X Corps) to an offensive mode.

But the Chinese proved difficult to find. During the lull their major formations had withdrawn some distance from the front line, most likely to regroup.

After a series of careful probes, a major UN counteroffensive began on January 25, but it proceeded cautiously. The primary goal was not to take real estate but to reduce Chinese defensive positions and in the process to kill as many of the enemy as possible—a goal that came to be known among the troops as "the Ridgway mission."

Lewis Millett, an ex-artillery forward observer who had turned himself into an infantry commander, took the Ridgway mission to

heart. Early in February, as his company was conducting a tank-
infantry probe as part of the general UN offensive, Millett found his
advance blocked by a company of Chinese who were holding on stub-
bornly to a small hill. Gathering his men, Millett led them in one
of the most ferocious bayonet charges in modern military history, a
feat that earned him the Congressional Medal of Honor and, later,
center stage in a three-dimensional display at the National Guard
Museum in Washington, D.C., where he now stands preserved for
posterity in resin and epoxy, rifle in hand, bayonet fixed, at the crest
of a miniature Korean hill.

The diorama in Washington shows him as he is about to kill
three Chinese soldiers occupying a foxhole directly in front of him.
The scene is accurate, Millett says, as far as it goes.

When you're fighting, it's confusing. You don't see everything that's going on. I killed the three Chinese in that first foxhole, and then went on. But I don't remember going on. I remember fighting, but I don't know what I did.

I know I went berserk. When you hit somebody in the throat with a bayonet, another one in the head, you got blood spraying up all over you, nobody's going to stay rational. In a bayonet charge, you're not rational in the first place. I think that's why the Vikings were so good. They'd go berserk. Nobody's thinking, they're just reacting.

The other thing about combat is, you can do things that would normally be impossible. The adrenaline gets in there, and you do things that are just physically not possible. During that attack I stuck a Chinaman and threw him up out of the foxhole on my bayonet and stuck him again on the way down. Well, you can't do that normally.

Then afterward, I was so weak. You could have touched me with your finger and I'd have fallen down. After it was all over I sat down and couldn't get up. I'd used up all this tremendous energy doing all these things, and I was completely drained. The whole company was like that. After we took the hill something started to happen on the right flank, and we all started to get up, not fast, not running, but slowly, like a bunch of sleepwalkers.

I didn't start out in Korea in the infantry. I was a forward observer with the artillery. But I was always on the front lines, and I decided that if I was going to be up there fighting all the time, I'd rather be in the infantry.

I guess it's in the blood. One of my ancestors, eleven generations ago, was killed in King Philip's War in 1675. My youngest son was killed in 1985, coming back from peacekeeping duty in the Sinai. Members of my family have been in every conflict in between. Both my great-grandfathers fought in the Civil War. My uncle fought at Château-Thierry in World War One. I was in World War Two and Korea. It's a tradition that goes back to the first Millett who served the King of Normandy in 1067.

When I decided to transfer to the infantry I went over and talked to Colonel Murch, in the 27th Regiment. We knew each other because my artillery unit had been firing support for the 27th all through the war.

I talked to Murch, and he said, "Well, the only job open is commanding officer of Company E."

I said, "That's my company."

This was December 1950, up around Uijongbu, north of Seoul. We were in the middle of the Eighth Army's big retreat. The Chinese had just come in and it was all we could do to get out of there.

In January we went into defensive positions around Pyongtaek, well south of Seoul. It was bitterly cold. I grew up in Maine, so I know what cold is. But this was *cold.*

There was lots of frostbite. One day one of my men came up to me and said, "You've got to relieve my squad leader." I said, "Why?" Well, turned out this guy had frostbite, and his toes were rotting off and they were stinking so bad everybody could smell him, even in weather that cold. I believe they had to amputate both his feet.

We had what's called a warming tent. I'd have one platoon out on line, another platoon out patrolling, and the third platoon in the tent, getting warm and eating. And we'd rotate around like that. But it was so cold that you could get frostbite before you ever got to the warming tent.

Things didn't turn around until late in January. General Ridgway took over the Eighth Army and at the end of January we went back on the attack. But there didn't seem to be any Chinese out there. We moved north in battalion-sized probes, ten and fifteen miles at a time, and there was no contact. Nothing. We were always braced to get hit, but there didn't seem to be anybody out there.

Finally, just north of Osan, we started to get resistance. My company was the lead element. We had some tanks with us, a hundred men on five or six tanks, and we'd ride out on the tanks until we started receiving fire, then get off the tanks, form a skirmish line and attack.

The first time we drew fire the Chinese were on a little range of hills. There weren't very many of them. Probably not more than a reinforced platoon. They fired some machine-gun bursts at us, some rifle fire, then they stopped. By this time we were within three hundred yards of them, and when we got up there . . . nothing but holes. They were gone.

The next day the same thing happened, only this time they fought. They were on some hills again, and we formed a skirmish line and attacked across the rice paddies. We attacked with the bayonet. We charged up the hill, and they shot at us for a while, but when we got near the top they broke and ran. We shot a lot of them in the back as they were running off the hill.

I think what might've shook them was the sight of our bayonets. A month or so earlier we'd gotten a combat bulletin that had been translated from the Chinese. It said that the American infantry didn't like to fight, that we relied on artillery and airplanes to do all our fighting for us. Particularly, it said, Americans were afraid of the bayonet.

That got me mad. When I read that I said to my men, "We'll see who's afraid of the bayonet."

I had all my men go out and get bayonets. We scrounged a lot, went back to supply and asked for some, stole a couple. We got sharpening stones from the Koreans, and we sharpened up the bayonets, and I started to teach them bayonet drill. The stuff I learned in the Canadian army. I'd been in the Canadian army for a while in World War II, before our country got into the war, and they had a very good bayonet drill. Very realistic.

The men took to it right away. They were very enthusiastic. But then I had a good outfit. Those fellas in E Company were fighters anyway. Other companies would poke fun at us, but we kept on with our drills, because I told the men, "Next attack we make, bayonets!"

The day after we overran that second hill there was no fighting for us, because we were out on the battalion flank. But the day after that, February the seventh, we really connected.

The road we were on ran north and south, with some flat land around it and then a hill mass rising up, maybe a hundred meters high, and running alongside the road. I put a platoon up there, marching single file along the ridgeline to protect my flank. I put the other two platoons on the flat ground next to the road.

After four or five hours we stopped to let another company catch up to us. While we were waiting there, some of the men in the platoon I'd put up on the ridgeline saw something they thought was strange.

The ridgeline had stopped, and in front of them it dropped down to a rice paddy. Across the rice paddy there was a hill that blocked their line of advance. They were looking at this hill, and some of the guys noticed that it had an awful lot of shrubbery on top. Most of the hills in that part of Korea were bare, like they'd been shaved, because the Koreans would cut down all the trees and shrubs for firewood.

Then somebody saw something move, a couple of figures, and they radioed me. "Enemy to the front."

I deployed my men. About that time somebody fired a round, and pretty soon there was firing back and forth. Long range, though. Three or four hundred yards. It wasn't very effective.

My platoon sergeant was close by, and I shouted to him, "Fix bayonets! We're going to attack!"

I jumped up onto a tank and fired the machine gun, to show the guys in the tank how I wanted them to shoot at the top of the ridge, just over our heads, so we could get up there.

Then I yelled, "Follow me," and we charged.

We ran across the frozen rice paddies. Eighty men on line, spread across maybe two or three hundred yards.

Halfway up the hill we really started to get it. At the bottom they couldn't see us, from where they were on the crest, but about halfway up they suddenly had us in defilade, shooting down into us. All these grenades going off, and with all the noise, I didn't hear this Chinese who was shooting at me. He was shooting right at *me*, with a .55-caliber antitank rifle. Has a shell about five inches long. Pierce about one and half inches of armor plating. A very big rifle.

I could see the dust kicking up all around me, but I didn't see right away who was shooting at me. Somebody was hollering, "Look out, Captain, he's shooting at you," but I was busy dodging all these grenades. I could see them coming at me, flying through the air. I'd jump over to the side, back, over to the other side, trying to get out of the way.

All the while I'm trying to think how to get up there and get that guy throwing the grenades, and finally he threw one I didn't see. He rolled it along the ground.

Bam. It put a hole in my shin.

Jesus, was I mad then. You ever get kicked in the shin? That's how it felt. Made me mad as hell.

Finally it dawned on me that if I charged just when this guy was getting ready to throw, I could run past the grenades and get up there in the hole with him before he could throw more.

And that's what I did.

I jumped in the hole with him and killed him. Ran the bayonet through his chest. Then I scrambled out and ran over to the next hole. The Chinaman in that hole was the one with the antitank rifle. I got him in the throat. Then I ran to the lip of the next hole. This one had a submachine gun, and when he turned around and saw me, he froze.

That saved my life. He could have shot me dead. But he froze. Not for very long. Maybe a second or two. And I can understand why. It surprised the hell out of him to see this guy with a big red mustache, wild eyes, big red face, screaming and yelling at him.

He should have killed me. But he hesitated just long enough for me to hit him first. I got him in the skull. It amazed me at the time, because, you know, you think of the head being hard. But it isn't,

114

not for a good sharp bayonet. It went right in, and I can remember thinking, in the back of my mind, Jesus, it's just like cutting cheese.

Once I got rid of those three I ran toward the center of the line, evidently going on and doing all kinds of crazy things. That's the part I don't remember. I only learned about that part when S. L. A. Marshall, the military historian, interviewed my company for one of his books. He talked to everybody in the company, myself included, and I was amazed when I heard them describing what I did. Killing all those Chinamen, using my rifle like a baseball bat, lifting that guy up out of his foxhole on my bayonet and whatnot. I have no memory of that at all.

In fifteen or twenty minutes it was all over. It didn't seem even that long. In a fight time gets compressed. I would have said five minutes, but it was closer to twenty.

Taking that hill we captured three heavy machine guns, and that's when I realized how lucky we'd been. When we broke over the top of the hill the Chinese started throwing grenades. They stopped firing their weapons to throw grenades, and that was a mistake. They probably panicked, but if they would have stayed with their heavy guns we'd have been slaughtered.

After that attack I was called in by the battalion commander and told not to do it anymore. "No more bayonet attacks," he said. "You're going to get yourself and everybody else killed."

Which was probably true. I was lucky they went to the grenades. That allowed us to get in on them. A lot of things come down to luck. That's why I'm alive today. I was just lucky.

I didn't know they'd recommended me for the Medal of Honor until they pulled me off the line in May. They would do that once the recommendation was approved at theater level and forwarded to Washington, so the person receiving the medal would be alive when the time came to give it to him.

I was surprised. I didn't expect it. There were a lot of guys on that hill that did as much as I did.

They flew me home commercial, on a Pan Am Constellation. Went home to Maine for a month, then down to Washington in late June. President Truman pinned it on in the Rose Garden.

People ask me about it all the time. How it was. If I was scared. They don't always understand my answer.

In actual combat I've never been scared. I've been frightened ahead of time that I wouldn't do a good job. But once a fight started I felt no fear. I just knew I wasn't going to die.

I'm not heroic. Heroism is when you're scared and do something despite your fear. I'm a warrior. I never felt fear in combat. But if I am a warrior, and I don't do what I think I should do as a warrior, that's what scares me. That's where the fear is.

CHAPTER 17

The Test

Goaded by the UN attack that had begun late in January, the Chinese quickly struck back. Massing seven armies along the central sector of the front, a huge force that remained largely undetected by U.S. intelligence, the Chinese high command pulled the trigger on February 11.

A South Korean division was immediately wiped out of existence. A number of American units were cut off and surrounded and had to fight their way out. Others were ordered to retreat before they could be enveloped.

Dug in around the village of Chipyong, facing the left flank of the Chinese attack, Colonel Paul Freeman's 23rd Regimental Combat Team was on full alert. Freeman's force had been in the area for about ten days, and there had been plenty of time to prepare the perimeter for defense. Still, aware of the odds against him—four thousand of his own men against an estimated twenty-five thousand Chinese—Freeman requested permission to withdraw.

The reply came from Ridgway himself: there would be no withdrawal. Chipyong must be held.

It was going to be a test of UN will and firepower against the awesome and up-to-now irresistible ocean of Chinese manpower.

On the night of February 13 Freeman met with his commanders. Lynn Freeman (no relation to Colonel Freeman), an executive officer in one of the rifle companies, was not at the meeting, but he remembers how the gloomy news quickly made the rounds: they were probably already surrounded by the Chinese and outnumbered at least six to one, but they were going to have to stay and fight. Help was on the way, in the form of an armored task force, but the Chinese would very likely attack before the task force could get there.

For the first time since he'd arrived in Korea six months before, Lynn Freeman began to have serious doubts that he would make it home.

Our battalion had been the last to pull into Chipyong, and when we got there my company immediately took up a reserve position around some old Korean farmhouses, with our CP in one of the buildings. We found out later that this was a rather precarious position, because during the early part of the fighting we took a lot of overs [rounds fired by the Chinese that actually went over various parts of the perimeter]. A number of our men were wounded this way before they ever got into the fight.

The area around Chipyong was very hilly. There were a few scrub trees on the hills, and as I recall there was snow on the ground. Our perimeter completely encircled the village, with the various companies dug in on the low hills. There were our three battalions [from the 23rd Regiment], the French Battalion,[1] and a company of rangers. The rangers stayed with us as part of the reserves. Everybody else was deployed on the line.

Inside the perimeter we had some tanks and heavy mortars and an entire artillery battalion, about two dozen big guns. And we had an enormous supply of ammunition. Colonel Freeman had made certain of that. So actually we had a lot of firepower.

---

[1] By this time the war in Korea had taken on a truly international flavor—all but two of the sixteen UN member nations committed to the war had troops engaged.

About an hour after dark it started. I heard a rifle shot that seemed a long way off. Then more rifle fire, then our machine guns opening up. A lieutenant came into our building and said, "Stand by. This is it!" He was a little excited. He had his shirt and boots on but not his trousers.

Actually that first attack was only a probe. The Chinese were trying to fix our positions. When the main attack came it hit mostly in the sector held by the French. We could see the French positions from where we were. They were on a hill on the west side of the perimeter, and we could see the flares go up and hear the whistles and bugles as the Chinese charged them.

Then suddenly we heard this ungodly howl. Somebody among the French had cranked up a hand siren. It surprised the hell out of the Chinese. After the siren went off the French troops jumped up out of their foxholes and went at the Chinese with bayonets and grenades. Ran right at them. It was really extraordinary to see. That busted up the attack right away, and their sector quieted down rather quickly.

There were four or five more attacks that night. Most of them hit the G Company sector. We thought we'd be thrown in, but G Company held.

When dawn came there were still Chinese in among the company's positions. Some were hiding in a ravine, and a rocket team fired a round in there and flushed them out. When they ran out into the open our men shot them down like a flock of quail.

We knew they were going to hit us again the next night, so we spent all that day getting ready for it. Digging all the foxholes and trenches deeper, clearing weapons, passing out ammunition, splicing any commo wires that might have been cut, resetting the trip flares along the perimeter. There were some airdrops of supplies, but not all the cannisters landed inside the perimeter. The Chinese ended up getting a lot of them.

All through the day we could see the air strikes coming in. The air force was using napalm, and sometimes we'd stop work and watch, because it was really something to see. The entire side or top of a hill would erupt in a big roiling ball of orange flames and thick black smoke. We took occassional mortar rounds all through the day, but I don't remember seeing a single Chinese. During the day they kept out of sight.

The second night started out like the first, with some probes. A squad of Chinese would sneak up close to the line and roll grenades into the foxholes, then get up and charge, trying to punch a hole in the line. They didn't succeed, and by midnight they'd quit fooling around and were attacking in force all around the perimeter. My company was still in reserve, and it was really tough. I would much rather have been in the middle of it, because when you're in reserve like that all you can do is sit there and wonder when you'll be going in. You can see all the firing going on, the tracer rounds, the artillery, the mortars exploding, the flares overhead. You can see all that, and you hear all the noise, and all you can do is wait for the call. There's too much time to think, and that's not what you want, because thinking can really do a job on your nerves.

The Chinese kept hammering at G Company's sector, and finally, around three in the morning, the pressure got to be too much and G Company pulled back off their little hill. The Chinese came in through the hole, and we lost our illumination for a while because the crews on the 155s had to abandon the guns when they came under fire. They'd been firing artillery flares all night to keep the perimeter lit up. We fought in complete darkness until they got some C-47s to come over and drop parachute flares, which put an eerie orange glow over the whole battlefield.

A platoon of rangers and a platoon from F Company counterattacked and tried to retake the hill that G Company had lost, but there were too many Chinese up there and the attack bogged down.

By now it was daylight, but the Chinese did not follow their usual practice and break off the attack. They continued their assaults all around the perimeter, concentrating on G Company's old positions. I'm sure they knew the Cav was coming [the armored task force from the 1st Cavalry Division], and they wanted to break our lines and finish us off while they still had a chance.

So they continued to attack in broad daylight, in full view of our air support, which just tore them up. They were taking horrendous casualties, but it didn't seem to mean anything to them.

That's when I thought we might not get out. When I saw that kind of fanaticism. I'd just had a daughter born a few weeks before, in January, and at that point in the fighting I began wondering if I was ever going to see her.

Finally we got the call, we were going to counterattack, and around the middle of the morning we moved out with the rest of the ranger company and tried to retake the hill where G Company's old positions were. As long as the Chinese held that hill they controlled part of our perimeter, and they could force a major breakthrough at any time.

We made several attempts to get up there. Our starting point was a road and a patch of flat land. Then we had to move up a gradually rising slope that had practically no cover on it. We were getting hit with small-arms fire, machine-gun fire, mortar fire, indirect fire from our own captured bazookas. It was murderous. There was a constant buzzing in the air from all the bullets. As officers we were trying to push our men forward, but the fire would get so intense that nobody could move. All the while we're firing our own weapons, and finally the ammo gets low and you've got to pull back.

That happened several times. Up about halfway, then back down. We were till trying to take those positions when the Cav came up from the south, about four in the afternoon, and as their lead tanks approached the perimeter the Chinese withdrew. God, we were happy to see those guys. In fact we cheered like hell.

Afterward I walked the perimeter, just looking around. I went down a little draw, and I'll never forget the sight. There were hundreds of burned bodies in it. The snow was burned off the ground and Chinese bodies were lying in heaps, all scorched and burned from our napalm, their arms and legs frozen in grotesque angles. Our air force used a lot of napalm on them, and it is almost beyond belief the way they continued to fight in broad daylight, so exposed like that.

But what I saw in that draw was only the beginning. We found hundreds and hundreds more, caught in draws and ravines where they'd been trying to hide.

I never saw such slaughter, before or since.

CHAPTER 18

The Killing Ground

The Chinese offensive of February 1951 broke like a wave on the rock of Chipyong, and almost immediately the UN resumed the attack with Operation Killer, which marked the beginning of a counteroffensive that would drive the Chinese and North Korean armies out of South Korea.

On March 15 Seoul was recaptured, and by the end of March Ridgway's divisions had reached the 38th parallel. Without pause the attack continued, and by the middle of April some of the UN formations were as much as twenty miles inside North Korea.

Meanwhile, and not unknown to the UN command, the Chinese were massing for their largest offensive of the war.

On April 22 it hit the UN lines along a forty-mile front: a quarter of a million men attacking in the now-familiar human-wave fashion. UN forces soon found themselves retreating again, but this time the withdrawal was conducted in good order. A new defensive line was quickly established just below the 38th parallel, Seoul did not fall to the enemy (an important psychological victory at the time), and perhaps most important, UN artillery and air strikes killed the attacking Chinese in astounding numbers while relatively little damage was done to the major UN formations.

By April 30 the offensive was over. Chinese losses were estimated at seventy-five thousand, against seven thousand for the UN, and by the first week in May Rigdway's forces started moving north again.

Digging into their massive reserves of manpower the Chinese launched yet another attack on May 16. Again, it came as no surprise, and although it temporarily dented the right flank of the UN line, once again the Chinese suffered horrific losses to Allied firepower. During the six days the attack lasted, more than three hundred thousand rounds of artillery were expended by UN forces, making it the biggest artillery "shoot" of the Korean War. And with scarcely a pause Ridgway launched another counterattack that by the early summer of 1951 took his army back to the 38th parallel for good.

The fighting in the spring and summer of 1951 was called the "yo-yo war" by the men on the front lines. Actually even the UN retreats during this time had been victories of a sort, since any territory that was lost was always quickly regained, while entire Chinese divisions continued to be sacrificed. But the fact that the fighting had taken a definite turn for the better—after the spring of 1951 UN forces never again permanently lost the initiative—was not readily apparent at the time. Most frontline troops felt that the war was essentially going nowhere, that neither side seemed to be winning, and that, as infantryman Ted White said, "The only thing a man could look forward to was just getting through it alive, so he could go home when his time came."

Ted White was sent to Korea right out of training, joining the all-black 24th Infantry Regiment in the middle of April 1951, just in time to take part in the tail end of Ridgway's first series of counteroffensives, the ones that carried names like Killer, Ripper, Rugged, and Dauntless. "We were there to kill Chinese," White recalls. "That's what they told us. The army was done with retreating. General Ridgway was in charge now, and he wasn't a retreating general. We heard it every day from the officers. 'Fix 'em, find 'em, kill 'em.' We went out every day and we attacked. Seems like that's all we did was attack. We hardly ate. We hardly slept. We just attacked. If I'd of known what I was getting myself into, I don't know as I'd of volunteered."

What happened was, me and a bunch of fellas decided to go down to the recruiting office and enlist. This was September 1950. I'd just turned nineteen. The war was a couple months old by then, and we decided we'd do something for our country, because none of us was doing much of anything else.

I had no idea what the 38th parallel was. I didn't understand what was happening in Korea. I wasn't even sure I knew where Korea was. All I knew was, there was a war on.

I went to Fort Jackson, South Carolina, for basic training. Stayed there for infantry training. Then I got sent to Korea. It was like I was here, and then I was gone.

The 24th Regiment was just north of the Han River, and on the day I joined the unit we were strafed and napalmed by our own planes. I came in with some other replacements, and the company we were assigned to (E Company) sent somebody down this hill to pick us up, and when we got to the top of the hill they told us right off to dig foxholes. As soon as we got ready to dig in about six airplanes came over and strafed us and dropped napalm. I didn't have a hole dug yet, so I hid behind a rock. There was a big boulder near where I'd started to dig, and I got behind it, and as this business went on I probably tried to crawl under it. I didn't know what was happening, because it was the first time I'd ever been under fire. The napalm burned some guys real bad. One was killed. He was lying there on the ground like a charred piece of wood. An officer finally got on the radio and told them to call it off.

After we dug our foxholes we left the hill. That's what usually happened. We'd move out and attack a ridge or a hill, dig foxholes to spend the night in, then move out again in the morning, or some-times even before we got all the way dug in.

Once we attacked four ridges in one day, one after another. Rumors had started that the Chinese were going to hit us with one of their big offensives, so after that we moved a little more careful.

We still advanced every day, but we did it slow, and that gave us a little more time to eat and sleep.

We ate C rations. I don't remember any hot meals. We ate everything cold, out of cans. There was stuff like franks and beans, corned-beef hash, spaghetti, ham and lima beans. There was always a lot of trading. Ham and limas I don't think nobody wanted. We gave a can to a Chinese prisoner once, and even he wouldn't eat it. On the other hand, everybody wanted the cans of fruit. Can of peaches, or fruit cocktail, it made your day.

I don't recall the hill we were on. We had taken this hill and we tried to make a perimeter around it. We strung up some barbed wire, and put out some mines and trip flares, and out in front of the barbed wire we put out some fifty-five-gallon drums of napalm. It was gasoline with napalm in it. You rig some TNT or a mortar shell as a charge, and you run your wires back inside the perimeter so you can set off the drums. When one of those drums blew up it would turn into a mass of flames thirty or forty yards wide.

So we must have known they were coming. Usually we didn't bother with that much preparation. Just your foxholes, and maybe a little barbed wire if you had it.

I didn't know too much about the Chinese being in the war. I got there in April of 1951, and the big Chinese attacks had come in November and December and January. A lot of the other fellas were new, too, so I didn't have people telling me what to expect.

When we got hit it was the start of the biggest battle of the Korean War. As I understand it, something like three hundred thousand Chinese attacked all across the front. Of course, at the time I wasn't thinking about no front except my own front. We could hear them coming, because they'd blow bugles and horns and whistles, trying to work on your mind. Then an artillery flare went up, a real bright light, and there they were. Thousands of them, kind of jogging across the rice paddies below us and up the sides of the hill. I remember telling myself, "Just survive, Theodore. Just survive. You gotta survive this somehow."

We stayed up on that hill for two nights. The Chinese wouldn't attack in the daytime because they were afraid of our planes. But at night we got them with artillery. That's what stopped them. I was just a rifleman, firing an M-1, trying to save my butt. What killed them Chinese was the artillery. It was a terrible thing to see. Bodies flying into the air, and pieces of bodies. When they charged they'd be so close together you couldn't miss.

But they had so many men. During the daytime you could see hundreds of bodies lying out there on the hillside, and you'd think, How could they take any more of that? But the next night they'd do it again.

Finally they just overpowered us, there was so many of them. We started to retreat. One company would be the rear guard while the rest of the regiment moved back to another position. Then a different company would hold that position while the rest of the regiment moved again.

Sometimes we'd take up a position and hold it for a while, until it seemed like we'd be overrun. But at the last minute we'd always get the word to pull back. Now what I understand is, that business was General Ridgway's idea. He was still out to kill as many Chinese as possible, and the longer a unit held on to a position, the longer the artillery could stay forward and blow the hell out of the Chinese. And we could see how much they were shooting. As we pulled back we'd pass old artillery positions where there would be piles and piles of shell casings. Thousands of them.

One time when it was my company's turn to be the rear guard we were sent up this hill, but we didn't even get to break the ground good when we got hit. We fell back off the hill and into a little valley with the Chinese right behind us. They were only a hundred yards away. Swarms of them, firing burp guns and rifles. It was the first time I saw them with helmets. Usually they had these soft caps with the bills, like padded baseball caps. They had brown uniforms and they were close enough to see the bandoliers of ammo flopping against their chests as they ran.

All I was thinking was, Dear Lord, please get me out of here.

There were five or six tanks in the valley, and we ran over to the tanks and crawled under them and fought from beneath the tanks for a while. But they came right through the tank fire even, and we left that position too. So did the tankers. They climbed out of those tanks and came along with us. The Chinese took the tanks, they took the valley, they took everything. And we came out straggling.

We fell back about thirty-five miles to Line Lincoln, just north of Seoul. That's where we made our final stand. But when we got back there we found everything was already set up. The trenches were dug, the wire was out, and the napalm and trip flares. As I understand it now, everything was planned. The whole retreat. They knew the Chinese were going to attack, and they had a retreat all planned out so as to kill as many of them as possible on the way back to Line Lincoln.

We had confidence we could hold Line Lincoln. The engineers had put a lot of work in it. They had long lines of trenches there that connected with each other, and bunkers with sandbags and heavy timbers for the roof. There were five or six different lines of barbed wire. There were mines and all kinds of booby traps and drums of napalm out there. There were even some searchlights. And there was artillery just behind us.

The Chinese hit the line twice, but none of the fighting was in my sector. In one of the battles the 35th Regiment killed more than a thousand Chinese and North Koreans. We heard they couldn't see the ground for a hundred yards in front of the wire, there were so many bodies lying around.

Then it got quiet. When we sent out patrols, they couldn't find anybody. They started sending out tank-infantry patrols that would go four or five miles out from the line.

The Chinese had pulled back, and after a week or so we moved off Line Lincoln and went on the offensive again. In the middle of our offensive the Chinese had another one of theirs. My regiment wasn't involved. That hit mostly on No Name Line, over to the east of us. The 2nd Division was over there, and the marines. That one was stopped even faster than the first one.

That was May. In June we were advancing again, taking hills, and one of the worst fights I was in took place about that time.

They put a squad of us out on a hill two hundred yards in front of the main lines. About twenty guys. We went out there and dug our foxholes, two guys to a hole, and then for every hole they gave us a machine gun.

Only twenty guys, and we get ten machine guns.

I'm thinking, Lord, what are they gonna do to us out here?

We had a machine gun in each hole, we had rifles, we had .45 pistols, and we had grenades. Plus, they zeroed us in with artillery. They told us, "You stay out here, and if you see Chinese you open fire. And you hold this hill."

Well, it dawned on us then. Somebody was planning to kill themselves some Chinese, and we were the bait. I learned later that another company had been ordered out to that hill, and they refused to go. They disobeyed the order, and they were charged with mutiny.

But we went. And not too long after it got dark—I don't recall the exact time—I saw the Chinese coming. I could see them against the skyline. The way they came strutting by, I could tell they didn't know we were there. They were looking up at the ridge two hundred yards away, where our main line was. They paid us no attention at all.

I woke the guy who was in the hole with me, and when the first Chinese got within about fifty yards of us I opened up with the machine gun.

That started it. We fought all night long. We didn't dare move out of our holes, because they kept sending artillery down on us. And even if we left our holes and somehow made it back to our own lines, we'd be shot by our own guys.

So we were there to stay. I had no confidence we could hold, but we *had* to hold. There was no place for us to go.

Actually I was too scared to think about being overrun. They kept coming in waves, and I kept firing. I fired my machine gun all night long. Everybody else was firing. And the artillery was dropping all around us. The artillery did a good job keeping them off us.

And all night long I'm thinking, These people are crazy. They're dying in droves, and they just keep coming on.

But all that night we didn't lose a man, and when they broke off the attack at daylight we could see what we'd done to them. There were dead Chinese all over the ground. Hundreds and hundreds of them. And they were only the ones their people couldn't drag away in the dark.

Everybody on that hill was recommended for a Bronze Star. I never got one, but I understand the recommendation went in.

CHAPTER 19

Tall Men

The title of this piece is metaphorical. In reality they came in all sizes and shapes, from diverse backgrounds, and for various reasons. It was only that peculiar blend of mental toughness and wild abandon, found in most elite units, that they had in common.

They were U.S. Army rangers. A company of them fought at Chipyong, but that action was not an example of the way rangers were supposed to be used in Korea. There was one ranger company, about 115 men, attached to each infantry division, and theoretically the rangers were to be used for long-range patrols behind enemy lines and for ambushes and hit-and-run raids. "But it hardly ever worked out that way," Douglas LaRue remembers. "We were irregular troops, unconventional, and the commanders of most of the divisions in Korea were conventional soldiers who had no idea how to use us properly."

In March and April of 1951, as part of the Ridgway offensives, the rangers took part in two major operations in Korea, and Doug LaRue was on both of them.

I was a four-time volunteer, as all the rangers in Korea were. We volunteered for the service, for the airborne, for the rangers, and for Korea.

I was eighteen when I joined the service, out of Bay City, Michigan. I had some problems there with the police. Petty stuff, nothing too serious, but I decided it would be best for me if I got out of the area for a while. So I joined the service and immediately signed up for the airborne. What the hell, they paid fifty dollars a month more than any other outfit.

I was in the 82nd Airborne Division at Fort Bragg when they asked for volunteers for the rangers. I volunteered, and was turned down. They had three or four times the number of volunteers they needed. But one of the men who was supposed to go had an appendicitis attack and was rushed to the hospital. A friend of mine was on charge of quarters that day, and when he saw them looking around for a replacement he said, "Hey, LaRue wants to go."

I was gone in fifteen minutes.

Ranger training was tough, but you expected it to be tough. What made it even tougher for me, I'd dislocated my shoulder in a parachute jump a few months before. It turned out to be a permanent injury. When I got out of the service I couldn't lift my right arm over my shoulder for six years. So I truthfully don't know how I made it through ranger training. But I did. It was something I wanted to do, and I did it.

We trained at Fort Benning, Georgia. The same place we took our airborne training. But this time they kept us locked away in a special area. They didn't want anyone near us, and they didn't want us to molest anyone else.

Of course it didn't work out that way. We'd sneak off at night, go into town and maybe bust up a bar. Some of the guys blew a hole in the highway bridge between Phenix City, Alabama, and Columbus, Georgia. They set off nineteen pounds of TNT. Everybody bought extra sidearms. Thirty-eights, forty-fives. We bought them from the police in Columbus.

Sometimes we'd fight with each other, just to be fighting. Fistfights. Knife fights. We'd play a game called spread bayonets. Two guys would stand facing each other, and they'd take turns throwing

Lloyd Kreider, a survivor of the Sunchon tunnel massacre, at the time of his testimony before the U.S. Senate's Subcommittee on Korean War Atrocities in December 1953. He was then a corporal in the 82nd Airborne Division. (Courtesy of Lloyd Kreider)

Members of Andy Barr's heavy mortar company trying to rest during the Eighth Army's withdrawal from North Korea. (Courtesy of Andy Barr)

The scene on the opposite side of the road: South Korean troops streaming south, away from the oncoming Chinese. (Courtesy of Andy Barr)

Korean orphans, one of the unpublicized tragedies of the war. Estimates vary, but some accounts state that as many as 100,000 homeless and parentless children wandered the Korean countryside or attempted to survive on their own in the decimated towns and cities. (Courtesy of Andy Barr)

Pat Scully's Fox Company did no trotting at Toktong Pass. Its 240 men dug in and held their ground for four days against repeated Chinese attacks, keeping the pass out of enemy hands and allowing two marine regiments to escape annihilation. (Courtesy of Pat Scully)

Above: Exhausted marines catch a few minutes rest during their breakout from the Chosin Reservoir. (Courtesy of Pat Scully)

Left: Harry Summers at the edge of the Chorwon Valley in April 1951. Twenty-four hours after his rifle company was relieved from these positions the Chinese began their spring offensive, and the unit that replaced Summers' company was annihilated almost to a man. (Courtesy of Harry Summers)

Lewis Millet just hours
after leading his company in
what the military historian
S. L. A. Marshall called
"the greatest bayonet
attack by U.S. soldiers
since Cold Harbor in the
Civil War." (Courtesy of
Stars and Stripes)

Theodore White was a
rifleman in the all-black
24th Infantry Regiment
before it was deactivated in
October 1951. (Courtesy of
Theodore White)

Marines from Bart Dauberman's company lived in bunkers like this one while manning the MLR, the network of trenches and fortified hills that by November of 1951 extended all the way across Korea. (Courtesy of Bart Dauberman)

Eastern Korea, November 1951. Bart Dauberman's Easy Company occupied this sector of the front until March 1952, when the entire 1st Marine Division was shifted from the east to the west coast. (Courtesy of Bart Dauberman)

Above: Jim Holton's command post during the battle for White Horse Mountain during the fall of 1952. As PIO chief Holton directed the press coverage of the battle, relaying reports to representatives of the major civilian news organizations who were still in Seoul, caught largely unawares by the suddenness, size and ferocity of the fight. (Courtesy of Jim Holton)

Left: One of Jim Holton's reporters, PIO man Bill Russell, complete with walking stick, typewriter, camera, tripod, carbine, bayonet, and two .45s. Presumably he also had a pencil there somewhere. (Courtesy of Jim Holton)

Stanley Weintraub beneath one of the guard towers at the POW hospital camp where he served as admissions officer. Weintraub later wrote a book, *The War in the Wards,* detailing his experiences with North Korean and Chinese POWs. (Courtesy of Stanley Weintraub)

A clipping from the *Washington Post-Herald*, February 1952, showing a smiling Nick Tosques (far left) as a prisoner of war in North Korea. Armed guards standing just out of camera range ordered the men to smile.

a bayonet at each other's feet. If the bayonet stuck in the ground, you had to move your foot to where it landed. The object was to get your opponent to spread his feet so wide he'd fall on his ass. Sometimes you ended up missing the ground and throwing your bayonet into a guy's foot, but that was part of the game. It was a test of nerve.

Every day started with a five-mile run. We did speed marches. We practiced demolitions, sabotage, map reading, communications, night raids, hand-to-hand combat. We trained with all kinds of weapons. The training week was about sixty hours. Some weeks it was closer to eighty, and after a while you just went numb. You did everything by instinct.

They picked the hardest, nastiest guys they could find to train us. We had a forty percent washout rate. You could quit any time you wanted, no questions asked. But when a guy quit they got him out of there fast. His stuff would be gone from the barracks when everybody else got back. Nobody was forced to be a ranger. You could leave anytime. But if you quit, they didn't want you around one second longer than necessary.

I was in the 4th Airborne Ranger Company, which shipped out for Korea in December of 1950. Sixteen days on a transport ship. When we got over there they put us in reserve at Eighth Army headquarters at Taegu. Each ranger company in Korea was supposed to be attached to an infantry division, which was supposed to use the ranger company for scouting and patrolling out in front of the lines and for raids. But there we were, miles behind the front lines, guarding Eighth Army headquarters.

We guarded the headquarters, guarded airfields, shot off all your old ammunition, ran maneuvers, made jumps, all to keep in shape. We wore Mohawk haircuts, just a strip of fuzz across the top of the head, and we always walked around loaded for bear—hand grenades, pistols, knives. We were getting in fights all the time. We took to stealing jeeps and trucks from other outfits just to keep in practice. After a few months we were awfully anxious to get into the fighting, and when we finally got the word, we were more than ready.

Our first operation was the Munsan jump. March 23, 1951. Operation Tomahawk. They didn't tell us anything ahead of time.

They don't tell you much in advance in the rangers. "We're going to leave at six o'clock tomorrow morning. Be ready." That's about the extent of it.

Later on I learned what it was all about. It was the first combat jump in ranger history. The Eighth Army was attacking north from Seoul to Munsan, on the Imjin River, and the 187th Airborne with the rangers attached was going to jump twenty-five miles behind the enemy lines at Munsan and cut off the Chinese and North Koreans who were retreating.

At Taegu we loaded onto old World War Two C-46s. It was a clear morning, but that's all I remember about it. Once inside the airplane you don't really see or hear anything. Your mind is on what's up ahead. What you're going to encounter at the drop zone. I was told we flew out over the Yellow Sea to come in on Munsan from the west, but we could have been flying over China for all I knew.

Until we hit the ground, it was no different from any of the training jumps we'd done. You just sit there with the engines roaring in your ears and wait. Then you get the command to stand and hook up. You hook your static line to the cable, you sound off for the equipment check, you move down the line, you stand in the door, you step out.

We jumped from about seven hundred feet. The static line pulls the parachute out of the pack so that it opens almost instantly. But you're traveling at least a hundred miles an hour going out of the airplane, and seven hundred feet isn't a hell of a lot of space. You feel the opening shock, and then *bam*, you're on the ground. But you had to come down fast like that so the enemy wouldn't have time to shoot you out of the sky.

When I hit the ground I banged my elbow, which you're never supposed to do. It's a cardinal sin to hit a bone. I hit my elbow on a rock, and my arm was numb for the rest of the day.

We lost our light machine gun. That was the one parachute that didn't open. It hit the ground and it was a mangled mess.

Otherwise the drop went about as planned. The drop zone had been bombed and strafed ahead of time, and there was almost no resistance. Just a little small-arms fire, and a few mortar rounds.

Our objective was a hill not too far from the drop zone. There were some North Koreans on it, and they died to the last man. We had a guy killed and eight or nine wounded trying to take that hill. After we overran their positions we piled the bodies on the crest and used them for seats.

We were still below the 38th parallel, and after the ground force coming up from Seoul linked up with us we patrolled north toward the parallel for a few days. Then they sent us back to Taegu. But we weren't back more than a few days when they hatched the Hwachon Dam operation.

Hwachon was one of the biggest reservoirs in Korea. The Chinese controlled the dam, and if they decided to open the sluice gates all at once they could flood a couple of rivers and that way knock out our bridges and maybe separate some of our units from each other.

So somebody decided that we were going to capture the dam. Neither side wanted to blow it up, because the reservoir provided water and electric power for Seoul, and at that time in the war both sides thought they were going to end up owning Seoul.

They gave the job to the 1st Cavalry Division, because they were the closest. And we were attached to the 1st Cav. Our job would be to go in there and disable the floodgates so that they couldn't all be raised at once.

It was important that we surprise the Chinese, so they decided that the rangers would cross the reservoir in assault boats. Whoever was planning this thing thought that if we paddled across the reservoir under cover of darkness we could land near the east side of the dam without being detected. We were supposed to be in position by dawn, when a battalion from the Cav would make an attack overland. While that was going on we'd rush the dam from the flank, get in there, do what we had to do, and get out.

Well, they found these plywood boats for us, but we couldn't get more than seven or eight men in each. And there weren't that many boats. My platoon had to wait until some of the boats got back from the first crossing. It was a long way over, probably close to a mile, and by the time we paddled across it was just getting light.

Then all this gunfire exploded. Some of the guys who had crossed ahead of us were climbing a hill just to the east of the dam when a bunch of Chinese opened fire from the hilltop.

They weren't supposed to be up there. But not only were they up there, they were well dug in. The Cav's artillery observer got killed in the first burst. Shot right between the eyes. I stepped over his body as we came ashore.

There were two machine guns up there. We knocked one out with a recoilless rifle and the other with grenades and then we took the hill. But we were still about five hundred meters from the edge of the dam. And now the Chinese knew we were there.

We could see more of them between us and the dam, and the word went along the line to expect a counterattack. All during the morning they dropped mortar rounds on us, and we were taking automatic fire and small-arms fire from three different directions. They were also sending more men across the dam. We had a sniper, the best shot in the company, and with an M-1 rifle and a scope he dropped about two dozen of those Chinese as they were running across the top of the dam. And he did it from a fantastic range. Something like a thousand yards.

About the middle of the afternoon, brother, did they hit us. It was a typical Chinese infantry attack. No covering fire. No effort to use the terrain. Just a headlong charge by an enormous mass of men.

There must have been five or six hundred of them, screaming and yelling and blowing bugles. But they didn't seem to have enough weapons. Maybe the first row would have weapons, and the next two or three wouldn't. The second wave would grab the weapons from the dead as they came on.

But there's only a hundred men in a ranger company, so we were in a pretty tight spot. I think the only thing that saved us was the artillery we called in. The shells landed practically on top of us. I don't think anybody ever had closer artillery support, ever. You could hold up a cigarette and get a light from the blasts.

Another thing that stopped them was their own dead. We killed so many that they had to climb up over stacks of bodies, and it definitely slowed the attack.

But finally we were ordered out of there. Our ammo was running low. One of our BAR men had been shot in the head and killed. Another guy was hit in the stomach and died of shock. There were wounded all over the place.

The whole operation had gotten out of hand. It was supposed to be a quick raid, in and out, but it was turning into a long drawn-out fight, and it didn't look like we'd ever get to the dam.

It was a tough day. When we got back that night to our bivouac I was so tired I fell asleep in a streambed with rocks the size of my fist under me, and I never knew they were there.

After the Hwachon operation, basically what we did for the next three or four months was patrolling. Foot patrols and tank-infantry patrols, spaced about a week apart. The high brass always wanted to know what the enemy was doing, and we would always go out and find them. We never had any problem finding the enemy. And the army divisions we were attached to loved using us for that stuff, because they considered rangers to be expendable. They would much rather get us killed than their own people.

But somebody had to do the job, and we didn't mind the patrols. What seemed senseless to us were some of the tank-infantry probes. We'd get orders to go out and take a certain ridge, and after we'd take the ridge we'd be ordered back. It was totally senseless.

One time we went twenty miles into Chinese territory. We were riding on tanks, and when one of the tanks hit a mine the Chinese opened up on us from a nearby hill. A colonel from the 1st Cav came up and ordered us to take the hill. So we deployed two platoons to take the hill and another to provide covering fire. I was running across a field to get in position when I heard something go smack. I looked down, and thought, "Oh my." A machine gun was shooting at me and a bullet had just shattered my rifle stock and put four or five little pieces of metal in my hand. A cheap Purple Heart.

We took the hill, and when we started back toward the tanks the Chinese artillery opened up on us. The tanks were ready to pull out. They were going to leave us there in enemy territory. Dorsey Anderson was our CO, and he held a gun to the tank captain's head and said, "Don't you move, or I'll blow your goddamn head off. You get my men on board these tanks, and my wounded, and then we'll leave."

We left with everybody, and the Chinese reoccupied the hill, probably before we were even out of sight.

We operated out of a base camp just behind the front. We lived in the ground, in dugouts covered with shelter halves.[1] Between patrols we played cards and fought. There was at least one fistfight every day, usually over something trivial. We lived on C rations and candy bars. We'd get a case of warm beer once in a while for a dollar, that said "Free" on it. The Korean women generally stayed away from us. A couple of them came up one time, but they kind of retreated in disorder and never came back.

In August of 1951 all the ranger units in Korea were deactivated. It was a total shock to us. The reason they gave was that we couldn't operate effectively behind enemy lines. How can you hide a guy with Caucasian eyes in a country where everybody has slant eyes? That was the reason they gave.

But we proved time and again that we could operate behind enemy lines. We did it all the time. Every patrol we went on was behind enemy lines. Guys would go out on their own, stay out all night and come back with a couple of pairs of Chinese ears.

I think the real reason for our deactivation was that the army brass didn't like having us around their regular units. We were different. We were too aloof. We didn't conform, and in the army that's the kiss of death. So they broke up all the ranger companies and shipped guys off to different units. Scattered them around.

I went to the 187th Airborne for a while and did nothing. It was a holiday. I left Korea in 1951 and was discharged from the service in 1952. I did a lot of heavy drinking just after I got out. It was a form of adjustment, I guess. But I was able to put the war behind me. I became a firm believer in the idea that once it's happened, it's history. And there's not a hell of a lot you can do about history. So I went back to college, got my degree, and went out and got a job with the IRS. But I'll always remember the rangers. We were

---

[1]A shelter half is a piece of canvas representing one half of a two-man army tent.

a hell of an outfit. And I admire and respect the young guys who are rangers today. I've been down to Georgia to see them train, and God, they're even meaner than we were.

CHAPTER 20

Heartbreak Ridge

In July 1951 truce talks began in the ancient Korean capital of Kaesong. (They would later be moved five miles east to Panmunjom.) There had been two major Chinese offensives in the spring, one in April and another in May. Both had been contained, and during them hundreds of thousands of Chinese and North Korean troops had been removed from the war by UN bullets and artillery and air strikes. U.S. commanders had finally learned how to deal with the enemy's manpower advantage. UN forces were never again even remotely in danger of being pushed off the Korean peninsula. The Chinese no doubt sensed this, and so talks began about a possible armistice.

There would be plenty of fighting ahead, two more years of it in fact, but once the talks began the character of the war changed. Neither side would ever again launch a major offensive. All along the line men on both sides began digging in for good, and it soon became clear that the war of movement was over and that something quite different was taking its place.

Exactly what that would be was not immediately apparent. During that summer of 1951 there was still some last-minute maneuvering going on (though few at the time realized its last-minute quality) as UN forces slowly punched their way into positions a few miles north of the 38th parallel. But these were, in the phrase of the day, "limited objective" offensives, designed to take a hill mass here and a ridgeline there.

Of course for the men on the ground who are doing the fighting, an attack is an attack. You are killed just as dead fighting for a "limited objective" as you are in a grand sweep of arms.

Sherman Pratt remembers one of those limited objectives. Later, and with good cause, it came to be called Heartbreak Ridge: a bad-luck piece of land that would eventually be fought over nearly half a dozen times without any appreciable gain by either side.

That summer I was promoted from captain to major, which meant I had to leave my rifle company, Baker Company of the 23rd Regiment. So they started looking around as to where they could assign a major. The battalion had only one job for a major, as battalion exec, and that job was filled.

One day I got a call to go down to regimental headquarters. I said, "What am I going to do down there?" The guy says, "You're going to be the regimental exec." I said, "Regimental exec? That's a light colonel's job. I'm just barely a major." The guy said, "Well, they don't have any more light colonels. So get down here."

The regiment had just gotten a new commander, a Colonel Adams. Adams was a very energetic, ambitious, active officer. He was not the kind of man who sat around the CP. He was out every day running up and down the hills, checking on his battalions, checking the positions, looking everything over for himself.

When I reported in Adams said, "Major Pratt, you're going to be my executive officer. As you know, the regimental exec usually handles the paperwork. But I'm going to use you in a different way. I want you out there with the fighting battalions. I can't be everywhere at once, and I want you to go where I can't be. I want you to be my eyes and ears."

Well, my heart just sank. I'd been a year on the line with a rifle company. I'd been through Kunu-ri and the big retreat in 1950, I was at Chipyong-ni in February of 1951 when our regiment and the French Battalion held off elements of six Chinese divisions, I'd been through the Chinese spring offensive against No Name Line. . . . When I got the call to be regimental exec I was envisioning a nice restful job back at the regimental CP, living in a tent, getting hot meals once in a while, being away from small-arms fire—the kind of relatively plush routine a staff officer normally enjoys.

Now I'm being told I'll be out on the line with the fighting battalions.

Of course I didn't let on how I felt. I was a major in the army, and it was "Yes, sir. Whatever you say."

At about this time we were given a series of hills to take. The 2nd Division had been in reserve and had been brought up to replace the 1st Marine Division around the Punchbowl, and the word came down that we were to extend our lines a few more miles north, which meant taking these hills.

Bloody Ridge, or what later became known as Bloody Ridge, was the first, and when that was taken we moved on to the next one. But very quickly the fighting took on an almost fanatical quality. By this time the North Korean troops holding these positions had dug an elaborate system of interlocking trenches and bunkers, they had obviously been resupplied and re-equipped, and they very clearly had been told not to give up any ground.

As the fighting was going on I was moving around to the various battalion command posts, checking on the progress of their line companies, making sure they had what they needed, but mostly giving them moral support. By just being out there I was letting them know that Colonel Adams and the rest of the regimental staff weren't sitting back in the rear somewhere sipping tall cool ones, they were on top of the situation. And being up at the battalion CPs, which were often quite close to the fighting, I could see what was going on with my own eyes.

I can fully understand how that place got its name, because it was just heartbreaking to watch. I could see the mortar rounds and artillery exploding among the men as they were trying to fight their way up these steep ridges. Even without binoculars I could see them scrambling around on the slopes, clusters of little figures that would occasionally be obscured from view by drifting clouds of smoke. Some of them would fall down and not get up. Others would fall, get up again, run a little, crouch down, run again. Sometimes a man would throw out an arm before he fell, or fall backward and roll down the slope. I could usually tell when some of them got up near an enemy bunker. Then you'd see them moving sideways, looking for cover, kind of circling around as they tried to get close, and there would be these little puffs of black smoke from the grenades the North Koreans would toss out at them.

I could see men trying to get the wounded off the slopes. Taking out the wounded was always a problem in these hill fights. It often took three or four men to get one wounded man down off the hill, and if you've got twenty or thirty wounded at a time, which was not at all uncommon, you had a lot of men who weren't doing any fighting. Helicopters hadn't come into their own yet, but it would probably have been too hazardous to use them anyway. In that mountainous terrain, you couldn't get the wounded far enough away from the fighting to be picked up safely. I saw the marines try it once, during an earlier battle, and they had three helicopters in a row shot down trying to get into the area where the wounded were waiting.

The French Battalion was with us again at Heartbreak, and at one point in the fighting I watched as they fixed bayonets and charged into that awful fire, straight up one of the slopes, until they were stabbing the North Koreans to death in their foxholes. As it happened, both General Ridgway and General Almond, the corps commander, were visiting the front that day and both of them saw that charge by the French. And they were absolutely astounded. It made an enormous impression on them, because Americans have never been enthusiastic about running forward and engaging the enemy in hand-to-hand fighting.

I was with the French at Chipyong-ni. They were superb soldiers, and they were all volunteers. Every one of them was in Korea because he wanted to be there. They were led by a man named Monclar, a general in the French army who had taken a reduction in rank to lieutenant colonel just to lead the battalion in Korea.

Monclar was an old man by then, but he was a fighter. He spoke pretty good English, and once when we were in the perimeter at Chipyong he overheard some of the guys griping about having to be in Korea. "What the hell are we doing here anyway? We should let the gooks have the stinking place." That kind of thing. Monclar walked right up to these guys and said, "Just a damn minute. This is the first time in five thousand years of recorded civilization that there has ever been an international organization to help preserve the peace. This is the first time an international army has fought to maintain law and order. If civilization lasts another five thousand years, that will not change the fact that this is the first time it's ever been done. And you people are a part of it. And you should be *honored* to be a part of it." And then he turned on his heel and walked away.

Monclar believed totally in the concept of a United Nations, and what the UN was doing in Korea. That's why he was there. But I think a lot of those French soldiers he had under him were old Foreign Legion types. They just wanted to be in a war. It didn't really matter what the cause was they were fighting for, just so long as they were fighting. You have people like that. They get an excitement out of war that they can't get anywhere else.

The fighting for Heartbreak Ridge went on for several weeks. I saw a lot of it, much more than I would have seen as a company commander, and what I saw only reaffirmed my thinking about medals. For every man who gets a medal, there are probably five or six who also deserve one but never get written up. A commander has to hear about a brave act, and then he has to write the man up for an award. But many acts of heroism are simply not witnessed. Or the commander, in the press of his combat duties, just doesn't have time to stop and write up the award. Or by the time he does get around to it the witnesses are gone. That doesn't mean that a man who gets a medal doesn't deserve it. But as I watched the battle for Heartbreak, I knew there were a lot of men out there who were earning medals they would never get.

It wasn't until toward the end of the fighting that you started to see the name "Heartbreak Ridge" appear in newspaper accounts. Before that it was just a hill with a number. It was a mysterious process, how those hills got named. Early in the war, when my regiment was still up in North Korea, I was expressing my concern about some high ground across the valley from our positions. Colonel Freeman, the regimental CO, said, "What do you mean?" I said, "Well, if the enemy gets up on that hill over there. . . . " He said, "Which one?" I said, "That one over there. The one that looks like a Chinaman's hat."

Freeman looked down at his map and said, "Well, that's Hill 325," or whatever the number was. Then he looked up and grinned at me. "But I like your name better."

Shortly after that you started to see the hill referred to in print as Chinaman's Hat. Now I don't remember if I heard that name from one of my men and just repeated it, or if I made it up myself. And I don't think Colonel Freeman would have referred to it by anything but its number. But somebody somewhere heard the name Chinaman's Hat, and it got into the newspapers, and the name stuck for all eternity.

Heartbreak Ridge was secured I believe on the twenty-third of September. And even while the mopping-up operations were still going on we moved in and immediately began improving on the Chinese and North Korean positions. Putting overhead cover on some of the trenches, strengthening the bunkers, improving fields of fire. What we were doing, though we didn't know it at the time, was establishing part of what would be the main line of resistance, or the MLR as it came to be called. Heartbreak Ridge became part of a defensive line that eventually stretched from the east coast to the west coast of Korea. After Heartbreak was taken, the order was to dig in and hold. There would be no more major offensives. The fighting from then on to the end of the war was to prevent the Chinese and North Koreans from taking over our positions. We dug in on the hills and ridges and we sat there for two more years, taking staggering casualties to no apparent purpose.

CHAPTER 21

Digging In

Throughout the rest of 1951 the digging continued all along the line, until an elaborate system of trenches and bunkers stretched literally from coast to coast across the peninsula. And as men on both sides settled down to await the outcome of the truce talks, and in the meantime to shoot bullets and lob artillery shells at each other, hill-tops and ridgelines took on the aspects of a permanent home.

Tom Clawson remembers what it was like to live on a hill in Korea. "Everything had to be hauled up the hill. Everything. Our C rations, our water, our ammunition, the mail. The GI was like a pack animal on those hills. With no roads, human leg power was the only way to get the stuff up there. Helicopters would have been ideal, but there weren't many of them around in those days. Korean laborers carried some of the stuff, but there was always something for us to carry too."

You spent hours every day improving your position, working on the foxholes and trenches and bunkers. But I never liked to get too fancy, because sooner or later we'd be shifted to a different position.

I lost all my personal gear that way, twice over. The sergeant would say, 'We're going out on a patrol, so leave all your personal stuff behind." Wallets, prayer books, letters, cameras, all that stuff had to go, because you didn't want to get captured with any kind of identification, or carry anything that wasn't absolutely necessary for your survival if you got in a fight.

Okay, you leave it all behind. Then you go out on your patrol. Most times you'd return to the place you started from, but the day would always come when you wouldn't. You'd come back and move directly into a new position.

But all the positions were always somewhere on the same ridge-line. I didn't realize it at the time, but when I got to Korea the war of movement had just ended. What they would later call the sitting war had taken its place. You had these two huge armies out there, and both sides started digging in to hold on to what they had. Eventually the trenches went right across the entire country. A no man's land developed between the two lines, and that's where we patrolled. Otherwise we just stayed on our hill.

My hill was Old Baldy. It was about sixty miles north of Seoul and about twenty miles north of the 38th parallel. It was called Old Baldy because the tremendous amount of artillery they'd dropped on the area when they were taking the hill had shaved the entire ridgeline bald. There wasn't a tree or a shrub left standing.

I think I should mention at this point that I didn't volunteer for Korea. I was drafted in May of 1951 out of my hometown of Cedar Falls, Iowa. I had two years of college by that time. In the summers I was a smoke jumper for the U.S. Forest Service out in Missoula, Montana. But I ran out of money and needed to work, so I didn't register for my junior year.

It didn't take long before I got a little card in the mail from my draft board. "Your friends and neighbors have selected you. . . . "

I can't say I wasn't expecting it. I was keeping a pretty close eye on the war, and when we lost so many men in the late fall of 1950 and early '51, they started drafting very heavily. But I had no thought, and I knew of nobody in high school or college who ever said to me, "We're going to try to avoid the draft," or go to Canada, any of that stuff. It was just not heard of back then. The Second

World War was over for only about five years, and we still had that sense of patriotic duty. I had five uncles on my mother's side of the family who were World War Two veterans. Kids would join the National Guard as juniors in high school. It was a whole different atmosphere then.

I took basic training at Fort Sill, Oklahoma. My advanced training was in fire direction for the 105mm and 155mm howitzers. But I ended up in the infantry. Murphy's Law. In the service you never get to do what they train you to do. Not as a draftee. I'd had seventeen or eighteen jumps with the Forest Service and I wanted to go into the airborne, but they needed bodies for the infantry and they wouldn't let me go.

I didn't know what unit I was going to be with until I got over to Korea. In Japan I was given an M-1 and a barracks bag full of clothes, and in Uijongbu, Korea, I was told where I was going to go: Baker Company, 5th Cavalry Regiment, 1st Cavalry Division.

But as a draftee I had no concept of a regiment, or a division, because you never saw a regiment or a division all in one place. All you knew was the company, about two hundred men, because that's where your life as an enlisted man was centered.

After the truck let us off at the front we still had to walk a long way to get to where the company was. And it was all uphill. There was me and a couple of other guys, and we had to carry big water cans up the hill along with our rifles and regular gear, because they had no water up there.

The first thing they do is assign you to a platoon. So the sergeant assigns me to a platoon, and then he says, "All right, now dig." So you dig your foxhole. And that's all they tell you. There's no orientation, you're not taken aside and told what to expect, or what's been happening, or what to do if the Chinese attack or the artillery comes in. That's what scares you the most when you're new. Nobody tells you anything.

Each company was assigned to a certain area on the hill. For the first day or two they tried not to put a new guy right up on the shooting line. You're kind of sitting back a little, watching, listening to the noises. I was scared, but I was excited too. The lights at night, the tracers and artillery, the men out there moving. I thought,

"This is combat." You hear about it all your life, and see it in the movies, and all of a sudden you're in it.

And boy, is it different from the movies.

In the morning, on the front lines, the first thing you do is police up your company area. A bunch of guys go around and pick up all the shell casings, abandoned weapons, dud grenades, old C ration tins, garbage. You pick up any kind of debris you find.

And you pick up bodies. That was my first detail, and it was nausea time for me. You'd be surprised how quick you get used to it, but the first time you see a body that's been ripped up by bullets, or blown up by a mortar shell, your stomach kind of flops over. Sometimes there wouldn't be a mark on them. That usually meant they'd been killed by concussion. We'd carry the bodies down the hill to graves registration, and they'd take over from there.

On a hill position like Old Baldy you're always on one hundred percent alert. That means you're awake all night and all day. At night you'd use the buddy system—two guys close together, in a foxhole or a trench, one guy sleeping for two hours, then trading off with his buddy. That's the only way you got any sleep. I did that all the time I was over there, and the pattern is still with me today, forty years later. I'll get up in the middle of the night, stay awake for a couple of hours, then go back to sleep.

It wasn't long before you lost track of time. There were no days of the week: they all blurred together. The only day you could be sure of was any day a chaplain showed up to hold services. Then you knew it was a Sunday.

It was a Sunday when I saw my first Chinese. My first live ones. I was on a machine-gun post. I had binoculars that day, the first time I had binoculars on the front line. We were all supposed to have binoculars. We were supposed to have pistols too, but we never got any of those. We were supposed to have a lot of things that just disappeared before they got up to the troops. They were always stolen in the rear areas.

I was looking through the binoculars and I saw a column of Chinese about half a mile away. They had on their quilted uniforms with the white coveralls, although there wasn't much snow on the ground yet. I had a sound power with me that was connected to the

CP. A sound power looks just like a civilian telephone but with a little knob on the side that you turn when you want to talk. I cranked up the phone and reported seeing the Chinese. I was asked for an estimate, and I told them five hundred. It was a wild guess. It might have been more, it might have been a lot less. I was pretty excited, and the tendency is to overestimate.

We watched them as they dogtrotted along the side of the hill, and we knew right away something was up. This was in broad daylight, and the Chinese never showed themselves in the daytime unless they wanted us to know they were there.

Turned out they wanted to hold us in position while they hit Chink Baldy, which was a smaller ridge leading off from Old Baldy. That's the kind of thing that was happening then. The Chinese would try to take a position, we'd try to hold them off. Meanwhile the MLR stayed pretty much where it was.

Mail was brought up almost every day. That's probably what we looked forward to the most. We even got hot meals once in a while, in thermal containers. Insulated green containers about three feet long and a foot wide. They'd fix the meals in a field kitchen, miles in back of the lines, and put the food in those containers and get it up to us, maybe not hot, but at least warm. Mostly though we ate cold C rations.

I don't know what the rats ate. There were rats in all the bunkers and trenches, and I don't know what they all found to eat.

I had one that kept bothering me at night. It would get into my foxhole, into a little room I'd dug in one wall to keep ammo and grenades and stuff in. One time it fell in there and it wouldn't stop squeaking, so I dropped a grenade in on him. *Phoom!* Talk about some pissed-off guys. Everybody thought the Chinese were coming.

Water was always short. Bathing was out of the question. If you had a little extra water you might wash up out of your helmet. Generally you got filthy quick and you just stayed that way.

That was life on Old Baldy. Filthy, lonely, boring, occasionally exciting, whenever the Chinese started acting up. There were a lot of firefights between patrols, and the artillery was always going overhead, both ours and theirs, but the Chinese didn't hit the hill in any strength until a year after it was captured, and by that time I was gone. I missed that fight, and I couldn't be happier.

CHAPTER 22

War Cruise

In Korea the land war commanded most of the attention, because that's where most of the action was. But the war was also fought, on the UN side at least, from the sea.

On the afternoon of November 4, 1951, four destroyers left the Seventh Fleet base at Yokosuka, Japan, for Korean waters. Officially they were known as Destroyer Division 122. The four ships would operate independently of each other, but with similar duties: to escort and guard aircraft carriers, pick up downed pilots, maintain the blockade of North Korean ports, and shell the Korean coast.

One of the four destroyers that departed Yokosuka that November was the U.S.S. Beatty, and among its three hundred fifty crewmen was a young machinist mate named Vincent Walsh.

Our first assignment was to join the carrier task force, Task Force 77. The carriers were launching planes for interdiction strikes, and we went on station with them. The destroyer screen and also the carriers were blacked out at night except for little red lights at the top of the masts, and the planes coming back from the strikes would home in on those lights. Our job besides the screening duty was to pick up any pilots who missed the carriers and had to ditch their planes.

After about a week we were ordered up to Wonsan to guard some minesweepers that were clearing the channel up there. Whenever enemy shore batteries opened up on them we'd do what we called a war dance. The tin cans and the sweeps would go around in a big circle, firing their guns in every direction, and that would usually quiet down the shore batteries for a while.

One morning while we were up there dawn broke and here's this guy in a sampan out in the middle of the channel, putting down a mine. The North Koreans would go out in these little sampans at night, drop a couple of mines, and try to get back before it got light. But dawn broke and the ship caught this guy still out there.

So we went to general quarters, believe it or not. This guy started rowing for all he was worth, trying to get back to shore, and we started firing our main batteries at him. It was like a giant playing with a little toy. There was this rock he tried to hide behind, but it disintegrated under one of our shells, and he did too. We were laughing. We thought the whole thing was comical. But of course when you kill somebody it's not comical, even when he is the enemy.

Shortly after that we returned to Japan to pick up supplies and mail. While we were there we threw a party for Japanese orphans at Christmas time. We were all thinking about home, wondering how long the war would last. I got letters from guys I'd buddied around with, and it seemed like the people back home were enjoying life, like there wasn't any war. Everybody was earning good money, getting a lot of overtime, getting promotions.

I didn't really resent that until I got out. After I got out I began to resent it, because nobody seemed to know we'd ever been there. It was a lot like when the Vietnam guys got out. People didn't care about the war. They weren't thinking about it. They just put it out of their minds. The attitude was, you were a sucker. The guys that stayed home got all the jobs.

After the Christmas layover in Japan we went back on station off Korea. There was a hand grenade factory up to the north of Wonsan that supplied the North Korean army, and we shelled that and destroyed it. We shelled a few other targets for the Eighth Army.

If we weren't on the bomb line firing at something we investigated small coastal boats. We boarded and searched several of those. It was really cold by now. Whenever we were underway the seawater would break over the bow of the ship and the spray would freeze in midair and hit you like a bucket of ice cubes.

My normal duty station was in the forward engine room. The forward engine room had a boiler room in front of it and another boiler room off to the side. So you had the heat from the boilers on two sides.

I was petty officer of the watch. I had a whole power panel to monitor. Dozens of gauges. You had to constantly take readings. The butter and egg box had to be kept at a certain temperature, the meat box was a certain temperature. We called them boxes but they were really small walk-in storage rooms. The meat box did double duty. If we pulled a pilot out of the water who was dead, we had to put him in the meat box to preserve the body until we could rendezvous with a tender.

On a later cruise we had occasion to pick up a dead pilot. They fingerprinted him and then he was wrapped in a piece of canvas and he went into the meat box. It made a strong impression on me, because that was my first exposure to violent death. I'd seen dead people before, but they were always resting peacefully in a casket, all dressed up and with their eyes closed. This guy, when he ejected, somehow or other it ripped his legs off. And it looked like someone had taken a meat cleaver to his head at the line of the helmet. I remember looking out from the whaleboat as we went out to pick him up, and I saw a shoe floating by with meat in it, and I thought, My God, this guy's gotta be in bad shape. But it was even worse than I thought. When we got to him we had to pick him up in pieces. We picked up the helmet and you could see the brains in it, and there were his eyes, just a pretty blue, and open.

I almost ended up that way myself. My general quarters station was in the magazine below the five-inch gun mounts, which were our large guns. There were two elevators down there, one to take the powder up to the guns, the other to take the projectiles. The projectiles weighed about a hundred pounds each, and they were what was called point detonating. They had a plastic cap, and when the plastic hit something it drove a pin back and caused the shell to explode.

One day we were down there while the ship was firing broadsides. When it did that, all the guns would fire at the shore at one time, and the ship would roll to one side and you'd lose your balance. I was loading powder into the elevator on my side, and across from me I could see this other guy loading a projectile into the elevator over there. Just as he was putting it in the ship listed, and when it did he dropped the shell.

Time froze. Suddenly everything seemed to happen in slow motion. As the shell was headed for the steel floor of the magazine the guy who dropped it put his fingers in his ears. Like that was going to save him, not hearing the explosion.

I remember thinking, This is it. They'll never find a speck of us when that thing goes off.

The shell was armed, but for some reason it didn't go off. It was an act of God. The same day they took us out of that station, because we just couldn't work with that guy after that.

In February we went back to Yokosuka, and then the *Beatty* sailed for home. I got out of the navy a year later.

Eventually I got over my resentment about Korea. About the way we were treated after we got back home. It wasn't as bad as Vietnam. At least we weren't spit on. We were just ignored. But it gave you the feeling you were a sucker to have gone over there, that going to Korea wasn't important enough to give up the chance to get a good job at home.

CHAPTER 23

A Wing and a Prayer

U.S. Navy carriers operated in Korean waters throughout the war. These floating airfields provided the ground troops with much of their close air support and also launched thousands of interdiction missions in an effort to disrupt the enemy's supply lines. Jim Service, who later rose to the rank of vice admiral, began his navy career as a pilot flying from the U.S.S. Valley Forge, which deployed off the east coast of Korea late in 1952 as part of Task Force 77.

Carrier life was a very regulated existence. Basically, for pilots, it was eat, sleep and fly. On a typical day the first flight would be up by three o'clock in the morning. You'd go to your briefing, get some breakfast, then man your airplane. At somewhere around five thirty, you'd get launched, in the black, and then make your rendezvous with the rest of the flight before heading off on the mission.

On the way out we would meet the night fighters coming in, and they would tell us, for example, that they had hit a motor convoy, or a train, and they would give us the coordinates. We would generally arrive over the target about forty-five minutes or an hour after the night fighters had hit it, usually just after dawn, and often as not we'd catch the enemy still scurrying around, trying to hide things. Or if the night strike had started any fires, that always acted as a kind of beacon for us. I was flying the F9F-5 Panther, a new jet airplane made by Grumman, and we had probably ten times the amount of weapons that the night fighters had, and we'd just pound the bejesus out of them.

As for the amount of targets we would encounter, it ran hot and cold. Like all orientals, the Koreans were very good at hiding the stuff during the daytime. They'd use caves, buildings of all sorts, straw thatch that looked like the roof of a hut from the air. But they did have to run at night, and our night fighters would invariably find them. And if those guys could stall a train, or hit the lead vehicles in a motor convoy, or in some other way block the road for a while, we could usually get in there and deliver the coup de grace.

Whenever the task force was far enough north there was always the anticipation of meeting enemy aircraft. Periodically we'd get reports that enemy fighters were working south of the border and close to the coast, and then your adrenaline level would go up quite a bit, because for a combat pilot, that's the dream really. To meet the enemy one on one in the air. The ultimate test. I think all of us were anxious to try our skills at air-to-air combat, but for most of us flying these interdiction missions, it never happened. We were usually too far south or east to encounter enemy fighters.

I flew just over seventy missions in Korea. Most were interdiction missions, but there were also armed reconnaissance missions, recce missions we called them, and CAPs, or combat air patrols.

I had a number of close calls, mostly from ground fire. Looking back, I find it hard to believe how naive I was. The first time I saw flak I didn't even realize what I was looking at. I thought to myself: God, all those funny little white clouds are sure in a strange place. Then I saw some big black clouds, really angry-looking ones, and I thought: Hey, I know what *this* is.

Each cloud represented an explosion, of course. The flak shell bursting in the air. The white and black were just different size shells. And many times you'd fly a mission over a target where you'd see hundreds of these little clouds blossoming all over the sky. Any single one of them could knock your airplane down, but you were simply too busy flying the aircraft to worry about getting hit. And there was also the age factor. At that age, twenty, twenty-one, twenty-two, you're bulletproof. Everything's an adventure. There's no thought of getting shot down yourself. It's always the other guy who runs out of luck.

Another threat to your existence as a carrier pilot was a bad landing. I had a few of those. On one occasion I was coming in and I got my signal to land from the LSO, the guy standing out there on the deck with the two signal flags. But the signal was a little late. My instinct was to fly off and come around for another try, because taking a late cut, as we called it, meant you were going to land awfully far up the deck. But the signals you get from the LSO (landing signals officer) are absolutely mandatory. When he says cut (land), you damn well better cut.

So I had no choice but to make the landing as best I could and hope I could avoid overshooting and ending up in the ocean, because you're not going to be in the water for long before you're completely incapacitated by the cold. If they didn't fish you out within minutes, it was goodbye. That was a greater fear, I think, than being shot down. Going into the drink. We lost a couple of pilots that way. Neither one was in the water long, but they both froze to death before we could get them back aboard the ship.

Ever hear that old expression, flying on a wing and a prayer? That's the feeling I had coming in.

I took the late signal, came in, touched down well forward, and although I succeeded in collapsing the nose gear on my airplane, it stayed on the deck. It was a heart-stopping moment for me, but I climbed out of the plane and in minutes the whole thing was behind me. It was just a close call, which wasn't anything serious. The only thing that was taken seriously by the pilots I flew with was crippling injury or death, because they were the only two things that could keep you from flying again.

And that's all we wanted to do, all of us. To be able to get up the next morning and fly an airplane.

CHAPTER 24

Grim Reaper

Despite its acknowledged effectiveness U.S. naval and marine air accounted for only forty percent of the interdiction missions during the Korean War. The air force flew the rest. Pilots like Bob Ennis went out regularly over enemy territory to blow up bridges, supply trains, railroads, truck convoys, dams, factories, anything considered by the planners and photo reconnaissance experts to be part of the enemy's infrastructure.

But Bob Ennis's role in Korea was a little out of the ordinary even for an air force pilot. He flew the B-26 Invader, a sleek two-engine bomber that had the speed and maneuverability of a piston-engine fighter. His plane was painted black, and every mission was at night. He flew fast and low and without the benefit of modern night-vision technology, but when a mission was successful his plane would materialize out of the darkness and be on top of an enemy truck convoy before the enemy knew what was happening.

It was close, nervy work, but it was exactly the kind of work Bob Ennis had been looking for.

I got my wings in 1950 and was sent to Japan to fly C-54 transports, ferrying troops and supplies between Japan and Korea. While I was doing that I met some people from the 3rd Bomb Wing who were flying B-26s on combat missions in Korea. I thought I should have some combat under my belt, rather than just flying transports out of Japan, and when my time with the C-54s was up I requested duty with the 3rd Bomb Wing.

I didn't have any flying time at all in B-26s. Everybody else at the wing came there via Langley Air Force Base in Virginia, which was the training center for B-26 crews.

When I reported in I was assigned to the 13th Bomb Squadron, and those guys were flabbergasted that I didn't have any B-26 time. But I knew the 13th Bomb Squadron was flying night interdiction missions, working over the roads and the railroads in North Korea at night, and that sounded interesting to me. And I knew the B-26 was a good airplane and I was eager to fly one.

Well, they had me, and they had to do something with me, so they gave me a couple of local checkouts. The transition from a C-54 wasn't too difficult. You're going from four engines to two, and from a pilot and co-pilot to just a pilot. Otherwise it's just another airplane.

Once they checked me out for solo they would assign me one or another of the airplanes in the daytime and I'd practice dive bombing and strafing and all the things you did with a B-26 on a night mission. When they thought I was ready they gave me a combat check, a couple of them actually, and then they turned me loose.

We flew mostly single-ship missions. A single B-26 would go out and cover a particular stretch of highway or railroad. But between our two bomb wings we covered every road and railroad in North Korea. Every road and railroad would have an airplane over it every night.

The North Korean convoys didn't use blackout lights. They drove with their lights on at night the way you would here in the States. But when they heard you coming they would quickly turn them off. And they had unique warning systems. They would put people on the mountaintops to listen for aircraft, and when one guy heard something coming he'd fire his rifle, and then the next guy down the line would hear it and fire his, and the warning would pass down the line. It was kind of crude, but it worked for them, because coming in on a run you'd often see a convoy where all of a sudden all the lights blink off on you.

But by that time, given a fairly clear night, you knew where they were. You knew where the road was, and you knew about where they were on the road.

I flew mostly over the roads. They gave the railroads to the more experienced pilots, because trains were not easy to get. But we did have a guy named Chuck Wolfe who was a locomotive ace. To be a locomotive ace you had to destroy five locomotives. Chuck got fifteen, so I suppose he was actually a triple ace.

What he would do, he would request to fly up the western coast of North Korea on bright moonlit nights. There was a rail line that ran along the west coast. Chuck would even know when the tides were out, and he'd fly low, right down on the mud flats, with the moon between his airplane and the coast, and when a train came along it would be silhouetted against the coastline.

Locomotives were not easy to get. We used to have a saying, "To get credit for a locomotive kill, you had to get the right wheels in the right ditch and the left wheels in the left ditch and the boiler in three separate pieces." It was that hard. They wanted absolute confirmation that the locomotive had been destroyed. That the North Koreans couldn't possibly use it again.

Well, when Chuck saw a train he'd glide in and lay a couple of bombs on the tracks in front of the train to keep it from going forward into a tunnel. Then he'd whip around and drop a few more on the tracks to the rear to keep it from backing up into a tunnel. Then he'd have plenty of time to work it over. While he was dropping the bombs he'd call a photo airplane in, to get photo confirmation of the kill. I've seen plenty of photos of trains that Chuck Wolfe had worked over, and his airplane is always in the pictures, diving down on the target or peeling off or whatever. Chuck was a crop duster in civilian life. He'd flown in World War Two, and after the war he'd gone into crop dusting. So I guess he was just a natural for the job.

The main thing I did as a pilot was listen to my navigator, because he kept track of where you were and the height of the terrain and where the natural obstacles were. He'd constantly feed the information to me, and when he said, "Hey, you'd better start pulling up," you sure as hell started pulling up.

On each ship there was the pilot, the navigator, and the gunner. The B-26 had two versions, one with a hard nose and one with a glass nose, and in the hard-nose ships the navigator sat right beside the pilot. In the glass-nose version the navigator would be out in the nose, with the pilot above him. The gunner would be in the waist, and he would operate an upper gun turret and a lower gun turret by remote control.

But the guns that did the damage were the fourteen forward-firing machine guns, which the pilot controlled. There were eight guns in the nose and three on each wing, and they could really blast the bejesus out of anything on the ground. That's an awful lot of firepower to be pointing in anybody's direction.

We didn't have a bombadier. We used dive-bombing and glide-bombing techniques. The B-26 was so fast and agile you could get down on the deck and kind of skip your bombs into a target. Normally we'd carry ten two-hundred-pound bombs, and the plane had a combat radius of about nine hundred miles.

We flew out of Kunsan, on the west coast below Seoul. We lived in corrugated metal huts. We had outdoor toilets. When it rained there was mud all over the place. It was pretty primitive, but our minds were on flying and we kind of took the living conditions in stride.

The general routine was to rest during the day and fly at night. But every crew didn't fly every night. When we weren't flying we had other duties. Some guys would be sent to armaments or supply or to some office somewhere. I was a briefing officer. I would help plan missions and brief air crews. But to anybody who wanted to fly that was just killing time.

We called ourselves the Grim Reapers. We had the hooded figure of Death, with his scythe, painted on our airplanes. The same crew didn't fly in the same airplane all the time, but the Grim Reaper was painted on every one of them, so it really didn't matter which one you flew.

I was very fortunate. I flew fifty missions in Korea, between January and December of 1952, and I don't think I was ever in danger of losing my airplane. But we lost planes all the time. Guys would get shot down, and some would make it back after bailing out, and others we'd never hear from again. They'd just never come back. In cases like that the aircraft probably ran into the ground, or hit the side of a mountain.

The North Koreans were cagey. They would sometimes string lights along the side of a mountain to simulate a truck convoy, and if you weren't careful you'd fly into the face of a cliff. At the very least you'd expend your bombs on a string of lights and not on a convoy. They would also run cables across the entrances to narrow valleys, the ones they knew we flew through, and if you hit those cables down you went.

They actually stood our wing down for two months, in August and September of 1952, because we were having so many losses. Losing guys always affected us very deeply, but you couldn't afford to think about it too long, because you had a job to do.

Sometimes we were given the job of flak suppression during the B-29 raids. Those were the hairiest missions I ever went out on. The bombers would be hitting targets up near the Yalu River at night, and we'd have to go in there and try to knock out some of the antiaircraft guns. Now these were also single-ship missions. It wasn't like World War II, where you'd go in with a whole flight of bombers. When we went after those antiaircraft guns we were all alone.

The North Koreans had searchlights up there, which didn't bother the B-29s because they were too high. But as they probed around with the searchlights they might pick up a B-26, because we were right down on the deck. And if you got caught in one of those beams the whole cockpit would light up so bright you couldn't see the instruments. You'd get disoriented, and there was a good chance you'd lose your airplane. We lost a number of them that way, and when you drew a flak suppression mission you'd kind of lose your sense of humor for a while.

I never had second thoughts about volunteering for Korea, even during the worst days when we were losing a lot of airplanes. But

I was never a tiger. I never took unnecessary chances. There's a saying, "There are no old, bold pilots." I would take any risk necessary to get the job done, but I tried not to be reckless. The odds of getting shot down or knocked down were bad enough already.

CHAPTER 25

MiG Alley

And then there are the fighters, the planes that attract most of the attention in any war. Korea was no exception. The air war in Korea produced forty American aces, including the first jet ace in history, and after the stalemate set in on the ground, jet to jet duels in the skies over North Korea provided some of the most exciting copy of the war for newspapers back home.

The war started with the Communists having the better plane. The MiG-15 quickly wrested fighter superiority away from the slower U.S. F-80 Shooting Stars. But then came the F-86 Sabrejet, and for the Communist pilots things would never be the same again, as the F-86s killed off Russia's best fighter plane at a rate of thirteen to one.

The advantage, however, wasn't all in the airplane. American pilots developed an edge over their enemy counterparts which they never lost.

"The more we fought those guys," Doug Carter recalls, "the better we seemed to get."

Carter flew one hundred missions in Korea, rather ironic for a young man who had never intended to fly airplanes in combat. He grew up in Bluefield, West Virginia, the youngest child of a self-made engineer, and was looking forward to being a doctor. "When the war in Korea started I was in college at the Citadel, in Charleston, South Carolina, studying pre-med. In May 1951, just before I graduated, my tactical officer, an air force major who had been a fighter pilot in World War Two, came up to me and said, 'Mr. Carter, how are you going to feel when you're up there at the Medical College of Virginia in Richmond, studying medicine next year, when all your classmates are over in Korea getting shot at?'

"I said, 'Sir, I'm going to feel very badly about that.'

"And he said, 'Sign here.'"

I signed, and the next thing I knew I was on my way to flight school.

Flight training was hard. I think every pilot goes through training with some weakness, and my weakness was flying on instruments. What we used to call an aural null. Flying an aural null was an emergency procedure. Your compass would be out, and you had to locate the sound of a radio beacon and use that to home in on the landing field and make your presentation and letdown. For some reason I found that very difficult to do. I'm not even sure I could do it today.

Other parts, the acrobatics and formation flying and the rest, I think I took to pretty readily. But I was not a natural flyer. I had to work at it. I'm not sure there are any natural flyers anyway. There are some people who become better pilots than others, but in my experience the guys who became the best pilots were the ones who really worked at it. You had to be blessed with some basic skills, but like your so-called natural athletes, you took your God-given skills and developed them through a hell of a lot of hard work.

We learned to fly in a variety of prop-driven airplanes and gradually worked into the T-33 and the F-80 and did our jet upgrade. That whole process took twelve months. Then we spent three months at Nellis Air Force Base in Nevada going through combat crew training. That's where you did your gunnery and dogfight-type training with the airplane you were going to fly in Korea—in my case, the F-86 Sabrejet.

They would pick the top ten percent of a class to fly fighters. They looked for guys who were aggressive in the air, a little bit bold, a little bit arrogant, the guys who showed the most discipline and who had the steel nerves.

I went into the service in June 1951, but with all that training I didn't arrive in Korea until October of 1952.

I was stationed at Kimpo, right outside of Seoul. By the time I got there the Chinese had been through once or twice, and we'd gone through it a couple of times, pushing them out, and every building had holes in it from machine gun and rifle bullets. We lived in these little barracks that had been built by the Japanese. Most had been bombed out or had shell holes in them, or the roof was missing. There were antiaircraft guns all around the field.

When I first reported for duty at Kimpo it was a very lonely feeling. There I was, twenty-two years old, a fuzzy-cheeked little second lieutenant, didn't know anybody, never been away from home before. I was a small-town boy anyway, and I'd been pretty homesick when I went off to college, which was only four hundred miles away.

It was a lonely feeling that was made even worse by the fact that in a fighter outfit you're not accepted right away. You come in there and you're just so much cannon fodder to those guys. You've got to build a reputation first, let them know that you're good, that you can do anything they can do.

My first mission was an orientation flight. I went up with one of the instructor pilots in the squadron, and we flew up and down the peninsula and picked up visual checkpoints on the ground. The various rivers and reservoirs in North Korea. We stayed well away from MiG Alley.

MiG Alley was essentially the airspace over the Yalu River. The most active MiG bases were there, just across the river in Manchuria. I believe there were at least a thousand MiGs distributed among those bases, and being on Chinese soil they were off limits. We absolutely could not strafe or bomb them.

And we could engage the MiGs only when *they* crossed the Yalu. We were warned repeatedly about that. *Do not cross the Yalu River.* Crossing the Yalu became a court-martial offense. But you didn't pay much attention to that when somebody was shooting at you. They threatened us with that all the time, but I don't know anybody who got court-martialed.

Most of the missions we flew were what we called Yalu sweeps. We'd go up and patrol over the Yalu and wait for the MiGs to come up and fight us. We flew in an enormous figure eight, always turning into the river. You didn't want to put your back toward the river because that's where they came across.

On my first sweep we didn't see any MiGs. Some days you saw them and some days you didn't. I was somewhat disappointed, because I was anxious to tangle with them. That's what I'd been trained for. I was scared. I don't know any pilot who isn't a little scared going into combat. And if you're not, the first time you see a guy blown out of the sky in front of you, you get a sense of your own mortality real fast. But I was totally confident. I felt totally prepared to fight the MiG.

On my second combat flight we all got shot at, but we didn't get a chance to shoot back.

It went on like that until my nineteenth mission. On that day I was with a guy named Ira Porter. He was flying number three in the flight and I was flying number four,[1] and we got into a big fight with about twenty or thirty MiGs, which by the way was not unusual. We were always outnumbered on these missions. So our four planes against their twenty or thirty was not something we were overly concerned about.

But during the melee the flight broke up into two elements.

Two was the minimum number of aircraft allowed to stay in a combat area. If a leader and his wingman got separated, both were to immediately effect a rendezvous somewhere. If they couldn't find each other they were to return to base. If for some reason one guy

---

[1] The basic fighting unit for the U.S. Air Force in Korea was a flight of four planes, with each flight composed of two elements of two planes each, and each element being made up of a wingman and his leader.

had to turn back, the other had to go with him. You were not allowed to stay out there by yourself.

Well, Ira got behind this MiG and the MiG pilot headed for the ground. He dropped from thirty thousand feet to probably two or three thousand. He flew across the Yalu River into Manchuria, and we didn't hesitate to go after him. This guy was jinking and turning and doing everything possible to get away. Ira had been firing at him for quite a while, and finally he fired out. Ran out of ammunition.

So I moved in behind the MiG.

By this time we were in the mountains, and he was twisting down through the valleys and over the hills and going around mountaintops like cops and robbers. I hit him with several good bursts, and finally I caught him with a burst right behind the canopy.

He lit up like a Christmas tree. It looked like he lost control of his airplane. He was in a hard left turn and the next thing I knew he hit the side of a mountain and disintegrated.

After he exploded in front of me, God, I was so damn excited. Seeing all that happen right in front of my eyes. It was like something you see in the movies.

As soon as he burst into flames on the mountainside we turned south to cross back over the Yalu River. And suddenly I didn't have any power. I called to Ira, "Hey, I'm losing power." We flew over the Suiho Reservoir, and God, that place was dynamite. There were all kinds of antiaircraft guns there. I could see the stuff coming up at me, like strings of little luminescent golf balls floating up and fattening to the size of baseballs as they went by the airplane. I was flying at about five hundred feet, and how they missed me I'll never know.

We crossed the Yalu and I'm still losing power. I can't get any altitude.

Finally, *finally* I realized I had my speed brakes out. Speed brakes on the F-86 were two large metal flaps that came out from each side of the fuselage, just behind the wings. During the fight with the MiG I'd put out the speed brakes so as not to overrun my target, and I got so damn excited I forgot I'd put them out. Once I retracted the speed brakes I was able to get back up to altitude and catch up to Porter.

But by now both of us were at bingo fuel. That was the term we used for just enough fuel to get from the Yalu back to base. Actually we were at bingo fuel while still on the deck. By the time we climbed to forty thousand feet we had practically no fuel and had to shut the engines off and glide.

When you shut off your engine you lose your radio too. You don't want to keep your battery on, because you need all that battery power to get an air start. So we agreed before we shut off the engines that when we hit ten thousand feet we'd start them up again. We didn't want to get any lower than that, because we wanted to have plenty of room to get an air start. And the lower you get, the more fuel it takes to get back to altitude.

We hit ten thousand feet and Ira gets an air start right off. I had to make three tries at it before my engine caught. In fact I was ready to bail out. We started climbing again, and I think we got up to around twenty thousand feet before we flamed out.

By this time we had the airfield in sight. Now it wasn't unusual to come back from a mission with empty tanks and make what's called a dead-stick landing. A landing without any power, where you would just glide in. We practiced those all the time.

We managed to land all right, and when we got in the group commander grounded Porter for ten days. Even though we'd shot down a MiG. Because as the element leader Porter was responsible for getting us back with enough gas.

But they let me go. Hell, I was so excited I was ready to go up and fly another mission. Later in my tour I shot down a couple of MiGs at altitude, but nothing was as exciting as that first kill.

Up at altitude, thirty thousand, forty thousand feet, once you see flames, once you know you've got a kill, you immediately break off. Because you're either trying to get another MiG or you're avoiding the ones trying to get you. You don't have time to wait around and watch the guy hit the ground. So a kill at altitude, though it was always a thrill, was not quite the same as getting a MiG down on the deck.

My tour lasted from October 1952 to May 1953, and during that time I scored two and a half kills, with a number of probables. Unless you saw fire or a parachute, and what you saw was confirmed either by another pilot or by the gun cameras, you were not credited with a kill. You could hit a MiG and have it throw smoke all over the sky, as happened to me with a number of my probables, but unless you and another pilot or the cameras saw flames, or saw the enemy pilot leave his airplane, you didn't get a kill, you got a probable.

Two and a half kills is not a lot. I think there were something like forty American aces during the Korean War, an ace being a pilot who shot down at least five enemy planes. But I was a wingman for most of my tour, which cut down on the number of opportunities I had to shoot, because a wingman's first responsibility is to protect his leader. As the leader is chasing down a MiG, you're clearing his tail, and you're also clearing your own. The leader is depending on his wingman, because once he locks onto a MiG he doesn't have time to look back over his shoulder both ways and see who's chasing him. He's depending on his wingman to protect him.

And to protect your leader you have to follow him through every maneuver—loops, rolls, high-G turns, Immelmanns—whatever he's doing. Consequently a wingman didn't get to shoot much himself.

As a wingman you tried to prove yourself in other ways. For example, I was on a mission once with a guy named Vermont Garrison. Vermont was one of my idols. A great fighter pilot. We used to call him the Gray Eagle. He'd been a POW in World War II. I was up on Vermont's wing, and we'd dropped our external tanks, which we always did whenever we encountered MiGs. But on this particular day I couldn't get rid of one of my tanks. It just wouldn't jettison.

The procedure was, when that happened you turned around and went back home, because you're putting yourself at a great disadvantage. With the tanks on you had significantly less speed and maneuverability.

Well, Vermont had gotten onto this MiG. And I said, "I can't drop my tank." He said, "Okay, we'll turn for home." I said, "I feel comfortable. I'll stay with you as long as I can."

And I stayed right with him. We went down on the deck, and he got this MiG right in the middle of Antung, which was their biggest fighter base. He was flying an F-86 that had the two extra

20mm cannon, and he couldn't have hit that MiG any better. We were only a couple of thousand feet over the town, and he blew that MiG right out of the sky.

That's just an example of how you proved yourself. Vermont was pleased with me because I had the guts to stay with him instead of turning for home. And he got a MiG. If I'd decided to go back, of course he would've had to go with me. I'll tell you, after that he thought I was Jesus Christ.

I flew a hundred missions during my tour, but not all of them were fighter sweeps. Sometimes we would fly cover for the fighter-bombers when they were hitting a particular target, just watching over them to keep them from being jumped by MiGs. We also flew escort for reconnaissance airplanes, mainly the marine Banshee and the F-80.

In general the enemy pilots were well below the quality of our air force pilots. That's the reason we had a thirteen-to-one kill ratio over there. Their pilots were simply not as good as us, and consequently they were not getting the most out of their airplanes. But once in a while you got a guy who could really hassle with you, and you were pretty sure he was not a North Korean, and probably not even a Chinese. He was a guy who knew how to handle an airplane in combat, very likely a Russian who'd flown against the Germans in World War II.

That was rare, though. Mostly the MiGs flew in huge groups, and they'd come in and dive down on you and fire from all kinds of angles where they couldn't possibly hit you. It was pure hit and run. They'd dive at you, fire a burst, then climb for altitude again, because the MiG-15 could climb faster than the F-86.

You could also say they had us outgunned. Six .50-caliber machine guns in the F-86 to three heavy nose cannons in the MiG. Those were the 20mm and 37mm cannons, which fired a very large shell. But their rate of fire was slower. You looked over your shoulder and you saw this little puff . . . puff . . . puff. . . . That was about the rate of fire of that 37mm. So they could climb faster, and they had heavier guns. Pilot for pilot, though, we had them beat hands down.

CHAPTER 26

One Man's War

Whatever hardships or danger they may have faced, men serving at sea and flying in the Korean skies at least enjoyed a certain freedom of movement. On the ground, meanwhile, the war remained in the stalemate that had set in during the fall of 1951, with the Communist and UN armies dug in along the entire width of the peninsula, glaring at each other across a few hundred yards of no man's land, and at this stage of the war, out there on the ridges and hilltops, a man often spent his entire tour of duty within a few hundred yards of his bunker or foxhole.

For the marines especially it was a frustrating experience. By training and inclination, marines are not partial to fighting defensively. There are no foxholes in the Marine Corps, only fighting holes, fine for holding an overnight perimeter or as temporary shelter during an attack, but not to live in. Many marine veterans of Korea would remember later how hard it was for them to sit in one place, sending out an occasional patrol, but otherwise simply waiting for the other side to do something, when all their training told them to carry the fight to the enemy.

Of course, the marines were defending only one sector of the MLR. In fact, they were in Korea with only a single division. U.S. Army units, South Koreans, and the various UN contingents made up the majority of the frontline troops. But whatever the branch of service or the nationality of the man involved, his life on the line was pretty much the same: he lived in a hole in the ground, fought off the lice and rats or tried to ignore them, considered himself lucky if he got a hot meal, read his mail and wrote his letters home, and at regular intervals got his gear together and his weapon ready and went out on patrol.

Still, some had it worse than others. And it was not always the terrain or the presence of the enemy that made life especially difficult. Beverly Scott spent some time in the Iron Triangle, a hill mass in central Korea, and on Heartbreak Ridge, and he remembers the experience as one of the most miserable of his entire life—a judgment that reflects not just the particular ferocity of the enemy in those areas, and the consistently bad weather, and the dreary living conditions, but also the fact that Bev Scott was a black officer in a white man's army.

I want to make something clear from the beginning. From the first day I went in the army I had no thought of getting out. I saw the army as something I could do extremely well. I fitted in. The army offered everything I like in life. I like order, I like structure, I like organization, I like discipline, I like judgment on the basis of performance.

And it was honorable. There was no better institution in American life, no better one anywhere, than the army for the black man in the forties and fifties. Things weren't perfect, but they were better than any civilian institution. You had more leverage in the army. You always had somebody you could go to and complain about bad treatment. A black man couldn't do that in civilian life. Especially in the South.

From almost my first day in the army I planned to go to officer candidate school. I got my orders for OCS around Christmas of 1945. Graduated in July 1946. A nineteen-year-old second lieutenant.

OCS was my first experience with living in an integrated society. There were no all-black officer candidate schools. Most of my bunkmates were white, and that was my first experience with meeting white people on a person-to-person basis. Previous to that all my experience with whites had been adversarial. Growing up in rural North Carolina, I'd done all kinds of menial jobs as a boy, and I was always subjected to insults and names. We had white neighbors living across the creek from our house, and all us kids did was fight.

OCS was the first time I'd ever competed with guys who had gone to Yale and Harvard and the various prep schools. It was a very enlightening experience. Frankly, it set the tone for the rest of my life, because OCS taught me that I could successfully compete with these people.

When the war in Korea broke out I was at Fort Knox, Kentucky, helping train black troops. I was an infantry officer, always had been. But in Korea they immediately began experiencing severe communications problems, because the men over there didn't know how to handle their radios or lay wire properly. They told us they needed school-trained communications officers. That became one of the army's highest priorities. So I was sent to Fort Benning, Georgia, to learn communications.

I graduated from Benning in December 1950, and a month later I was in Korea as a commo officer with the 25th Infantry Division.

Basically what I did was try and teach the infantry officers in my battalion[1] the basics of radio communications. Few of them accepted what I told them. It might have been partly because I was black and they were white, but mostly it was them not wanting to admit they were doing things wrong. But they were. They always tried to talk with the radios out of range. And they didn't understand the business of laying wire.

The radio operators seldom had any training. A company commander would grab hold of a rifleman and say, "Here, you carry this radio." That was all the training they got, and consequently most radio operators didn't know good procedure, didn't know how to keep the transmissions short, or how to tune the radio so it was

---

[1] 1st Battalion, 24th Regiment

zeroed in on the proper frequency. I tried to bring some professionalism to the battalion's communications, and eventually it got that way.

The 24th Regiment was the only all-black regiment in the division, and as a black officer in an all-black regiment commanded by whites I was always super sensitive about standing my ground. Being a man. Being honest with my soldiers. I felt that the black soldiers were depending on me to look out for them, that if I didn't look out for them nobody would.

Most of the white officers were good. Taken in the context of the times, they were probably better than the average white guy in civilian life. But there was still that patronizing expectation of failure. White officers came to the 24th Regiment knowing or suspecting or having been told that this was an inferior regiment.

And there were always the really outright racist sons of bitches. But you didn't deal with those people. You maintained a strictly professional relationship and had no interpersonal dealings at all with that kind of officer.

I served as the 1st Battalion communications officer all through the spring and summer of 1951, when the 24th was on the line constantly. The 24th fought well. As a commo officer I was not in a foxhole on the front line, but I was damn close to it, and I saw no instances of the mass cowardice that some people claimed the regiment displayed earlier in the war. Those men did their jobs as well as any white unit fighting at that time.

In September we got word that the 24th was going to be deactivated. Nobody told us why, the order just came down. It was probably inevitable, though, that the regiment would be broken up, because by now General Ridgway was pushing hard for real integration in the army. And there were other generals around who may not have cared much for integration, but who refused to believe that all-black units could fight, and who wanted them disbanded for that reason.

Anyway, they pulled us off the line about the middle of September and moved us back in reserve. While we were back there we started turning in our equipment. Everyone in the 24th was transferred to the remaining regiments in the division, with the 24th being replaced in the division by the 14th Regiment from Japan.

I was transferred to the 14th, and right away I experienced some problems. People in the 14th didn't want anybody from the 24th. I was a technically qualified communications officer, which the 14th said they needed very badly, but when I got there, suddenly they didn't need any commo officers.

Then their executive officer said, "We got a rifle platoon for you. Think you can handle a rifle platoon?"

What the hell do you mean, can I handle a rifle platoon? I was also trained as an infantry officer. He knew that. I was a first lieutenant, been in the army six years, almost all that time in the infantry. If I had been coming in as a white first lieutenant the question never would have been asked.

In any case, I became the first black platoon leader in the 14th Regiment. I was the only black officer in the battalion. I never had any problems with my men; they were mostly Hispanics, and when they saw that I knew what I was doing, and wasn't going to get them killed or shot up unnecessarily, they relaxed and accepted me.

My relationship with the other officers was cool. Especially with the company commander. For a while I wasn't talked to. I was watched very closely. I should have been made the executive officer of the company, since I outranked all the other lieutenants, and it was customary to have the second-highest in rank as the company exec. But I wasn't given the job.

I saw right away it was going to be pretty tough for me.

It was now the fall of 1951. We'd just moved to the Iron Triangle area. Three towns arranged in a triangle around a long valley, the valley surrounded by steep hills.

That valley had been one of the main invasion corridors to the south, but the truce talks had started, and now they were digging in. Every morning we'd see fresh piles of dirt on the ridges. You never saw the Chinese, but you saw the dirt. They were always digging, and they churned out that dirt like worms.

We were digging in too, until what you had were two armies facing each other from opposing trenchlines. Between the two trenchlines there was maybe five hundred or six hundred yards of no man's land. And what the war came down to for us was patrolling that no man's land.

It was a miserable time. Just a miserable, miserable time. We lost men almost every day, killed or wounded, and it was hard to see the point. The lines stayed exactly where they were.

After we'd been in our positions for about a month, word came down that we were going to make this big attack. We were going to attack all the way up the Iron Triangle to Pyonggang, to straighten out the line, and I'll tell you, we truly believed that was going to be our last action of the war. We were absolutely convinced we would never survive an attack like that. The Chinese were not going to be dislodged on those hill masses. It would have been impossible to get them out of there. We'd been patrolling those hills for a month, and we'd never gotten more than halfway up any one of them before taking heavy fire and a lot of casualties.

But the order came down that we were going to attack. We were pulled back off the line, re-outfitted, issued fresh ammunition, we recalibrated our weapons, we spent about two days—cold, wet, miserable days—rehearsing the attack. And you never saw so many long faces, including my own. We felt certain we were being ordered to our deaths.

At the last minute, for reasons unknown to us, the attack was called off, and I don't think I could begin to describe the relief we felt. I read later that there had been a breakdown in the truce talks, and that this attack was to be part of a major offensive all along the front. But new overtures were made in the talks, and the attack was called off.

Shortly after this we moved to Heartbreak Ridge. We had to cross a valley to get there, and the entire road through that valley, over two miles of it, was covered with camouflage netting. It was like a long dim tunnel, and it was very depressing to see, because it meant that we were going into positions where the enemy would be looking down our throats.

It turned out to be even worse than that. Our trenches in that sector were only about twenty meters in front of theirs. We were eyeball to eyeball. Just twenty meters of no man's land between us. We couldn't move at all in the daytime without getting shot at.

Machine-gun fire would come in, grenades, small-arms fire, all from within spitting distance.

It was like World War I. We lived in a maze of bunkers and deep trenches. Some had been dug by previous occupants of the ridge. Some we dug ourselves. There were bodies strewn all over the place. Hundreds of bodies frozen in the snow. We could see the arms and legs sticking up. Nobody could get their dead out of there.

On Heartbreak it was just a matter of holding our positions. We'd send out a patrol once in a while, but only at night. It was suicide to move around in the daytime. Many times they'd attack us at night, so nobody slept after dark. You stayed wide awake. During the day we'd get shelled by artillery or mortars, or get sniped at, so you never got any real sleep.

Added to that, we were fighting North Koreans. There was a distinct difference between fighting them and fighting the Chinese. The Chinese were normal soldiers, in the sense that when they saw they couldn't do something they'd pull back. The North Koreans would come at you even when they couldn't do anything. Even when they knew it was hopeless and that they were going to be killed. They'd come right into your hole, try and shoot you or stab you or bite you if they didn't have a weapon. Just fanatical as hell. Maybe thirty or forty of them would come straight at us in a kind of banzai attack, where they'd all get killed, but it was just to distract us while more of them were trying to sneak around us somewhere else. And they were vicious people. They mutilated bodies. They shot prisoners. Just nasty, nasty people.

Heartbreak Ridge was bad news any way you looked at it.

But I finally made exec while I was up there. We had a new CO by that time, a big Polish guy from Pennsylvania who was making a real effort to be fair. A replacement came in, a lieutenant named Stevens who had been wounded in World War II on Okinawa and who'd been called up from the reserves. He was a nice guy, a real handsome guy. We all called him Steve. When he came to the company our exec was moved up to battalion, and I was made the executive officer while Steve took over my old platoon.

At this time the army required that we have one hot meal a day. I suppose it was for morale purposes. Conditions on Heartbreak were so miserable otherwise. You could choose either breakfast or supper—that is, you could eat your hot meal before the sun came up or after it went down. But to get to the mess tent you had to walk down the reverse slope of the hill, and the North Koreans were always lobbing mortar rounds over there. It was just random fire, but it was something you had to be careful about.

Steve and I got to be pretty close friends, and since we both preferred to eat our hot meal in the morning, each morning we'd walk down the hill together. And as we walked down we'd talk about various issues, or about the platoon, things that needed to be done, or the personalities of the men, who you could rely on and so forth.

On this one particular morning, I guess it was a week or two after Steve got there, I couldn't get my razor going. I used an electric razor plugged into an old radio battery, and the battery was acting up, so I sent Steve on ahead of me.

Finally I got myself shaved, and as I was walking down the hill a big blast blew apart the mess tent. A mortar round had landed right on it. The explosion killed a number of cooks, and it also blew Steve's legs off.

He'd been sitting at the mess table, where I'd have been sitting if that battery hadn't acted up, and the blast just kind of sheared him off below the hips.

I was one of the first to reach him. I helped get him out, and he was a mess. He survived the wound, but he didn't want to, because as we were taking him out he saw his legs still lying there under the table. He'd been a newspaper reporter from Vallejo, California, and I think he eventually went back to his work in Vallejo, but after they took him away I never had any contact with him again.

By this time, March of 1952, I had been in Korea longer than anybody in the division. You needed thirty-six points to rotate. You got four points for every month of line duty, so after nine months on line you had thirty-six points. I think I had something like fifty-two points by this time, but they kept telling me, "Well, we don't have a replacement for you."

That was nonsense, so one morning while I was back picking up the company payroll I stopped by the Inspector General's office and complained about being treated unfairly. I left a note asking that they look into my case and find out why I couldn't rotate home when I'd been there longer than anybody in the division.

The next time I went down there I got word from the IG to report to Yongdungpo to go home.

I didn't even go back to the company. I called my platoon sergeant and some of the other guys on the telephone, told them goodbye and left.

CHAPTER 27

Behind the Wire

As the outpost war continued to exact its daily toll of lives, the truce talks ground on in Panmunjom, a small village just below the 38th parallel and about forty miles northwest of Seoul. The talks had begun on July 10, 1951, and from the moment the two sides sat down the sessions were characterized by bitter haggling.

On August 22 the Communists broke off the talks and the delegates did not meet again until October 25. A month later, on November 27, 1951, agreement was finally reached on a truce line, but the talks immediately bogged down again on the next major issue: the exchange of prisoners of war.

By the summer of 1951 the UN was well aware that many of the prisoners it held, both Chinese and North Korean, did not wish to return to their Communist homelands, and President Truman himself had vowed publicly that no POW held by the UN would be forced to go back against his will.

Technically this violated the Geneva Convention. "Prisoners of war," that document states, "shall be repatriated without delay after cessation of hostilities."

But the Geneva Conventions of both 1929 and 1949 had assumed as a matter of course that prisoners of war would wish to return to their home countries. The men who had drawn up the documents, and the governments that had signed them, apparently had not envisioned a situation where POWs would not want to go home.

The Communists, of course, quoting the Geneva accords like scripture, demanded that all POWs be repatriated without delay.

Harry Truman stood his ground, and the issue deadlocked the truce talks. The war dragged on. In the meantime a young college instructor from Pennsylvania was about to enter the drama.

His work with prisoners of war would involve Stanley Weintraub in one of the most controversial episodes of the Korean conflict: the screening of all POWs held by the United Nations to find out whether or not they actually wanted to return to Communist-controlled China or North Korea. Weintraub was directly involved in the screening process, and he considers it the spark that set off the prisoner-of-war riots in May of 1952 that saw Communist prisoners on Koje Island actually capturing the camp commandant, General Francis Dodd, and holding him for ransom. A number of U.S. soldiers and scores of prisoners were killed before the riots were put down.

Weintraub, now a widely respected biographer and cultural historian and the author of more than forty books, remembers the experience as formative. "I think about it all the time, not just the uprisings but the entire process that put us in such an awkward and embarrassing position. It's probably why I'm so interested in writing books about war. I'm fascinated by why we do what we do. The bungling. The stupidities.

"Even the very process that got me to Korea in the first place still amazes me."

I was not old enough in World War II to be drafted. Some of my friends went into the service, but I was not draftable. I missed it by something like three weeks. So when the Korean War started I was very high up. I was working on a master's degree at the time, at Temple University in Philadelphia. I knew I would be drafted. I knew there was no way I could get a job after a master's degree.

No one would want me. I'd be too high up on the draft list to be of use to anybody. So I figured I'd better go into the service if I could, and go in as a gentleman rather than as a private.

The army still had a special regulation then which stated that direct commissions could be given to qualified scientists in an emergency. Korea qualified as an emergency. So they asked me, "Are you a scientist?" I said, "Does a bachelor of science degree make one a scientist?" And they said, "That's fine. Sign right here." I said, "Don't you even care what science is involved?" And they said, "Oh no. A bachelor of science degree is a bachelor of science. That makes you eligible."

It was a BS in education. I had gone to a teacher's college. I had no science worthy of the name. But they filed my application, and before long I got the commission. April 1951. But it was only effective if I signed up for immediate active duty.

I signed it, and I was called up. Immediately.

I reported to Fort Sam Houston, Texas, in June of 1951. By now the war in Korea was a year old. At Fort Sam we had to do some marching, and go through the infiltration course at night. We had to go through gas mask training, and I learned something useful there, because later in Korea we had to use gas on the rioting prisoners. The training lasted six weeks. Then I had a week's leave, spent at home, and I was on my way.

While we were crossing the Pacific we were given news handouts and bulletins about what was going on in Korea. We were told the war was now pretty much a static affair. But people were still getting killed there all the time. And we knew we could be among those.

There was no euphoria whatever about going over. There wasn't any idealistic commitment felt by people there. I was gung ho for it more than the others, because I think I was more aware of the history. I had seen what had happened with the encroachments of Stalin in eastern Europe, and I realized it was likely to happen in the Far East as well. I felt the domino theory was a logical theory then, although I don't recall hearing the term used.

We landed at Yokohama, and we went from Yokohama by train all the way south to Sasebo. At Sasebo we boarded a flat-bottomed ferry boat. We knew we were approaching Korea while the boat was still miles out to sea. You could smell Korea. The fecal odor was clear, miles out. They put human excrement on their fields for fertilizer. The pervasive smell of Korea from then on, for me, for the next eighteen months, was that fecal atmosphere.

At the replacement depot in Pusan I was told that a particular major was going home and I was to take his place as admissions officer of the POW hospital, just off the main road between Taegu and Pusan. I hadn't the faintest idea of what I would end up doing in Korea, but I hadn't expected that. I knew nothing about hospitals. I had no experience in administration. I had no experience with bureaucracy. I had graded freshman papers at Temple. That was the only paperwork I had ever done. But such was the logic of the army.

I discovered once I got to the hospital that it didn't look like any hospital I had ever seen before. There was one old school building, and hundreds and hundreds of huge tents. All the surgery was done in the school building. It was slapdash. I think the only reason the prison camp was put there was because they had all these prisoners in the area, and they merely went out and put barbed wire around them.

We had about two hundred thousand prisoners. Most were sent to the island of Koje, off the southeast coast about twenty miles below Pusan. The Chinese prisoners were sent to the island of Cheju, which I understand is now a popular vacation spot, a very posh place for Koreans to go on holiday. They had to separate the Chinese from the Koreans, because so many of the Chinese had been forcibly impressed into the Communist armies, and were totally hostile to any kind of propaganda from their own side. There were a lot of fights between the militant Communists and these reluctant "volunteers" who had joined the army at the point of a gun. There were also fights between the Koreans and the Chinese, as two different nationalities. So it was necessary to separate them.

The healthy people were sent to Cheju or Koje. The wounded and sick were kept at the hospital. But all prisoners were interrogated and processed at the hospital first.

Processing the prisoners turned out to be one of our most naive episodes, because our knowledge of foreign languages was so lousy in this country. We were unprepared, totally, for being in Japan, and then for being in Korea, and then for having the Chinese come in. We were incompetent in all three languages. So we needed to use POWs as our interpreters. We picked people who appeared smart, and who had some knowledge of English. It was a good job for them. They ate better. They had more privileges. But many of them were also the most militant of the Communists among the prisoners. Many of them were trained agents. North Korea was allowing trained agents to be captured as POWs. These people were under orders to organize the hardline Communist prisoners and cause any kind of disturbance they could in the various POW camps, with the aim of provoking a violent reaction from our side which could then be used for propaganda purposes.

We found this out too late to do us any good. We didn't realize this was the case, that they were duping us, until the mutinies, when these people we had chosen to help us became the leaders of the various prison-camp insurrections.

As admissions officer I supervised the screening process. We screened all incoming prisoners to see if they were well. If they appeared sick we had to determine if they were merely malingering. Very often they would fake an illness to avoid work, or avoid being sent off to Koje Island, which already had a bad reputation. Moscow Radio would claim, for example, that we were doing medical experiments on the prisoners at Koje. I don't think this was true, but many of the prisoners obviously believed it.

The prisoners came to us in big six-by-six trucks, unless they were very seriously wounded. In that case they would come in by helicopter or ambulance. There wasn't much helicopter use then. Some, but not much. Helicopters didn't come into their own until the Vietnam era. When you see the television show "M*A*S*H" and you see all the helicopters coming in, it's not Korea. What they've done is transpose onto the Korean War something that was technically not there.

The prisoners came to us in a constant stream, perhaps a hundred a day. We also had stacked in front of the admissions tent, like a pile of cordwood, the bodies of DOAs. These were prisoners who had died while en route to the hospital. We would have to give them identities, which usually was "Unknown Korean," and a fingerprint. We were required to forward all these identities to the Geneva Convention officials, to show we were handling prisoners of war properly, and disposing of the dead properly.

But our touchiest problem came not from disposing of the dead and wounded, as might be expected, but from getting rid of body parts.

In a hospital in the West the common procedure is to take amputated body parts and incinerate them. But we were not allowed to incinerate body parts. Under no circumstances were we allowed to incinerate anything. The world had just gone through, a few years earlier, the business of Belsen and Dachau and Auschwitz, where you had mass incinerations of bodies. So we were not allowed to burn body parts, for fear that we would be accused of crimes against humanity by the Communists. Even the smell of cremated body parts, we were told, would be bad.

But we had to dispose of them somehow, and it became my job to arrange that. It wasn't difficult. We would gather up a bunch of arms and legs, wrap them in canvas, and send Digger, a sergeant who had been an undertaker in Kansas City, up into the hills with a POW work party, and he would dig a big hole up in some inaccessible spot and bury them. We buried arms and legs all over the Korean countryside. My feeling is that someday archaeologists will go to Korea and will dig up a place where they'll have nothing but six or seven left legs, and they'll wonder what kind of strange cult was involved.

There had been unrest on the POW islands, particularly Koje, for many months. There was always a real militancy on the part of the hardline Communist prisoners to indoctrinate the others, and to keep them indoctrinated at a high level. If people resisted this indoctrination they were killed, but usually in a manner that would not be too obvious. Sandbagging the back of the head was a favorite, as I recall. You would find the body at the compound gate at dawn, and there would be almost no marks.

But the real violence began when it became clear to these hardline Communists, early in 1952, that we were going to separate the prisoners who did not want to return to North Korea or China. We were going to allow them, in effect, to make their own choice about where they would go.

The Communists had demanded all along that all POWs must be repatriated. Many prisoners didn't want to go back, but the Communists ignored this and insisted that we live up to the Geneva accords and send everyone back. We began screening all the prisoners, to find who actually did want to go back, in April of 1952, and that was the spark. That's when everything exploded, and the mutinies and insurrections began, led of course by these hardliners.

At our hospital we had to call in the 15th Regiment of the 3rd Division to help. The 82nd Airborne was sent to Koje. There was violence. We shot prisoners. We tear-gassed prisoners. We had to use flamethrowers to burn down the tents and get inside their fences. It was surrealistic, because you don't ordinarily think in terms of attacking patients. We had one ward of patients—about three thousand of them—who were all orthopedic cases. People either on crutches or with casts on their limbs or amputees, in some cases double amputees, with no legs, who were busy marching around with spears and homemade pikes made from the aluminum sides of a stretcher, and grenades made from gasoline and casting plaster—stuff they had been filching for months and hiding. They had all kinds of weapons prepared. And these hardliners were prepared to fight to the death. There were a few shot, not a great many. Basically we went at them with concussion grenades, with flamethrowers, and with tear gas. It was violent. I was directly involved in some of it. But eventually the uprisings were put down, although in propaganda value they represented a great victory for the Communists.

CHAPTER 28

Piece of Cake

The United States suffered 160,000 casualties in the Korean War. For the South Korean army the figure was 850,000, and most authorities consider that a conservative estimate. This enormously higher casualty figure would seem to suggest that South Korean troops did their share of the fighting, and perhaps more than their share of the dying. But there are American veterans of Korea who will argue to this day that South Korean troops did no fighting worthy of the name, that the only thing South Korean formations ever did was break and run.

This they did do, from the first day of the war and with distressing regularity thereafter, until finally, in the spring and summer of 1952, all twelve South Korean divisions were in turn pulled off the line and given intensive combat training by the U.S Army. When they returned to the battle line some of these units remained untrustworthy, but most conducted themselves very well indeed, holding up time and again in combat with the Chinese, who constantly probed those sectors of the front held by South Korean units in the continued belief that the South Koreans would quickly fold.

There had never been any shortage of individual bravery among the South Korean troops. What they had suffered from was poor leadership and an almost criminal lack of training and modern equipment. But not many Americans noticed this, because not many ever got to know the South Korean soldiers as individuals. An exception was a young high school teacher from Virginia named Blaine Friedlander.

I had no idea what I was getting into. Not an inkling.

When the group of replacements I was with landed at Pusan they put us on a train. When the train got up to Taegu they ordered us off and put us in some tents. Nobody told us anything. I had assumed, up to this point, that we were being sent to join the infantry.

A three-quarter-ton truck came by, and we were blindfolded and put in the back of the truck. They closed the canvas flaps and we rode around for a while, and when we got off they took us into a little Korean house. We had to fill out forms, they fingerprinted us, they interviewed us. By now I knew I wasn't destined for the infantry, but it was several more days before I finally learned what was going on.

We were being assigned to KMAG, the Korean Military Advisory Group, and we were in the process of being given security clearances.

KMAG people lived and worked with South Korean army units. Everybody who was cleared had to sign a contract with the State Department, that we would be under State Department rules and regulations, and under the Korean army's rules of warfare. We were no longer American soldiers. For all practical purposes we were Korean soldiers. Or maybe partly Korean soldier and partly State Department employee. I never quite figured it out.

I was cleared, I signed my contract, and I was sent up to the front lines. I rode up in a truck filled with cases of American beer. The driver stopped along the way to pick up his Korean girlfriend, and she went along with us. We drove over the mountains to the east coast, near the Japan Sea, and as we approached the front lines

I saw sheet lightning. I'm sitting there wondering why there's sheet lightning on a clear night, until finally it dawned on me that that was artillery I was looking at.

The next morning I joined the 11th ROK Division. I was to be one of the communications people. There were forty Americans working with the division, twenty in the field and twenty back at the division CP.

The ROKs[1] did not have a good reputation. I was told in Taegu, in complete seriousness, that if I heard "HA" transmitted in Morse over the radio three times, that meant Haul Ass. That the enemy was attacking and the ROKs have bugged out. We were not allowed to use the letters HA for a call sign or anything else. They were reserved to protect the American lives in these ROK units, because all you ever heard was how the Koreans had bugged out every time they were attacked.

Well, they had, early in the war. But they weren't trained. Once they were trained the South Koreans were terrific soldiers. They fought as well or better than any American soldiers. For a long time they just did not have the proper equipment and training and while they were in that state, green and poorly equipped and poorly led, they were slaughtered by the hundreds and thousands. But they were brave soldiers. There were numerous instances when South Korean soldiers would strap explosives to their bodies and throw themselves at enemy tanks, because they didn't have antitank guns or tanks of their own and that was the only way they could stop them.

Anyway, KMAG was considered to be a very dangerous assignment, because the South Korean troops were supposed to be so undependable. The word was that KMAG really meant Kiss My Ass Goodbye.

Eventually I was made the commo chief for the 9th ROK Regiment. I was only a PFC, but I lived like a king. I don't recall ever doing my laundry, I don't recall ever cleaning my quarters, or shining my boots or cleaning my rifle. All those things were done for me.

---

[1]South Korean soldiers were almost universally called ROKs (pronounced "rocks") by Americans, the acronym coming from Republic of Korea.

I had five or six Korean soldiers who went with me everywhere. I do remember trying to clean my weapon once, but they took it out of my hands and said it just wasn't done. Their job was to see that I was treated with every courtesy—that's exactly the way one of them put it—and it would be discourteous of them to have me clean my own rifle or wash my own clothes.

I became friends with all of them. One was a graduate of a high school in Pusan, and he could speak English as well as any American. The others also knew some English, and they would try and teach me Korean. We had many, many discussions. How this war stacked up to the American Civil War, what the educational systems were like in the United States and Korea, the different philosophies behind the two cultures.

I don't want to imply that we sat around all day talking. Most of my time was taken up with radio work and with whatever other jobs were assigned to me. We worked seven days a week. The division was in some fights while I was there, but they didn't give up any ground.

The South Koreans proved to be excellent fighters once they had proper training and good leaders, but they had their own standards of discipline, which by American standards were very harsh. In the ROK army, physical beatings were common. Officers would routinely beat enlisted soldiers for minor infractions of the rules, and several times I saw senior officers punch junior officers with their fists. One soldier who was caught with a dirty rifle was made to stand all day in a barrel of water, in the dead of winter. Another who went AWOL (Absent Without Leave) to see his family was caught and brought back in irons. He was ordered to dig a hole, with his entire battalion watching, and when he finished he was ordered to kneel in front of it. The battalion commander walked up behind him, shot him in the back of the head with a .45, and kicked him into the grave.

I knew this man. He came from a town not far from where the regiment was stationed, and I'd met his family. He had a wife and three children, and all he'd wanted to do was visit them for a few hours. But I was powerless to save him. I couldn't do a thing for him. I had to stand there and watch like everybody else. The rules for KMAG people were very clear: we were there only to advise and train the Koreans. Under no circumstances were we allowed to interfere with their methods of discipline. That was their business.

It seems callous, the way the Koreans treated each other, but you have to keep in mind that what we as Westerners might view as callous was simply an accepted standard with them. When they broke the rules, they expected to be beaten. That soldier who went AWOL knew that if he was caught, he'd be executed. It was simply their way of doing things.

I was able to accept all this much more readily than the average GI, who was always shocked to encounter such behavior, because I saw firsthand the kind of life the average Korean had. If you were familiar with the way they lived, the routine hardships they experienced as civilians, you couldn't really be surprised at the strictness of ROK army discipline. We would call it brutal, but the average Korean soldier came out of a brutal environment. The poverty was unbelievable. The Koreans I served with were given one uniform, one pair of sneakers, one canteen of rice a day with maybe a little kimchee[2] and a pack of cigarettes. They earned about eight cents a day. But they were still better off than most civilians, who had no money, no food, no clothes, nothing at all.

If nothing else, my experience with the Koreans gave me a sense of perspective. I quickly saw that, compared to them, my own life, even in its worst moments, had been a piece of cake. And that made me admire them all the more, because despite the grinding poverty and the harsh life most of them experienced, they never seemed to lose hope. In the midst of these incredible hardships, they could still smile and laugh.

Once I was able to communicate with them I realized they were not a bunch of faceless gooks, but people who cared very deeply about their country, who knew its history and who also knew a surprising amount about *our* country, much more than the average American knew about Korea. They may have been brutalized, but they were not an army of dumb peasants. They were individuals. But you had to get to know them, and be able to talk to them, to realize this.

---

[2]Cabbage pickled in a uniquely Korean manner.

Most Americans never got close. In fact, most of the Americans I met over there had an ingrained prejudice against Koreans that automatically blocked any attempt at understanding.

When the time came for me to leave Korea they flew me down to KMAG headquarters at Taegu, and then I was put on a train to Pusan. In the barracks at Pusan the other soldiers started making loud remarks about me. I was wearing my KMAG patch, and they didn't like Koreans. And as far as they were concerned I was a gook too, because I'd been with the ROK army. Right now they might be the closest of friends, but my memory is, the American soldier hated the Korean soldier. And the dislike was automatic, because some of the guys making those remarks had never come near a Korean outfit. They hated Koreans by reflex action.

What the Korean soldier thought about the Americans . . . well, maybe the best way to explain it is to share a memory I have. Around Christmas of 1951 I remember being on the line when the 9th ROK regimental band came by and played Christmas carols for me. They were going around to every American who was up there and serenading each individual American with Christmas songs. And after they finished playing the songs they broke ranks and came up to me, one by one, in a long line, and shook my hand and thanked me personally for being there.

I'll never forget that. It was all they had to give, so they gave me that. A touch of home.

CHAPTER 29

Pressman

Jim Holton also spent time among the South Koreans, and in his case also, familiarity bred not contempt but a new respect and appreciation for the ROKs. Holton had worked for the Associated Press before being called up from the reserves shortly after the war began, and he served in the States for more than a year as an army public information officer (PIO) before being rather abruptly ordered to Korea, where he suspected he was going to be handed over to the infantry.

I sat for a week in a replacement camp in Taegu, just above Pusan, waiting to find out if I would be given another PIO job or sent off to the infantry. This was just after Christmas of 1951. I had spent Christmas in Tokyo, and now I was in Taegu, awaiting my fate.

It was bitterly cold. I was staying in a building without windows, a kind of schoolhouse. Dust was everywhere. There was a terrible stench to the place. But mostly there was the uncertainty about where I was going. That colored everything.

Finally I got the word that I had a PIO assignment at IX Corps headquarters in Chunchon. That was about one hundred fifty miles north of where I was.

To get up there I had to ride on a Korean train. It was the morning of New Year's Eve. I think it took about twelve hours for the train to get up there, and it was extremely uncomfortable. The seats were wooden benches, apparently made for the Japanese. Koreans were bigger than Japanese, and in these tiny seats even a Korean would have been uncomfortable. For a Westerner like myself it was torture.

Chunchon had been a fairly large city before the war, but it was nothing but rubble when I saw it. I was picked up in a jeep and driven to a big tent city just outside the town. By now it was about eleven o'clock on New Year's Eve. I reported to the duty officer, and he had a soldier show me to the tent where I was going to be living. I had a bottle of bourbon I'd bought in Tokyo and saved, and I shared it with the two other PIO officers in my tent. Well, the word got out that a guy with a bottle of booze was in the PIO tent, and rather quickly quite a lot of people showed up. That was our New Year's Eve celebration—a bottle of bourbon and a bunch of thirsty guys in a tent.

I started work the next morning. As a military journalist working out of an army public information office I was assigned to provide press coverage to American and South Korean units on the central front.

Actually I never did go to a frontline unit, in the year and a half I was there, that was American. All my visits to the combat areas were to Korean units. And very quickly I got the unofficial blessing of both Eighth Army and the ROK high command to wander around as I saw fit among these Korean units, because they badly needed press coverage to restore their reputation.

The reason they needed press coverage was because the civilian correspondents in Seoul would not cover a fight involving Korean troops. Seoul was about sixty miles south of us, and I would go down there to the press billet and talk to people I knew from the AP, trying to get them interested in what the South Korean army was doing, and they would just laugh in my face. No one had any confidence in the South Koreans as fighters. There was even an animosity toward them, especially among the correspondents who had been there in the early days of the war, and who had found themselves repeatedly surrounded by North Korean troops when South Korean units had bugged out. This had happened so many times that the South Koreans had a very bad reputation with the civilian press.

What they didn't realize was that this was a different army. This was not 1950, this was 1952. Virtually all the ROK units had been pulled out of the line, re-equipped, refitted, and intensely trained by General Van Fleet [the Eighth Army commander who succeeded General Ridgway]. The ROKs hadn't been tested in combat yet, at least not on a large scale, but I could see that the South Korean units I was covering were well disciplined, well led, and were going to put up a good fight when the time came for them to fight. It was just something I couldn't convey to the reporters in Seoul.

Part of the problem was that they simply didn't get around much, even to American units. They spent virtually all their time at the press billet in Seoul. This was an old Japanese-built apartment house. Every major news organization had an apartment there. They had a well-stocked bar. They had a dance hall. There were a lot of Korean women coming and going. And meanwhile the correspondents were getting virtually all their information from the daily briefings held by Eighth Army PIO. With the war in a stalemate they were able to get by quite well on what they were being told in these briefings. As much as the public wanted, they were able to do right there in Seoul.

I had very quickly come to admire the Koreans. I'm of Irish extraction myself, and maybe because of that I could empathize with them. The Koreans in fact have been called the Irish of the Far East. The same background of poverty, the long history of subjugation. They had a melancholy sense of life, and a kind of resignation. Very much like the Irish in many respects.

I think too that my getting so involved with the Koreans, becoming almost a kind of spokesman for them, was a reaction to the hostility I experienced among my civilian colleagues in the press.

201

They simply didn't want to give the Koreans credit for anything. In their minds the Koreans were incapable of fighting, and we Americans were there fighting their battles for them, and saving their country for them. Nothing was further from the truth, but there was no way I could persuade them otherwise.

They were persuaded finally, by the performance of the South Koreans in battle. By that spring [1952] the ROKs were back on the line in division strength. And it was apparent that the Chinese were going to hit these divisions, to test them and see if they would break, as they had early in the war—when, I should add, they were facing a Soviet-equipped and trained North Korean army with almost no training or modern equipment of their own.

The first big test came in the spring of 1952. An ROK division successfully fought off a series of Chinese attacks. The action wasn't on a large enough scale to attract the attention of the media in Seoul, but it happened in our corps area, and I went up there to do a story.

I was with the Koreans all through that spring and summer. There were more skirmishes with the Chinese. The ROKs continued to do well. But as usual nobody came up from Seoul to report on this.

Occasionally we would have some big names in the business visit our sector, but these people were not resident journalists. They were only passing through. Margaret Bourke-White showed up and spent a week with us. I guided her all over the central front. Punch Sulzberger, with his father, then president of the *New York Times*, spent several days with us. Edward R. Murrow was there for a little while.

Most of those visits took place during a long lull in the fighting. But by late summer it became apparent that the lull was going to end.

Suddenly there were no patrols coming from the Chinese side of the lines. Everything was unnaturally quiet, and we strongly suspected that the Chinese were massing for a major attack, maybe to try and crack the line and hit Seoul again before winter set in.

But what exactly were they up to? What we suspected was one thing, but for military planning purposes, we were totally in the dark.

Then one day a Chinese officer walked into one of our outposts with a briefcase full of plans.

And in due time the Chinese did attack where the captured plans said they would.

It was the start of a really horrific ten-day battle for a hill called White Horse Mountain. No American frontline units were engaged. The fighting was entirely between South Korean and Chinese troops. It was real head-on combat, and it was at White Horse Mountain that the South Koreans proved themselves to the world. They held their ground against something like twenty-six consecutive assaults by the Chinese. I know they made believers out of all those skeptics in the Seoul press corps.

I covered the battle with my PIO staff. It caught the correspondents in Seoul completely by surprise, and they never did get anybody up there. But this was a really big fight, and they desperately needed firsthand reports. Since we were the only ones on the scene, we took it upon ourselves to keep Seoul informed. Ultimately we were responsible for I think ninety percent of the material that the wire services filed about that battle.

I kept observers out on the front line in relays, and they would phone back eyewitness reports on the progress of the fighting. From my CP I'd collate the reports and then phone them in as poolers to the Seoul correspondents. We kept this up day and night for the entire battle.

One day during a lull I decided to go up to the front and see things for myself. So I got a jeep and a driver and my Korean interpreter and we went up and drove around the battlefield. Talked to the ROK commander, took some photos, that sort of thing. And just as we were about to leave, artillery started coming in. It got heavier and heavier until finally we were sealed in the dugout. I never did get out of there until the next morning. It was calculated by somebody that twenty thousand rounds landed on our hill during the night, which is a hell of a lot of artillery and mortar fire.

It was bad for me, because there was nothing for me to do all night except lie there and take it. The door of the dugout kept coming open, and I could see these lurid orange flashes as the rounds hit, one practically on top of the other, and of course they constantly shook the dugout, and dirt kept falling from the ceiling, and I kept thinking, *What the hell am I doing here?* I didn't have to be there.

I think that was just about the longest night of my life. What got me through it was the thought that lots of other people had endured that kind of thing, many of them more than once. And if they got through it, then I could get through it.

When the fighting finally died away I had a chance to go down to Seoul and talk with some of the guys in the press billet, and all I heard was, "Boy, you fellas sure saved our ass. That was a terrific thing you guys did up there, sending us all those reports."

That made me feel pretty good, to hear that. That all the work we did was worth it. But even more gratifying to me personally was how their attitude toward the Koreans had changed. Now all I heard was, "What you were telling us was true. Those guys sure can fight." They even wanted to go up to the Korean corps areas and do feature stories about individual Korean soldiers.

The only sad thing about it was that it took a major bloodletting like White Horse Mountain to make those people change their minds.

CHAPTER 30

On Her Majesty's Service

White Horse Mountain might have been strictly a South Korean-Chinese fight, but in all other respects it mirrored what the war in Korea had become by the end of 1952. The two opposing armies were now dug in for good, with both sides stabbing at each other in major or minor ways while awaiting the outcome of the truce negotiations in Panmunjom, which by now were well into their second year.

The major point of disagreement among the negotiators was still the prisoner-of-war issue, and until that issue was resolved the fighting would continue in the same old way: the Chinese constantly probing the UN line, looking for weakness, the UN formations bracing for the attacks, and occasionally hitting back with local counterattacks of their own, but never on the scale of the Chinese assaults. For by now large-scale attacks by UN forces were politically impossible.

As 1953 began, American commanders especially remained confident of their ability to smash through the Chinese lines and sweep the enemy from Korea with a major offensive, but this was not to be. The American public was tired of the war, and though it might put up with a sustained defensive effort until a truce agreement could be reached, any action that would generate thousands of casualties— as a major offensive certainly would—was simply out of the question. The order for such an attack would have to come from the White House,[1] and any U.S. president who approved it would be committing political suicide. A push to the Yalu would also mean risking an all-out war with China, and very possibly with the Soviet Union—a risk both President Truman and most of America's allies found totally unacceptable.

For the men on the battle line, then, there was nothing to do except dig in deeper and wait for the hoped-for truce. Meanwhile life on the line continued much as it had since the stalemate first set in: the troops living in a kind of tense boredom, watching for Chinese activity, trying to stay alert in the quiet sectors, sending out patrols, and occasionally engaging in firefights.

By now there was British, French, Australian, Canadian, Dutch, Philippine, Thai, Ethiopian, Colombian, Turkish and Greek infantry manning the MLR. There were Scandinavian, Indian and Italian medical units. There was a South African fighter squadron. There was a New Zealand artillery regiment. None of these countries sent anywhere near the number of troops the United States had sent, but the men they did send were usually the best a particular country had to offer.

The Commonwealth Division was especially well regarded. In the summer of 1951 all British, Australian, Canadian and New Zealand units then in Korea were combined into one division, which quickly built a reputation for professionalism and steadiness under fire.

Within the Division, the British had two infantry brigades, an armored regiment and supporting artillery and engineers. The armored regiment, as 1953 began, was the 1st Royal Tank Regiment, which had sailed for Korea several months before.

The regiment was in position along the MLR when a nineteen-year-old trooper, Victor Poole, arrived from England to join them.

---

[1]Because the United States was bearing the overwhelming burden of the war, in both manpower and money, Washington very early in the conflict insisted on direct military control, and got its way with its allies.

I arrived in Pusan just before Christmas of '52. I had no idea where I was going, in the sense that I didn't know where my regiment was posted, but I knew at least which regiment I was going to join. That was one of the biggest differences between the British and American armies in Korea. Most of the Yanks who went over there went over as individual replacements. They didn't know what unit they would be with until they got there. But in the British army, in most cases, a regular soldier is told which regiment he is going to when he enlists. And your regiment then becomes everything. Absolutely everything. Pride in the regiment is instilled in every British soldier almost from the first day of service. The traditions and history of the regiment become yours simply from the sustained indoctrination you get.

And in combat this could make a very great deal of difference, especially if things got a bit sticky. In Korea I got along very well with Americans, indeed I often went out of my way to meet them. But a lot of the Yanks I came into contact with over there seemed to have a very individualistic attitude. They were watching out for themselves, first of all. It struck me rather forcefully that they didn't seem to have much sense of unit pride, which can really be like a kind of glue that will hold a unit together when things get especially rough.

An exception to that, I would say, were the American marines. We had the marines on our left flank in Korea, and they were quite something. If you made the mistake of calling them soldiers, they'd let you know right away that they weren't soldiers, damn you, they were *marines*.

But I must say, if it hadn't been for the Americans we'd have damn well starved over there. Their food was far superior to ours. Our food was left over from the Second World War, and it hadn't been good then. Some of those cans and packages had been sitting in England for years before they sent them out to us.

We were also extremely low-paid compared to the Americans. They got I think ninety or a hundred dollars a month, counting their combat pay, and we were getting about a fourth of that. You might expect we'd be resentful, but we weren't, because the Yanks were always so generous.

Unlike the Americans, the British had wet canteens (servicemen's clubs where beer was served), but we never had money to pay for the bloody beer. So we'd always try to invite some Americans to one of our canteens, because they would always buy beer for everybody who happened to be in the place.

As I said, I'd landed in Pusan around Christmas of '52. This was after a thirty-one-day sea voyage from England through the Mediterranean and the Suez Canal to the Indian Ocean, to Singapore and Hong Kong and then up along the China coast to Korea. I was in a replacement draft with about twenty other men, and in Pusan we boarded a train and went north. We spent close to eighteen hours on this damn train. No heat. Nearly freezing to death. The damn thing seemed to stop every five minutes, and the fastest it went was about twenty miles an hour.

We were met at the railhead by some New Zealanders, transport people, and taken by truck up to where the 1st Royal Tank was on line. At that time the left flank of the Commonwealth Division was at The Hook,[2] and the right flank was over at a hill we called Gibraltar. There were three infantry brigades in the division: 25 Brigade, which was all Canadians; 28 Brigade, which had two British battalions and one battalion of Australians; and 29 Brigade, which was all British. The 1st Royal Tank Regiment supported only the two British brigades, since the Canadians had their own tanks.

I ended up in C Squadron. There were three fighting squadrons and a headquarters squadron in the regiment, with roughly sixteen to twenty tanks in a squadron. These were the new Centurions. A damn good tank. It was heavily armored, with a 19mm cannon on it.

But at the time I was in Korea all the tanks were dug in. We never fought tank to tank. In all the time I was there I never saw an enemy tank, except once, a destroyed one that was sitting all blown apart in the middle of a river. The British army used its tanks like artillery. We'd dug these big pits and put the tanks in them, and pack sandbags around the tanks, and they would sit there sometimes for months. The infantry would give us shoots, like they would artillery, and we would always be firing in support of the infantry.

_____

[2]A series of ridges near the western coast of Korea above Seoul.

Shortly after we moved up to the line I was out with some of the lads, just looking around, when all of a sudden it sounded like a couple of bloody express trains passed over our heads. An instant later, about a hundred yards to our left, we saw two enormous explosions. It was Mr. Chinaman, introducing himself.

Then just behind us, about a quarter of a mile, there was a great tremendous eruption: a battery of American 155s going off, replying to Mr. Chinaman.

That was my first whiff of the war, and it wasn't very pleasant. But we were soon to see a lot worse, when the Chinaman hit us at The Hook.

In the interval, though, it was nothing but sheer boredom, sitting on those forward positions, just watching and waiting. A good ninety-five percent of your time was like that, just sitting there, waiting. The other five percent was sheer terror. That was the five percent of the time when the enemy decided to test your sector.

When the Chinese hit us at The Hook in May of '53, I was in the transport troop of C Squadron, driving a resupply truck. The boredom on the line had been too much for me, so I'd volunteered to drive trucks. We took up all the ammunition to the men in the forward positions.

The battle started with artillery and mortar barrages, around the seventh or eighth of May. We didn't think anything of it at first, because you got that kind of stuff from time to time. But as the days passed the shellfire started to intensify. By about the middle of May it was coming in with hardly any letup. The men on the hill just had to hunker down and take it. Of course drivers like myself had to go up there every so often through the shot and shell to resupply them, and trucks were hit. Men were blown to bits. But I never got a scratch, and I saw then what a tremendous role luck plays in combat. Getting through combat has nothing to do with how strong a man is or how tough he is or even what kind of training he's had. If you're in a certain spot at the wrong time, you get killed.

I might drive down a road through shellfire and make it, and the next man might drive down the same road, doing everything I did, only two minutes later, and he gets it. Men would leave one bunker to go to what they thought was a safer one, and get killed. Another man might move and then watch the place he'd moved from get blown up a minute later. It's all luck.

The last battle of The Hook reached its climax on the night of the twenty-eighth of May. On that night all bloody hell broke loose. The Black Watch, a very famous British regiment that had already fought a terrific battle for The Hook back in November, was still there early in May, but sometime between the eighth of May and the twenty-eighth the Black Watch was relieved by the Duke of Wellingtons. And the Dukes ended up taking a horrible beating.

I'd just come back from a resupply run to The Hook when it started. Suddenly you heard this great bloody eruption of gunfire. Before, it had been all artillery and mortar bombs, but now there was this rising crescendo of small-arms fire that just got to be really terrible as the night went on. There was no letup. And of course the artillery and mortar fire was still coming in also. My regiment had two tanks up on The Hook proper, and three others on the saddles to either side. And every one of those five tanks had multiple hits. Some had their bins blown off the turret. Some had their treads and wheels blown off. All of them were scorched black from artillery and mortar bombs. None of the crews were killed, but they were all badly disoriented from the concussion.

Eventually the infantry positions on The Hook were overrun. I went up there the next morning, after the Chinese broke off their attack, and it was a horrible thing to see. The men in the forward positions had dug deep trenches and underground tunnels, and a lot of them had been buried in their positions by the tremendous volume of artillery. Our boys were still digging them out, many still alive, still holding tightly to their grenades and Bren guns, because all night long there had been vicious close-quarter fighting going on in those tunnels and trenches, even as the artillery and mortar bombs were crashing down.

As we were digging those men out, with their noses and mouths full of dirt, half suffocated, many of them wounded, Chinese bodies all around them, I remember thinking, How could men take what they took? To stay there in those holes and trenches all night long, getting shot at and getting buried alive, and still fighting back. You see, they weren't professional soldiers. A good percentage of those men in the Dukes, I'd say at least fifty percent, were draftees. But they were well led, with officers and NCOs who had tremendous regimental pride.

The Dukes were so badly mauled that they had to be pulled off the line and replaced by another British battalion, but they refused to give up the hill. I'm convinced they would have died to a man for that hill. And in the end, after the truce was signed, we had to give back the bloody thing anyway.

Chapter 31

Pork Chop Hill

The last few months of the war saw some of the fiercest fighting since the spring offensives of 1951. As the negotiations at Panmunjom reached a critical stage the Chinese launched a series of attacks designed to test the UN's will to fight and to gain as much additional territory as possible before the truce was signed. Most of the attacks came against outposted hills like Old Baldy, The Hook, Carson, Vegas, and Reno—all were fiercely contested, and some were lost.

And then there was Pork Chop.

Officially, on the military maps, it was Hill 255. That was its elevation in yards. Seven hundred sixty-five feet, which is not much hill to look at. But for some reason the Chinese couldn't stay away from it. In March of 1953, and again in April, and once again in July, they tried to make Pork Chop Hill their own. Charles Brooks was there in April and in July, especially in July, when the fighting went on for four straight days.

I was trapped in a bunker. The Chinese were great infiltrators, and what they had done was dig themselves right to the base of the

213

hill, and when the attack came they were on us before we could do anything about it.

We were hit with an artillery barrage first, but that's not the kind of warning that it might seem to be. We'd often get artillery fire and nothing would come of it. Sometimes it would last up to half an hour, and then it would just stop.

But this time, when the barrage lifted, they were already there, on top of everybody. We knew they were down at the bottom of the hill, because every night we could hear them digging, and every night the digging got closer. We called air strikes in on them repeatedly, navy Corsairs would come in and drop napalm and five-hundred-pound bombs so close we'd have to stay in our bunkers until the strike was over, but it didn't seem to have any effect on the Chinese. They were like moles. They dug caves into the sides of their trenches and you couldn't blow them out and you couldn't burn them out.

My company happened to be on Pork Chop that night only by dumb luck. Pork Chop was one of a group of hills on what they called the outpost line. There was Pork Chop, Erie, Arsenal, Old Baldy, one they called Alligator Jaws, and Snook. They were all out there in no man's land, about half a mile in front of our main line, and the companies would take turns going out. We'd go out to Arsenal for a few weeks, come back to the MLR for a while, then go out to maybe Erie for another week or two, then back to the MLR again. The outpost duty was rotated because nobody liked going out there. Those hills could easily be cut off and overrun, and they were always coming under artillery and mortar fire.

I was a squad leader, and that night there were six or seven of us in my bunker waiting out the barrage. When it finally lifted one of the guys poked his head out the door and said, "Christ, they're in the trenches!"

We looked out and saw Chinese all over the hill. It was eleven o'clock at night but everything was all lit up. They were dropping parachute flares from airplanes and shooting them up with artillery and mortars, and there were even searchlights mounted on tanks that were parked along the MLR half a mile behind us. It was as bright out there as a football stadium at night.

We couldn't get out of the bunker. Every time somebody stuck a leg or an arm out we drew fire. So we knew they'd overrun at least our part of the hill. Since I was a squad leader my bunker had the sound power in it, and I could talk to the commander. But all he could tell us was that we'd have to hold on until they could counterattack.

The bunkers were very solidly built. They were made out of sandbags and heavy timbers and rocks and they were known to survive direct hits from artillery and mortars, so we felt pretty secure in there. They had apertures in them where we could fire our weapons, and all we could do was fire everything we had and try to keep the Chinese away. It was like a movie where you see the soldiers popping away at the Indians from inside a fort, except that you're only too aware that it isn't a movie. But not scared. Strangely enough you're too busy to be scared. Your adrenaline's going like mad, and as long as you can move around and fire back at the enemy you're generally all right. It's when you have to lie in a hole under an artillery or mortar barrage, helpless, that's when you're really scared.

We held out all that night without losing anybody. We could see the Chinese outside, kind of just wandering around the hill, so they had definitely captured at least part of it. Every so often a few of them would come poking around, probably looking for survivors, and we'd have ourselves another little fight. What we tried to do was keep them away from the apertures so they couldn't throw grenades in on us, but they got a few in, and one guy had his feet blown off. He sat on an old ammo box and didn't make a sound all night. Just kept staring at his feet. They were still there, but they were barely connected to his legs. I think if he'd of moved his legs the feet would've fallen off. He must've been in shock but there really wasn't anything we could do for him.

Just after daylight they threw a satchel charge on top of the bunker, which gave us a jolt. That's about twenty or twenty-five pounds of TNT. But it didn't do anything to the bunker. It was pretty solidly built. If you can't dig a hole next to one of those bunkers and set the charge in it, you're not going to do much damage, because the explosion isn't going to blow down.

215

I kept reporting in with the sound power, so our commander knew we were there, and he knew we were holding our own. He told us the Chinese had part of the hill, and that they were calling for reinforcements, and as soon as they got there and everybody regrouped they would counterattack and try and get our part of the hill back.

I couldn't help thinking, That's exactly what had happened in April. Only then I wasn't on the hill, I was part of the counterattack.

I don't know which was worse. When we counterattacked in April it was one o'clock, two o'clock in the morning. Snow was on the ground, and as we moved out of our blocking positions to the assault positions we could see the Chinese in the light from the flares, running all over the sides of the hill like a bunch of piss ants. Then the sarge yells, "All right, let's go!" And everybody's moving, kind of half running and yelling and screaming and shooting at everything that moves. We ran straight into the Chinese, shooting and yelling until they just weren't there anymore. It's just a tremendous mass of confusion. And it really doesn't sink in, what you're doing, until it's all over, hours later after you get pulled off the hill to regroup. That's when everybody sits around talking to each other about it, about how lucky you are to get through it without getting shot.

But now I was on the other end. I was the guy on the hill who got overrun, and somebody else was going to make the counterattack. We knew it probably wouldn't come that first night, but it didn't come all the next day either.

We could see the Chinese through the apertures. They were all over the hill. After they threw that satchel charge on the roof I thought they might make a real effort to rush us, but nothing happened. Our own artillery was coming in by now, and maybe that was keeping them busy.

But there was always somebody out there, and there was always somebody coming around, looking into the apertures, trying to see who was in there. And every time somebody came around, they'd toss a grenade in. We'd kick them into a corner behind an ammunition box and just turn our backs, because that was all we could do. They sounded like giant firecrackers going off. If we got them behind one

216

of the metal boxes most of the shrapnel would blow straight up, but they didn't always go exactly where we kicked them, and by the end of the day all of us had been hit.

I turned away from one grenade and it blew a load of shrapnel into my back. It felt like a spray of hot embers hitting me.

Actually we were lucky. They were using these small fragmentation grenades. They looked like a small can on top of a wooden handle. If they'd tossed a concussion grenade in there, what we called a watermelon, it would have taken us all out.

So by the second night we were all wounded. We were out of ammunition and grenades. We were low on water. And we'd lost contact with our CP. The wires must've been cut. We didn't have any information, and we didn't know what was going on, so we decided we'd try and get off the hill on our own.

We told the guy who'd had his feet blown off what we were going to do, and he agreed with it.

I said, "When we get to the bottom of the hill I'm going to tell whoever's in charge that you're still up here, and to make a sweep up here and get you out."

He didn't say anything, but I think he knew he was a goner.

We couldn't take him with us, and he knew it. We didn't have a stretcher, and even if we did, we couldn't carry a man out that bunker and down the hill on a stretcher without making a target out of him. All we could do was give him a rifle and all the ammunition we could spare, and wish him luck.

We waited for daybreak, and then we worked our way out of the bunker and through the trenches toward the reverse slope. We moved in single file, and every time we went around a bend in one of the trenches I expected to come face to face with Chinese. There were dead bodies all along the way, both ours and theirs, and we could hear firing going on over on some other part of the hill, but we were moving away from it, and we got all the way down the reverse slope without seeing a single Chinese.

We came off the hill and crossed the stretch of no man's land into our own lines. That's why we waited for daylight, so we wouldn't get shot by our own people as we came into the lines. They had an emergency aid station set up right there on the MLR, and I got some treatment for my back. They tried to take out as much of the shrapnel as they could. Then they put me in an armored personnel carrier that took me to the battalion aid station. I was operated on again, just lying on my stomach on a table while they tried to take out the shrapnel they could see. Then I was put on a truck and sent farther back to a MASH. The surgeons worked on me there, and then I was evacuated to a hospital in Japan. That's basically where I recuperated, but they flat out said that they'd never get all the metal out.

Back at Pork Chop they eventually did counterattack, but they never got that hill back. After three or four days the attacks were called off because the casualties were getting too high and somebody finally decided the hill wasn't worth the effort. I never did find out what happened to the guy we left behind in the bunker. I like to think he made it out, but I kind of suspect he didn't.

CHAPTER 32

Living with the Enemy

In Korea one of the worst fears of the combat soldier was being taken prisoner. The North Koreans gave notice almost from the first day of the war that captured Americans would not be treated as human beings, much less as prisoners of war. They gave such notice not through any formal announcement, but simply by their actions. Whenever territory that had been overrun was recaptured from them the bodies would be there, sometimes in shallow graves, many times simply lying about on the ground, almost always with the hands tied behind the back. The Chinese were less inclined to kill their prisoners, but judging from what was done to them later, that was only because the Chinese authorities thought they might be able to use the soldiers they captured to embarrass the Western capitalist warmongers.

Being a prisoner of war in Korea was a relative matter. Some men were prisoners literally for only a few minutes before being released unharmed and sent on their way. Others escaped after days or weeks in captivity. Most spent months in various prison camps.

For Nick Tosques the ordeal lasted two and a half years. And during that entire time Tosques could have brooded, if he had been so inclined, about whether he even belonged in Korea, for he had been drafted into the service not once, like most men, but twice.

I was drafted the first time in 1946. In 1947, after I'd put in about thirteen months, the army had a reduction in force and I was let go. Then, in July 1950, shortly after the Korean War broke out, a notice appeared in the newspapers saying that anybody drafted between 1945 and 1950 who had served less than thirteen months was subject to be redrafted. I had put in just under thirteen months, and sure enough, toward the end of July I was called back in again.

I was sent straight over to Korea. When I got my draft notice and reported to Fort Dix in New Jersey, they told me I'd already had basic training. Things weren't going so well in Korea, and they needed replacements fast. So anybody who had already been in the service was sent over on a plane, without any kind of training.

At Fort Dix they told me I was going to be assigned to an ordnance outfit, but when I got to the replacement center at Camp Drake in Japan they lined us up and it was "You, you, you, and you . . . are going to the 555th Field Artillery Battalion."

I said to the captain, "I never had any training in artillery."

He said, "You'll learn."

The 555th, they called it the Triple Nickles, had just been hit hard. They'd been overrun and lost a lot of men and a lot of their guns.

That very night they put the four of us on a train. We went to Sasebo, over on the west coast of Japan, and then we took a boat to Korea.

At that time, early September of 1950, they were still fighting in the Pusan perimeter. There were fire missions every day, and I had to learn real fast.

The first thing I had to learn was how to put the shells together. They came in two sections. You had the shell, and then you had the shell casing. Inside each casing there were nine powder bags. The range of a 105mm howitzer was seven and a half miles, and if all nine bags were in there the shell went seven and a half miles. If the forward observer called for a shorter range, you'd put in fewer bags.

Charge six, six bags. Charge four, four bags. Charge three, three bags. If it got down to two, which it did just before I was captured, you knew they were mighty damn close.

I learned how to load the gun, I learned how to fire it, and I learned everything fast, because if you didn't, you didn't survive. The North Koreans kept punching holes in our line, and many times we'd have to fire at point-blank range.

We were supporting the 5th Regimental Combat Team, and after the breakout from the Pusan perimeter we went up with them almost to the Yalu River.

Up at the Yalu the word was, "You'll be having your Christmas dinner in Japan, and then it's back home to the States."

Next thing we knew, we were back below the 38th parallel. And the only people going home were the guys with serious wounds. The Chinese had come into the war, and Christ did we take a beating. I never saw so much stuff go up in smoke during that retreat. Tons and tons of C rations, ammunition, equipment, gasoline. Anything we couldn't carry back with us we burned.

After a couple of months we were back on the offensive. In April of 1951 I got picked to go on ten days R and R [Rest and Recuperation] in Tokyo. When I came back from that, I was told that my name was on the list for rotation.

I thought, Boy, isn't that something. I go away, I come back, and I get another piece of good news.

I'm supposed to go home in two weeks. A couple days later the Chinese started their spring offensive. They decided they were going to push us back below the 38th parallel again.

I was still thinking, Well, I'm going home.

All we were doing now was firing and firing and firing. Day and night. In shifts. But we couldn't stop them.

On the afternoon of the twenty-fifth of April our CO came out to the gun positions and said, "Pack up and leave. We're getting the hell out of here."

Up ahead we could see the guys in the 5th RCT leaving their positions. They were jumping on trucks and heading back toward us. We hitched up our guns and jumped on our own trucks and joined them on the road, but I don't think we went more than a mile when we ran into a roadblock. The Chinese had gotten in behind us and knocked out an American tank and put it across the road. Both sides of the road dropped off into rice paddies, so when we came to the roadblock we had to stop. And as soon as we stopped the Chinese opened up from the hills all around us.

Machine-gun fire. Mortar fire. Rifle fire. It poured in on us like rain. We unhooked our guns, swung them around, and fired point-blank—open the breech block, aim down the barrel, ram the shell in, and fire. And hope you hit something.

Some of the Chinese moved in close enough to throw hand grenades. There were explosions going off all around my gun. Somebody yelled, "Nick, look up!" I looked up and I saw the grenade coming, and the last thing I remember is taking a flying leap.

Next thing I knew, it was night. I don't know how long I was out, but it had been daytime when I jumped away from that grenade. I remember pinching myself. I thought I might be dreaming. All around me are dead and wounded men. The trucks are on fire. I didn't know which way to go, so finally I got up and went over to a guy who was moaning.

He'd been hit in the gut. He was in a half-sitting position, trying to hold his intestines in with his hands. I took a fatigue jacket off a dead body and tied it around the guy so it would cover the hole in his gut.

"Pal," I said, "I can't pick you up. Not like that."

He wanted a drink of water. I knew you weren't supposed to give water to somebody with an abdominal wound, but this guy wasn't going to make it anyway, so I found a full canteen and gave it to him.

I said, "I'm going to try and get help."

Up the road a little ways I ran into three or four guys from the 5th RCT. They were huddled together along the road. One guy was wounded in the arm, and he was crying.

I said, "Look, we have to get the hell out of here."

They looked at me, and one of them said, "What outfit are you from?"

I said, "The Triple Nickles."

They kept looking at me, and another one said, "All right, where do we go and how do we get out of here?"

I didn't have any more idea than they did how to get out of there. All I could think of was to go south, the direction we'd been going when we were hit. But no matter which way we tried to go, we would hear Chinese talking. Out in the dark ahead of us and all around us.

So finally I said, "Look, get rid of your rifles, lie down, and play dead."

But what the Chinese did was go around and stick all the bodies with bayonets. Not to kill the wounded, but to see if anybody was still alive. They knew that someday there was going to be peace talks, and they wanted as many prisoners as they could get.

I got jabbed in the butt, very lightly, but enough to make me flinch. Then I heard, "Getuppu! Getuppu!"

No use pretending now, so I got up. And I was amazed. I'm only five foot eight, but I was looking down on this Chinaman. At that moment I wasn't really afraid. I looked down at him, and I remember I kept saying to myself, "Damn, he's only a kid."

He looked like a very young teenager. Fourteen, fifteen years old. It was a moonlit night, and he spotted the watch I had on. That came off. I had a ring, and he wanted that too. But I couldn't get it off because my finger was swollen.

The guy behind me whispered, "Nick, you'd better get it off, because if you don't, he's going to chop your finger off."

He wanted that ring. He stood right there as I was fooling around with it, trying to get it off. Finally he raised his rifle. I started spitting on my finger, trying to work it off. I did an awful lot of spitting before it finally worked free.

He was just like a kid with a new toy. The watch and the ring. He went around smiling at everybody.

It wasn't until daybreak that I realized the fix I was in. It didn't sink in right away that I was a prisoner. I thought maybe, just maybe, they'd take our stuff and then walk off and leave us, and then we could keep moving south. But by daybreak I saw it wasn't going to happen that way.

They kept us right there for a day or two. We slept on the ground, but of course there wasn't much sleeping. We could hear gunfire off to the south, and every once in a while we'd have to get up and run like hell to avoid being hit by our own artillery, which was still throwing shells back at the Chinese.

On the first day they brought in an officer who spoke English, and the interrogations started. During basic training every soldier is told: If you're captured, you give only your name, rank, and serial number. But you can say that for only so long. You see some of the other guys getting hit in the back or the kidneys with a rifle butt, and hit hard, and you start thinking about what else you can say without really telling them anything.

This Chinese officer asked me, "What outfit?" I didn't tell him. But when he said, "Those trucks, and those big guns, were you with them?" I said, "Yeah."

Only that. "Yeah."

Then he asked me where I was from. I said Washington. I didn't say Washington D.C., or Washington State. Just Washington.

He didn't press me. I saw that if I just gave him an answer, he'd move on. It didn't have to be an exact answer, just so it looked like I was cooperating. There were a lot of interrogation sessions, but I don't think anybody actually told them very much.

Over the next couple of days other prisoners were brought in, and when we got to be a fairly large group they told us we were going north to a POW camp.

We walked single file along the roads, and it got to the point where if you had to go to the bathroom you did it right in your pants, because there was no stopping unless they wanted to stop themselves. I can remember some of the men saying, "I've got to go," and stopping to drop their pants, and suddenly you'd hear a shot, and you wouldn't see that guy anymore.

We moved mostly at night, because during the day we were constantly under attack by our own planes. There wasn't much food. They gave us a kind of dry powder. You held it in one hand and sprinkled a little water on it until it turned to mush, and then you ate the mush out of your hand. Sometimes we got raw sorghum, and once in a while a piece of seaweed.

The march north lasted around sixty days. I was captured on the twenty-fifth of April and it was toward the end of June when we got to Camp Number One, at Changsong, North Korea. But nobody knows for certain. We lost track of the days. That's my best guess, the end of June.

We had no news during the march. For all we knew the Chinese had captured all of South Korea. And we had no idea where we were going, except that it was a POW camp. Some guys thought they were taking us to China. I was thinking maybe Manchuria.

Camp One turned out to be just a collection of old Korean mud huts and a few wooden buildings. There was no fence. After we were there a few days, during one of the lecture sessions when they would ask if there were any questions, somebody asked about that.

"Why isn't there a fence? Where's the barbed wire?" And the interpreter said, "We don't need barbed wire. Your faces are the barbed wire."

The first thing they did was break us up into small groups. Ten men were put into each little room. Not in each hut, but in each room. The rooms were about the size of a large closet. You couldn't move without touching somebody.

They took our clothes and gave us thin blue uniforms. We were all filthy, nobody had had a bath for two months, but we were not allowed to bathe. Everybody had body lice. They were in your hair, in your clothes, all over your body, and there was only one way to kill them: one at a time, between your thumbnails.

Right away the interrogations started. They interrogated us every day, and also at night. They'd take us out in groups, sometimes at two or three in the morning. You never knew when they were coming for you.

They found out, though not from me, that I was from Washington D.C., and then I was interrogated something awful. Hour after hour. What street is the White House on? Where is this building located? Where is that building located? Like it was a big military secret. You could get it from a guidebook, what they were asking. But I couldn't remember where everything was. I'd never paid that much attention to the streets these buildings were on. And when I couldn't answer, *whap*, I'd get hit with a rubber hose on the back of the neck.

Pretty soon I was telling them anything, just to keep from getting hit. That building's here, that other building's there. What the hell, how are they going to know? Well, somehow they found out I was making the stuff up. *Whap.* The rubber hose again. I guess it never occurred to them that I was telling the truth when I said I couldn't remember. I was from Washington D.C., and in their minds everybody from Washington was supposed to know where all the government buildings were. And also what the government was doing.

Then there were the lectures. We were given lectures every day. "You're capitalists. Your government lies to you. The rich people don't care about you, that's why they sent you over here to die. Your government makes war to oppress the Korean people." That kind of baloney.

We had to learn about communism. The only way to live. The only way to go. How under communism everyone is equal. We had to listen to that stuff every single day.

We'd get up early every morning for roll call. After the head count we'd get our bean juice. It looked like milk but it was actually water that they'd boiled soybeans in. Some guys drank it and some guys didn't. In the evening they would give us a cup of gluey rice. It tasted like laundry starch. Everything they gave me, I tried to get down. Sometimes it came up and sometimes it didn't, but I tried to eat everything. Other guys kept pushing their food away, and they lost weight and got sick and died of disease or malnutrition.

They had a makeshift hospital. If you got sick they threw you in there, put your food in there, and if you ate it you ate it and if you didn't you didn't. There was never any medicine. I don't think they had enough for their own people.

The mornings were for hard labor. We'd be marched up into the hills to chop wood for them. All the huts were heated with firewood. We had to cut down the wood, chop it into sticks, and carry these big bundles of sticks down to the camp.

The afternoon was study time. We'd study about how Mao Tsetung and his bunch got rid of Chiang Kai-shek and all the capitalists in China. How capitalism was no good. How the working man was exploited. How communism was the only way to go. And we had guys who turned. Who fell for that baloney. Not right away. But it was pounded and pounded and pounded into us. Every day. Every day. Capitalism no, communism yes.

Like most of the others, I went along with it. Yeah, yeah, yeah. You're right. You're right. But in the back of our minds all we're thinking about is home. About getting back, going to work, and buying what the hell we wanted.

After each study session we'd be sent back to our huts to discuss communism, but what we'd do, we'd put one guy on watch and then we'd talk about anything *but* communism. What kind of work did you do at home? What kind of car did you drive? Did you have any girlfriends?

But you couldn't completely ignore the lessons, because in the mass study sessions they would ask what you learned. What are you studying? Do you know how your government lies to you? That your Harry Truman lies. That he will never get you home.

There were times when I did lose hope of ever getting back. After a few months in the camp they told us that peace talks were starting. But nothing happened. They would get us in formation on the parade field and tell us the talks were going well, and we'd think, Great, another month and we're out of here. Then they would get us out there a month or two later and tell us that the talks had broken down, that the Americans didn't want peace and that we were never going home.

After that happens three or four times, what are you going to believe? Months go by, a year, two years, and we're still there. Some guys didn't even believe there were any talks, that the Chinese were just playing with our minds.

A lot of guys got very depressed. A few even committed suicide. It got to be too much for them. They finally lost hope permanently, and when that happened you were a goner.

One thing that cheered us up was the dogfights. Our camp was only a few miles from the Yalu River, right under MiG Alley, and we could see the MiGs and our jets dogfighting almost every day. They were too high for us to see which planes were which, but one day they brought in a captured pilot, and he told us to listen to the rate of fire. The MiGs had a slower rate of fire than our jets, and you could hear the difference even on the ground. After that we'd cheer like hell every time a MiG got shot down. Then the guards would come running up, waving their rifles and yelling at us not to cheer, or they'd shoot us.

We took them seriously. They had already executed a guy who had been giving them trouble, and we had to witness the execution. We were going about our business when suddenly they called us out and put us in formation. Then they brought the guy out and put him up against a wall. The firing squad was already out there waiting. I remember praying to myself, that he'd die right away and not suffer. I saw movies before I went to Korea, about the Germans and Japanese putting prisoners in front of a firing squad and shooting them, but to actually see it happen was a terrible shock. No movie can possibly prepare you for it.

The guy wasn't blindfolded. He might've refused to be blindfolded, because we'd heard about executions taking place in other camps, and the word was they gave you a blindfold. He had his hands tied behind his back, and he just stood there looking at them until they shot him.

I think it was late in 1952 that we started getting mail. It wasn't everything that was being sent to us, but every so often they would pass out some letters. I got one from my mother that started off: "Dear Nick, Elizabeth died. Ha. Ha. Ha."

The Chinese opened all our mail first, and when they saw that they called me to headquarters and wanted to know why my mother was laughing about somebody's death. What kind of person would laugh at another person's death? They kept me there for hours, and I just couldn't get it across to them that Elizabeth was a car. My father had a 1936 Ford that he'd kept all those years, and my mother always called it Tin Lizzy. But no matter how I tried to explain it, they couldn't understand.

I remember the first time they told us the war was over. We didn't believe it. They had to keep repeating it, because by this time we didn't trust anything they said. Then they took all the sick and wounded out of the camp and told us they were going to be exchanged. We still didn't believe it. We thought: Are they really going south, or is this some trick? Maybe they're just sending those guys to another camp.

They passed out new uniforms and new blankets, but they'd done that before, every time they announced a "breakthrough" in the peace talks. When the talks would break down again they'd take the blankets and the uniforms back.

Finally they divided the camp into two sections. One section left first. Then my section left a couple of weeks later. We still didn't think we were going home. The trucks took us north to the railroad station. They put us into boxcars, and then the train started moving south.

Now we're thinking, Hey, maybe this is it.

Maybe.

We rode south for a few hours. Then they took us off the train and put us on trucks again, because the rails had been knocked out.

But we were still heading south.

The Chinese kept us in a holding camp on their side of the line for two days. They gave us the usual rice, but added a few little things. A little can of pork, which nobody ate. We figured we could survive a couple more days on rice, and they could stick their pork up you know where.

After two days we got into the trucks again and headed south. All along the way we were passed by other trucks headed north, filled with Chinese and North Korean soldiers who were being exchanged.

When we got to the truce area I jumped off the truck and caught my trousers on a handle. Tore them right down the seam. As I crossed the line I had to hold my pants up with both hands. There were all kinds of officers waiting on our side of the line, but I couldn't salute because I had to hold up my pants. A colonel said, "Don't worry about that, son. Just get across that line."

Some of the guys, when they crossed, they fell on their knees and kissed the ground. One guy turned around and gave the Chinese the old thumb bit with the nose. Me, I was busy holding up my pants.

We were given haircuts and showers, and then they had a meal for us. All the officers waited on us. They were the cooks. They dished out the food. Anything we wanted, and as much as we wanted. Big steaks, cooked right there in front of us. How do you want them?

I got a tray and piled it with food. I sat down, I took one or two bites, and that was it. I couldn't eat any more. My stomach had been empty for two and a half years, and it would be another year before I could eat a normal-sized meal again.

But otherwise I didn't have a lot of trouble adjusting. I thought, I'm here, I'm back, I'm walking, I'm alive. I saw a lot of hell, a lot of suffering, a lot of dying, but I made it back, and in my book that's enough to be grateful for.

CHAPTER 33

The Last Patrol

On June 25, 1950, Paul Leyva was at a picnic in the country, a cool green spot a few miles outside Chicago. It was just the guys on his block getting together on a hot summer Sunday, to eat and drink and flirt with the girls, and even after he heard the news of the invasion on the radio Leyva continued to enjoy himself. Exactly one month earlier, on May 25, he had turned eighteen, and he had dutifully reported himself to his local draft board. "But it was peacetime, and I wasn't worried. Even after I heard the news about Korea I thought, Well, this thing will be over before they ever get around to calling me. I just went on with my life. Baseball, picnics, going to dances, just like any other eighteen-year-old kid.

"But the war didn't end. It kept dragging on and on. Around the neighborhood guys only a year older than me started getting drafted, and I knew my turn would come.

"It came on December 5, 1952. And even though I was expecting it to happen, I couldn't believe it was happening."

I was inducted out of Fort Sheridan. They put us in companies of 150 men each, and they took 149 out of my company and sent them to Indiantown Gap, Pennsylvania, to be in the infantry. I was sent to Fort Knox, Kentucky, to be in tanks.

I couldn't believe it. I'd been drafted with five or six other guys from my neighborhood, guys I'd known since grammar school, and I thought, Hey, this is neat. Then all of a sudden they go one way and I go another. All of a sudden I'm alone.

But I didn't mind being in a tank battalion. At least I wouldn't have to walk. At Fort Knox we trained in phases. A certain number of weeks on the cannon, a certain number of weeks on the driving, a certain number of weeks on the maintenance. We trained on an M-4, an old World War II tank. It was a good little tank, but it was old-fashioned. They told us that when we got to Korea we'd have newer ones to fight with.

But when I got over to Japan they gave me an M-1 rifle. I thought, Jesus, I'm going to be back in the infantry. I'd never fired an M-1 rifle. On the ship going over to Korea the guys taught me how to break it down and put it back together again, but I didn't get any training with it. They spent all that time training us to drive tanks, and now I'm going into the infantry.

We landed at Inchon, where the replacement depot was, and I just couldn't believe this was happening to me. I couldn't believe I was in Korea. I thought, Hey, I should be back on the corner with the guys.

There was about three thousand of us came in on the ship. They put us on trains, and when we got to the replacement depot, not too far from Inchon, we were put into these big squad tents for the night. Next day they called us out and lined us up. I still had my rifle, but this guy from Alabama, a big country boy, came up to a bunch of us and said we're going to a tank battalion.

So I was back in tanks.

Nine of us rode in a truck up to Kumhwa, in the Iron Triangle area, and joined the 64th Tank Battalion. When I got to my company they took my rifle back and gave me a .45, which all tankers carried.

And then they assigned me to a tank.

They assigned me as a loader. There were always five guys to a tank: the gunner, the loader, the driver, the assistant driver, and the tank commander, who was always a sergeant and who sat up in the turret. But we could change jobs if we had to. All of us were trained to drive the tank and all of us were trained on the gun.

By now we're in May of '53. The war's got only three months to go, but we didn't know that at the time. The truce talks had been going on for what . . . almost two years? We didn't really expect anything to happen. There had been too many false alarms already. So we really didn't pay any attention. To us it was all propaganda. As far as we were concerned, the war could go on for two or three more years.

My company was a bastard outfit. Artillery on wheels. We supported the South Koreans. We supported the Greeks. We supported the Turks. They moved us up and down the line, wherever they needed some cannon fire. And there would always be the reconnaissance patrols, where we would have to go out and just keep going until we got hit.

My first combat came on a recon patrol. This is late May, early June. Both sides were dug in, and every so often the Chinese would try to take a hill or an outpost on our side of the line, or just try and push our lines back, testing us to see how much ground we'd give up.

They'd just made one of these attacks, and headquarters didn't know exactly how far they had penetrated our lines. So we were ordered to go out and find them.

But they found us first. We were behind a little hill, camouflaging our tank with branches, when they opened fire on us with machine guns. So we jumped in and buttoned up and got the hell out of there before they could zero in on us with their mortars.

A week or so after that I had my tank blown out from under me. We were moving up to the MLR in single file with three platoons. Fifteen tanks. In the summer you had to stay on the roads or you'd bog down in the rice paddies. And the roads were too narrow to drive on except in single file. So we always had to move in a line, one tank behind another.

233

We were laying fire on a hill that had already been scorched and burned and blown apart by napalm and artillery. But the Chinese were still up there. They started firing mortars at us, and pretty soon, *blang*, my tank gets hit. Nothing happened to the tank, but the concussion loosened the oil lines and the engine caught fire.

The platoon leader called over the radio, "Get out of there." So we scrambled out of the tank and jumped on a couple of other tanks as they were turning around.

We left the burning tank there. By now the Chinese were walking the mortar rounds up and down the line of tanks. The Chinese were very good with mortars. Mortars are usually not an accurate weapon, because what you're doing is lobbing the shells high up in the air and letting them fall on something. It's like throwing a baseball over a high fence and trying to hit something you can't see. But the Chinese were very good. They would use their mortars against relatively small targets, like a tank, and more often than not they'd hit it.

So we pulled back out of range. One of the tanks was covered with blood, and I went over to see what had happened. They pulled a guy out of it, the tank commander, and he was split in two. Half his body had fallen on the driver, and his legs had stayed in the turret, where he was standing. Before he could button up a mortar round landed right on the tank and the concussion had blown him in half.

I watched as they put him on a stretcher. His eyes were open, and he was twitching, and I thought, Jesus, he's still alive. But of course he couldn't be, because that's all there was of him, from his waist up.

Then the lieutenant comes up to me and says, "Paul, you have to go back and get your tank."

I thought, *Shit.*

"You and Dawkins," he says.

Me and Dawkins were the new guys, see. And I'm Mexican and he's black. So they gave us asbestos gloves and we jumped on a tank retriever, which is like a combination tank and tow truck, and went back up the road about half a mile to where our tank was still burning. We hooked up a tow line and brought the tank back in, all without getting shot at, which I thought was a miracle. I thought the war was going to end for me and Dawkins right there.

They gave us a new tank the next day. We went out on more patrols. They shifted us around constantly. We'd spend a day, maybe two days in one position, and then we'd be moved somewhere else. When we weren't up on the line or moving to another position or going out on a patrol, we did maintenance on the tanks. We pulled maintenance constantly. Everything had to be ready to go at any time. A certain number of gas trucks were assigned to each company, and every time we got back from a mission we had to refuel. An M-46 tank could carry three hundred gallons of gas, but we were lucky if we got three miles to the gallon.

On the thirteenth of July the Chinese tried another big push, and we were moved up from a reserve position to the MLR again. That's when we lost another tank. It happened on the same road where we lost the first one. We were moving up in single file, and just as the lead tank went out of sight around a bend they hit us. We could hear the guys in the tank calling over the radio, "We're hit! They're all around us! Get them off us! Get them off us!"

We immediately got orders to pull back. Once we got back out of range we sent out a patrol with a retriever to get the tank back. Only one guy got out, the Korean loader. Every tank crew had to have one Korean in it. This guy's name was Park, and he came running down the road, bleeding from the head and waving his shirt and yelling, "It's Park! Don't shoot! Don't shoot! It's Park!"

We got to the tank and it was all burned out. The Chinese must have used a flamethrower on it. We never found the other four guys. No bodies, nothing. They just disappeared.

About a week after that we were shifted over to Sniper Ridge. They were expecting another big push, and we just sat there waiting for it. I remember how the Chinese would play music every night over loudspeakers. The one song that still sticks in my mind is "China Nights." They'd play music, and blow their signal bugles, trying to mess around with your mind. And it worked. Nobody got any sleep.

All kinds of rumors were flying around that an armistice was going to be signed, but we didn't believe any of that. We'd heard all that before. We stayed alert, but the Chinese didn't come, and after we'd been there a few days two tanks from my platoon were ordered to go up along the outpost line and see if they could draw fire. My tank was one of the two. I thought, Shit, here we go again. I'd already had a tank shot out from under me, and I didn't have much confidence that I'd survive another hit. A guy only has so much luck.

As we moved up we passed some marine positions. They were dug in alongside the road, and we could see their big recoilless rifles mounted on jeeps. We kept going until we were out in front of everybody. When we didn't draw any fire they ordered us to stay in place facing this hill where there was a fork in the road. They told us that's where the Chinese would be coming.

We stayed up there all night, the longest night of my life. From behind us they were sending up flares, one after another, and they told us that when the Chinese came we were to keep firing until ordered to pull back.

There was no infantry in front of us. There was nobody on our flanks. We were out there all alone, and I thought, Paul, this is goodbye. This is the last patrol you'll ever go out on, because you're never going to get back from this one.

But nothing happened, although in fact that did turn out to be my last patrol. In the morning we pulled back and were moved to another position, just across the road from an artillery battalion. All day and all evening they'd been firing. *Boom. Boom. Boom. Boom.* Then, at exactly ten o'clock that night, everything stopped.

We were told the armistice had been signed, but nobody believed it until about an hour later when a trailer truck showed up filled with hundreds of cases of beer. The beer was warm, but what the hell, who's going to complain at a time like that?

Epilogue

The armistice agreement ending the Korean War was signed at Panmunjom on July 27, 1953, at ten o'clock in the morning. Exactly twelve hours later, as stipulated in the agreement, the cease-fire went into effect.

The guns fell silent, the fighting was over—two years and seventeen days after the truce talks began, a little over three years after the conflict started with the North's invasion of the South.

Within a month of the signing of the truce agreement most of the prisoners of war were exchanged. Many of the soldiers on the battle lines were sent home, where the majority found that their experiences in Korea were of no interest whatsoever to the general public. In the United States especially, the public had long since put the war out of its mind.

People were able to do that rather easily in the early fifties, largely, one suspects, because there was no television then to bring the war into their living rooms. They were not subjected each evening to the sight of American boys fighting and dying in a faraway

Asian land, or to antiwar protesters in the streets at home, had there been any. In fact, no one had actively protested the war in Korea. It was simply ignored until it went away.

It has been largely ignored ever since. World War II and Vietnam have each generated an avalanche of novels, memoirs, histories, documentaries, and movies, while the brutal three-year infantry war that was fought more than forty years ago on the Korean peninsula seems destined for popular oblivion, its proud but aging veterans struggling to the end of their days simply to get a national memorial raised to commemorate their service.

The Korean War was a long time ago now, in a place that was once far away, but is far away no longer. Many of the men whose accounts are contained in this book have since revisited Korea, these days not much more than twelve hours away on a jetliner, and each who did remarked on the same two things—the enormous changes that have taken place since they fought there, and the long memories of the Korean people. One man in particular, who had fought long and hard with the 2nd Infantry Division, and who was revisiting Korea with a group of fellow veterans, was not ashamed to admit that tears flowed from his eyes as he was repeatedly stopped and thanked on the streets of the towns and cities by ordinary Koreans of all ages, even schoolchildren too young to have personally experienced the war.

We remember what you did for us, they would say to him. And we are grateful.

Biographies

ANDREW BARR was born in Arlington, Virginia, and enlisted in the army in 1946. He served in Korea until October 1951, achieving the rank of captain at the age of twenty-two. In 1953 he resigned his commission to enter the real estate business in Arlington.

CHARLES BROOKS enlisted in the U.S. Army in 1952, and after service in Korea returned to his hometown of Willow Street, Pennsylvania, and began working as a carpenter, a trade he still practices.

DOUG CARTER entered the U.S. Air Force shortly after graduating from The Citadel in 1951. Between 1953 and 1958 he served with tactical flying units throughout the United States and Europe. In 1969 he was posted to South Vietnam and flew 227 combat missions in Southeast Asia. He retired from active service in 1980 and now serves as the director of officer placement for The Retired Officer's Association in Alexandria, Virginia, and resides in nearby Springfield.

WILLIAM CHAMBERS was born in Borger, Texas, in 1928. He worked a variety of jobs after his service in Korea and upon retirement settled in Lancaster, Pennsylvania.

THOMAS CLAWSON was born and raised in Iowa but moved to Minnesota after his discharge from the army. He graduated from the University of Minnesota in 1961 and worked in park acquisition and development until his retirement from state government. He lives now with his family in West St. Paul, Minnesota.

ROBERT ENNIS graduated from West Point in 1949 and became an officer in the U.S. Air Force that same year. After his tour in Korea he served in various capacities at bases in the United States, Southeast Asia, Thailand and the Philippines. He earned a master's degree at the Air War College in 1976 and retired from active service in 1978. He is now a management consultant in Alexandria, Virginia.

UZAL ENT retired in 1980 after a career as an officer in the National Guard. Until 1992 he worked for the Pennsylvania Department of Public Welfare as a supervisor of its Voice Telecommunications Services Unit. Born in Sunbury, Pennsylvania, he now resides in Camp Hill, where he devotes most of his time to writing, woodworking, and oil painting.

ROBERT FITZGERALD grew up in the small factory town of Ballston Spa, New York, and worked for the Delaware & Hudson Railroad until his enlistment in the army in 1948, shortly after his seventeenth birthday. After his capture by the North Koreans in July 1950 he spent more than three years as a prisoner of war, regaining his freedom in August 1953 during Operation Big Switch. He was discharged from the army in October of that year, and until his marriage in 1964 he struggled alone and not always successfully with the alternating fits of depression and rage that were the legacy of his years in captivity. In 1964 he began the counseling and treatment that eventually led to a full recovery. He lives now with his wife Anne in Rennselaer, New York, where together they have raised seven children.

LYNN FREEMAN is a retired army officer. A native of Portland, Oregon, he now resides in Concord, California, where he retired for a second time after spending eighteen years in county government.

BLAINE FRIEDLANDER graduated from the University of Virginia in 1948 and after his army service he earned a master's degree in education at George Washington University. He taught English and history in high school until 1955, when he left teaching to earn a law degree at Georgetown University. He has been an attorney in the District of Columbia and Virginia since 1959, and currently resides in Falls Church, Virginia.

WILLIAM GLASGOW spent thirty years in the army, enlisting as a private in 1944 and serving in duty stations all over the world until his retirement as a colonel in 1974. He now makes his home in Alexandria, Virginia, his hometown, where he writes about the American Civil War and local military history.

JAMES HOLTON began his journalism career as a reporter in his hometown of Reading, Pennsylvania. After infantry service in World War II, he was hired by the Associated Press, served in Korea, then was recruited as a news writer by NBC News in New York. He spent twenty-seven years with the network, serving in all phases of news coverage. He now lives with his wife Ruth in Reinholds, Pennsylvania.

LLOYD KREIDER was raised in a Mennonite family on a farm in Lancaster County, Pennsylvania. After his army service he worked as a pharmacy technician in hospitals in the Lancaster area, where he now lives with his family.

DOUGLAS LARUE has a degree in business administration and spent thirty years with the Internal Revenue Service. Born in Bay City, Michigan, he now lives in Freeland, Michigan, and spends much of his time traveling.

FRED LAWSON is a native of Waynesville, Ohio. He enlisted in the U.S. Air Force in 1946 at the age of seventeen, then transferred into the Marine Corps in 1950. After his discharge from the service in 1952 he returned to his home state and became a manager for the J.C. Penney Company. He now lives with his family in Xenia, Ohio.

PAUL LEYVA is a native of Chicago. He continues to work full time for a family-owned clothing company in the city and avidly collects books about the Korean War.

LEWIS MILLETT was born in Maine and raised in Massachusetts. He enlisted in the army air corps in 1940, went AWOL in 1941 to join the Canadian army in order to get into World War II, and after Pearl Harbor, transferred back to U.S. service. He is a graduate of Bates College in Lewiston, Maine, and served as a Ranger advisor in Vietnam and an instructor in unconventional warfare. He lives now with his family in Idyllwild, California.

VICTOR POOLE was born and raised in southern Wales and joined the British army in 1949 at the age of eighteen. After completing his five-year term of enlistment he returned to his native Wales and finished his apprenticeship as a millwright. In 1966 he and his wife emigrated to Canada. They now reside in Welland, Ontario, and travel frequently in the United States.

SHERMAN PRATT has been a career army officer, a practicing attorney, and an administrative assistant on Capitol Hill. During the Second World War he commanded one of the two rifle companies that captured Adolf Hitler's mountain retreat at Berchtesgaden. A native of Arkansas, he now resides in Arlington, Virginia, where he remains active in community affairs.

ROBERT ROY is a native of Massachusetts. He attended high school in Worcester before enlisting in the army in 1949. After the Task Force Smith action he continued to serve in Korea until his rotation home in May of 1951. He was discharged a year later and worked for several large companies in the Albany, New York, area until his retirement in 1986. He and his wife Ila now live in Wyantskill, New York.

BEVERLY SCOTT was born in Statesville, North Carolina, and attended Bluefield State College in West Virginia before entering the U.S. Army. He received his commission as a lieutenant in 1946.

After his tour in Korea he served at duty stations around the world. He was a senior advisor to the Thai army in Thailand and South Vietnam from 1963 to 1965, and served on the staff of the Army Inspector General in Vietnam in 1968. He now makes his home in Alexandria, Virginia.

ROBERT (PAT) SCULLY spent thirty years in marketing after serving almost nine years as a U.S. marine in China, Japan and Korea. A native of Brooklyn, New York, he currently resides with his wife in Haddonfield, New Jersey, where he remains active in Marine Corps affairs.

JAMES E. SERVICE spent two years at Penn State University before entering the naval air cadet program in Pensacola, Florida, in 1950. A pilot throughout his navy career, he also served as commanding officer of the carrier U.S.S. *Independence,* as Commander, Naval Air Forces, Pacific Fleet, and as president of the Naval War College in Newport, Rhode Island. He retired from the U.S. Navy as a vice admiral and now divides his time between homes in California and Idaho.

EDWIN SIMMONS is a retired Marine Corps general who is now the director of Marine Corps History and Museums, a position he has held since 1972. He is a native of New Jersey, born in the small town of Paulsboro in 1921; a graduate of Lehigh University, class of 1942; with a master's degree in journalism received in 1955 from Ohio State University. He currently lives in Washington, D.C.

RICHARD SUAREZ was born and raised in San Francisco, where he still resides. After his service in Korea he held a variety of jobs until settling down as a carpenter and cabinet maker, and he remains active in both trades.

HARRY G. SUMMERS, JR. was born in Dayton, Ohio, and lived in Kentucky and Canada before enlisting in the army in 1947. He was an infantry squad leader in the Korean War, a battalion and corps operations officer in the Vietnam War, and a U.S. negotiator with the Viet Cong and North Vietnamese in Saigon and Hanoi in 1975. He has been an instructor at the Army War College and is the author of the book *On Strategy,* a controversial analysis of the U.S. military failure in Vietnam.

NICHOLAS V. TOSQUES was born in New York City but moved to Washington, D.C. in 1938, at the age of ten. After his return from Korea he worked for a number of years in the printing industry, including fifteen years at the Bureau of Engraving and Printing in Washington. He now resides with his wife in Dagsboro, Delaware.

VINCENT WALSH has worked for Philco-Ford, IBM, and General Electric as a technician and engineer. He was born in Philadelphia, raised in the nearby suburb of Willow Grove, and now resides with his family in Huntingdon Valley, Pennsylvania.

STANLEY WEINTRAUB is a native of Philadelphia and a graduate of Temple University. He has written over forty books and is the recipient of a National Book Award nomination. Now residing in State College, Pennsylvania, he is Evan Pugh Professor of Arts and Humanities at Pennsylvania State University.

THEODORE WHITE was born and raised in Washington, D.C. After his service in Korea he began his career as a furniture sales representative in the District of Columbia and Maryland.

ARNOLD WINTER was born in North Dakota. As the son of an oil-field worker he attended twenty-one different schools throughout the western states before graduating from high school in Denver, Colorado, in 1948. He enlisted in the Marine Corps in 1949 and was sent to Korea in 1950. Hospitalized for frostbite during the Chosin Reservoir campaign, he received a medical discharge in 1952. He has worked as a minister, shipyard worker, carpenter, and remodeling contractor, and now lives with his family in Cornville, Arizona.

GEORGE ZONGE lives in Stormstown, Pennsylvania. After retiring from his second career with a local electronics company he began devoting a major portion of his time to veterans affairs.

For Further Reading

A number of excellent books deal with the Korean War. The most thorough is Clay Blair's *The Forgotten War* (New York: Times Books, 1987). Less detailed but more readable are T. R. Fehrenbach, *This Kind of War* (New York: Macmillan, 1963); Robert Leckie, *Conflict* (New York: Putnam, 1962); and Harry J. Middleton, *The Compact History of the Korean War* (New York: Hawthorn Books, 1965). The story of the U.S. Marines in Korea is told in Andrew Geer, *The New Breed* (New York: Harper and Row, 1952). A highly personalized view of the war can be found in Marguerite Higgins, *War in Korea* (Garden City, N.Y.: Doubleday, 1951); Keyes Beech, *Tokyo and Points East* (Garden City, N.Y.: Doubleday, 1954); and Martin Russ, *The Last Parallel* (New York: Rinehart, 1957). The Allied occupation of Korea is ably dealt with in Bruce Cumings, *The Origins of the Korean War* (Princeton, N.J.: Princeton University Press, 1981). Providing a readable political overview is Joseph C. Goulden, *Korea: The Untold Story of the War* (New York: Times Books, 1982). A fascinating account of the Korean conflict from the

British side is Max Hastings, *The Korean War* (New York: Simon & Schuster, 1987). One of the best memoirs to come out of the war is Matthew B. Ridgway, *The Korean War* (Garden City, N.Y.: Doubleday, 1967). Invaluable for reference is Harry G. Summers, Jr., *Korean War Almanac* (New York: Facts On File, 1990). Not dealing with the war, but useful as an introduction to Korea and the Korean people, is Russell Warren Howe, *The Koreans* (Orlando, Fla.: Harcourt Brace Jovanovich, 1988).

Index